CARDIFF
CAERDYDD

The UCAS Guide to getting into

TEACHING AND EDUCATION

For entry to university and college in 2013

370.7141

378.41 UNI

Published by: UCAS Rosehill New Barn Lane Cheltenham GL52 3LZ

Produced in conjunction with GTI Media Ltd

© UCAS 2012

UCAS, a company limited by guarantee, is registered in England and Wales number: 2839815
Registered charity number: 1024741 (England and Wales) and SC038598 (Scotland)

UCAS reference number: PU037013
Publication reference: 12_051
ISBN: 978-1-908077-13-4
Price £15.99

We have made all reasonable efforts to ensure that the information in this publication was correct at time of publication. We will not, however, accept any liability for errors, omissions or changes to information since publication. Wherever possible any changes will be updated on the UCAS website (www.ucas.com) and the GTTR website (www.gttr.ac.uk)

UCAS and its trading subsidiary, UCAS Media Limited, accept advertising for publications that promote products and services relating to higher education and career progression. Revenue generated by advertising is invested by UCAS in order to enhance our applications services and to keep the cost to applicants as low as possible. Neither UCAS nor UCAS Media Limited endorse the products and services of other organisations that appear in this publication.

Further copies available from UCAS (p&p charges apply):

Contact Publication Services PO Box 130 Cheltenham GL52 3ZF

email: publicationservices@ucas.ac.uk or fax: 01242 544806

For further information about the UCAS and GTTR application processes go to www.ucas.com or www.gttr.ac.uk

If you need to contact UCAS or the GTTR, details can be found at www.ucas.com/about_us/contact_us or www.gttr.ac.uk/aboutus/contactus

UCAS QUALITY AWARDS

Contents

Foreword

THINKING ABOUT TEACHING?

Finding the course that's right for you at the right university or college can take time and it's important that you use all the resources available to you in making this key decision. We at UCAS and the GTTR have teamed up with TARGETjobs.co.uk to provide you with *The UCAS Guide to getting into Teaching and Education* to show you how you can progress from student to a career in teaching. You will find information on teaching as a career, entry routes and real life case studies on how it worked out for others.

Once you know whether you want to teach in primary or secondary schools, or the Lifelong Learning sector, you can use the institutions' profiles to see where you can do your teacher training. Most institution profiles include entry requirements so you can check if getting in would be achievable for you. There's also advice on applying

through UCAS and the GTTR, telling you what you need to know at each stage of the application process. There are six easy steps to applying through UCAS and getting a place at university or college.

We hope you find this publication helps you to choose and make your application to a course and university or college that is right for you.

On behalf of UCAS, the GTTR and TARGETjobs.co.uk, I wish you every success in your research.

Mary Curnock Cook, Chief Executive, UCAS

At TARGETjobs we champion paid work experience for UK university students. Find internships and placements across all sectors, plus take part in the TARGETjobs Undergraduate of the Year awards.

TARGETjobs.co.uk

the best possible start to your career

Introducing teaching

It could be you...

... enabling a toddler to learn through play — early years education

... congratulating a child on reading their first book — primary school teacher

... engaging a teenager to do well in exams — secondary school teacher

... sharing in your students' A level and university success — higher education teacher

... helping an immigrant to speak their first words of English — TESOL teacher

... and lots more besides. Could a career in teaching be for you? The aim of this guide is to help you decide.

A CAREER IN TEACHING?

- Choose from a wide range of exciting teaching career options. See **Which area?** starting on page 26.
- Hear it from the horse's mouth. Read what recently qualified teachers have to say about their careers in our **Case studies** from page 43.
- Learn about all the abbreviations and special language in teaching in the **Jargon buster** section on page 22.
- Make your UCAS or GTTR application stand out from the crowd. Read **How will they choose you?** starting on page 89.

TEACHING IN CONTEXT

Mention a career in teaching to those not in the know and, chances are, you might get the tired and negative response, 'Those who can't, teach'. Or you could be told that you will end up wasting your time and your degree on unteachable, unmotivated students when you could be earning big bucks in a flash City job instead.

Teaching is a vocation. Most people who go into it do so because they want to make a difference to someone's life, whether at the very beginning of their learning experience, such as primary school children, or later on in further or adult education. That is one of the joys of the profession: there is a huge variety of learners out there. You just need to find the group that suits you best. Sharing your love for your favourite subject is also another big attraction, as is the potential to see reluctant learners blossom.

If you're interested in a possible career in teaching, this guide can help point you further in the right direction. Read on to discover:

- the main roles on offer
- the qualifications and skills you will need
- study and training options at undergraduate and postgraduate level
- advice and personal experience stories from recent graduates working in teaching.

Why teaching?

Choose a career that is...

VARIED

Teachers come from all walks of life and have studied all sorts of things. Some will have done a degree in teaching (BEd) and others will have chosen another subject and then taken a special postgraduate qualification later. There is no specific teaching 'type': the only prerequisite is a willingness to share knowledge with and inspire your learners, whatever their age.

CREATIVE

The National Curriculum might tell you **what** to teach but you can decide **how** to teach it. By using your creative powers to design fascinating lessons, you can motivate even the toughest of critics. ICT is used a lot these days to help create classes that are more interactive for students, encouraging participation, but a teacher who can deliver facts and information in an interesting and engaging manner will be valued by schools and students alike.

INFLUENTIAL

Think back to your school days. We can all remember teachers we disliked, whose classes we dreaded for fear of boredom. But can you remember a teacher who made a lasting impression on you? In what way did they bring their subject alive in your mind? Did this motivate you to study it at a higher level, perhaps? A class is only as good as its teacher, so if you have the ability to inspire others and share your love of learning, this could be the career for you.

WELL PAID

Compared with something like investment banking, of course, teaching will look poorly paid. However, when considered next to more 'normal' pay structures, teachers do pretty well. From September 2011 Newly Qualified Teachers (NQTs) received £21,588 in England and Wales (£27,000 in inner London), comparing favourably with the average starting graduate starting salary of £25,000. As you progress, so does your salary. At the top end (point six) of the main pay scale teachers currently earn £31,552 (£36,387 in inner London), while the upper pay scale offers salaries of up to £45,000. Advanced skills teachers can earn up to £64,036, and those taking up leadership positions (eg head teachers and deputy head teachers) can earn between £42,379 and £112,181 depending on their experience, level of responsibility and location. Additional benefits are excellent too, such as great pension schemes and generous holiday allowance.

STIMULATING

Students can be unpredictable and this is what keeps the job so stimulating. From the highs and lows of a five-year-old learning to read, to a teenager who finally grasps a concept in your class and wants to ask you everything you know about it, you will be kept on your toes as learners progress and their thirst for knowledge increases. Can you anticipate their next question?

DEDICATED TO PERSONAL DEVELOPMENT

If you do decide on a career in teaching, you can rest assured that you will receive excellent training, whatever training route you choose. This could be an undergraduate (BEd) degree or a postgraduate (PGCE) qualification, or carried out mainly in schools (school-centred initial teacher training, SCITT, or graduate teacher programme, GTP). See page 53 for more details about routes into teaching. You will always receive support in learning classroom, planning and management skills, and be shown how to lead your students, whatever their age, to achieve to the best of their abilities. Training doesn't just stop on qualification though; you will be encouraged in your own professional development throughout your career as a teacher, through support at school and from any teaching union you wish to join.

WHAT DO TEACHERS SAY?

'I love the 'light bulb moment' when something clicks for a child or when I hear them talking enthusiastically in the playground about one of my lessons they have enjoyed – this makes all the hard work worthwhile.'
Charlotte Johnson, primary school teacher, page 44

'Speak to as many teachers and get into as many classrooms as you can to see how the profession works and whether you could fit in. Make the most of your time on teaching placements; this is the best opportunity to try techniques out in a supportive atmosphere. Be prepared to accept feedback and advice and then act on it.'
Claire Chalmers, English teacher, page 46

'Don't go into teaching unless you are passionate about it – this would be a very stressful job if your heart was not in it! If you want to progress, be proactive in your first few years of teaching and go out of your way to take on additional responsibilities.'
Daniel Markham, head of design and technology, page 48

'Contact local schools to shadow teachers to see both whether teaching is for you and to get valuable experience for your teacher training application. On placement learn how to manage your time well – it is important to find a good work-life balance.'
Jonathan Whybrow, trainee secondary teacher, page 50

'Being part of a child's life and watching them develop is invaluable. It could be something as simple as a child who has never initiated communication in English before asking me a question in English – it is these moments I treasure.'
Katy Helen, pre-kindergarten teacher in Cambodia, page 52

www.ucas.com

www.gttr.ac.uk

Focus your career with the TARGETjobs Careers Report. Using biographical data, information about your interests and insightful psychometric testing, the Careers Report gives you a clear picture of jobs that match your skills and personality.

TARGETjobs.co.uk
the best possible start to your career

A career in teaching

A career in teaching

A career in teaching is a popular career choice amongst graduates, and in the wake of the recent recession, there has been a marked rise in the number of people interested in entering the profession. There were over 35,000 people starting initial teacher training courses for the 2011/12 academic; an increase of nearly 50 per cent over the previous year. The Teaching Agency attributes the profession's popularity to:

- salary
- content of work
- quality of training and development programme
- the opportunity to use the knowledge they gained during their degree at work
- work/life balance.

WHERE THEY WORK

Where you work will depend on which education sector you choose. There are, broadly speaking, three main areas, which then break down into smaller sub-areas, as follows.

School education

Every child in the UK has the right to a free school place and parents are legally obliged to ensure their child is educated. Around 90 per cent of children in England and Wales are educated in the maintained sector, in schools that are state funded, follow the National Curriculum and are inspected by Ofsted. There are four main categories of school:

- **Community schools** – run by the local authority, which takes care of employing staff and deciding on admissions criteria, and owns the land and buildings. Community schools aim to develop links with the local community.

- **Foundation and trust schools** – in a foundation school a governing body is responsible for recruitment and admissions criteria, and usually owns the land and buildings. A trust school is also a foundation school, but which has formed a charitable trust with an outside partner.
- **Voluntary-aided schools** – these tend to be faith schools, although children do not have to belong to the particular faith to apply. A voluntary-aided school is similar to a foundation school in that it is run by a governing body with a similar remit.
- **Voluntary-controlled schools** – these are similar to voluntary-aided schools but run by the local authority instead of a governing body. The land and buildings are usually owned by a charity, such as a religious organisation.

Other types of state school include academies, grammar schools, faith schools, city technology colleges and specialist schools that focus on a particular subject area.

Most UK schools are mixed, although some are still single-sex, more typically in the private sector. Children aged 4 or 5 to 11 attend **primary schools**, and attendance at these is compulsory from the beginning of the term after their fifth birthday, although many children start in pre-school from age three or four.

Secondary schools educate children aged 11 to 16. Most of these schools are all-ability, although some areas (not in Wales) still have grammar schools that require pupils to pass an entrance examination.

In England, The Qualifications and Curriculum Authority (QCA) advises ministers on the National Curriculum requirements. The National Curriculum sets out the opportunities that pupils should be given in each subject. The core subjects for 5 to 16 year-olds are English, mathematics and science. In Wales, the Qualifications and Curriculum Group in the Department for Education, Lifelong Learning and Skills is responsible for the National Curriculum. In Wales, there is also an additional core subject, Welsh. At present, the National Curriculum is divided into four Key Stages.

- **Key Stage 1 (KS1)** for children aged 5 to 7
  From 2008, a new phase was introduced in Wales, the Foundation Phase, to cover pupils aged 3 to 7.
- **Key Stage 2 (KS2)** for children aged 7 to 11.
- **Key Stage 3 (KS3)** for children aged 11 to 14.
- **Key Stage 4 (KS4)** for children aged 14 to 16.

Around one fifth of children have **special educational needs**, such as mild dyslexia and behavioural problems, but most of these can be educated in mainstream schools.

There are around 2,300 independent schools in England and 2,500 in the UK as a whole. Independent schools in England must all be registered with the Department for Education and have their standards monitored by Ofsted or another approved inspectorate, although they are allowed to set their own admissions policies and curriculum; in fact, most do teach the National Curriculum. Independent schools educate just over seven per cent of all British children (rising to 18 per cent at sixth form level).

Further and adult education

Over 500 colleges in the UK provide further and adult education to more than 4 million students. Most of these are aged 16 to 19 but some are older. Courses range from A levels and vocational qualifications to evening classes and distance learning, and are offered for academic, career and leisure purposes. The range of subjects on offer is incredible: from first aid, car maintenance and aromatherapy to basic literacy and numeracy, and advanced mathematics.

Learning normally takes place in a variety of venues, including further education (FE) colleges, colleges of technology (or technical colleges), sixth-form colleges, tertiary colleges, agricultural colleges and specialist colleges.

Higher education

Higher education normally refers to learning that takes place in universities or colleges that are governed by an Act of Parliament and enjoy academic freedom. They can appoint their own staff, choose which students they would like to admit, decide which courses they wish to offer and award their own degrees. The number of universities has increased dramatically since 1992, when polytechnics were given degree-awarding powers and were allowed to call themselves universities. Higher education also covers a number of different areas, including prison education, museum and environmental education, sports and outdoor education, and English Language Teaching (ELT), incorporating teaching English either as a foreign language (TEFL) or as a second language (TESL).

EMPLOYMENT OPPORTUNITIES

Society will always have learners and, consequently, will always need teachers. Jobs are available in all areas of the UK, although naturally more occur in larger towns and cities than in rural areas. If you wish to specialise in a particular teaching area, such as special needs provision, this might only be available in certain schools.

A teaching career can offer a flexible working life, depending on which area you wish to work in. Part-time and temporary work are always available to cover sickness and maternity leave, for example. Teaching English as a Foreign Language (TEFL) and to Speakers of a Second Language (TESL) can offer different working hours, such as in the evenings and at weekends, to fit in with the commitments of their learners. Many people are also attracted to a career in TEFL because of the travel opportunities.

Career progression is also pretty good in teaching. Those who work hard and are committed to their profession can progress to senior posts, commanding great respect and a healthy salary package.

TRENDS

As with all areas of work, the teaching profession is witness to a number of trends that can be affected by what is going on generally in society.

Developing diversity

Since teaching is a public-sector profession, its recruitment procedures are subject to government scrutiny and targets. Currently, the Teaching Agency (TA) is trying to encourage two main groups into the world of teaching to reflect the pupil population in UK schools more accurately.

- **Men** are under-represented in education as a whole, but in early years and primary education in particular. In 2011/12, 38 per cent of those entering secondary teacher training were men, but men only made up 18 per cent of the teacher trainee intake for primary level teaching. However, men currently occupy disproportionately more senior level posts in schools.
- **Black and Minority Ethnic (BME)** represented around 12 per cent of the trainee intake in 2011/12. More needs to be done to attract BME applicants into teaching. Each year the Teaching Agency works with individual providers to negotiate BME trainee recruitment targets.

Subject shortages

If you have seen any advertising for teaching, you may have noticed that there are particular areas which suffer from teacher shortages, especially at secondary level.

In England and Wales, subjects that are currently short of teachers include mathematics, physics, chemistry and modern foreign languages. Tax-free bursaries are available to eligible trainees in these subjects, the amount awarded reflecting the demand for teachers in particular areas. Bursaries also vary according to what class of degree an applicant has gained. In 2012/13 trainees with a first class degree will be eligible for a tax-free bursary of £20,000 for an initial teacher training course in chemistry, physics, mathematics, or modern languages; the figure is £15,000 for a 2:1 degree and £12,000 for a 2:2 degree. Physics trainees with a first or 2:1 degree can also apply for an Institute of Physics scholarship worth £20,000. For primary initial teacher training, and for the other shortage subjects at secondary level (art and design, design and technology, economics, engineering, English, dance, drama, geography, history, information and communications technology (ICT), computer science, classics, music, biology, physical education and religious education) applicants with first class degrees receive a bursary worth £9,000 or £5,000 with a 2:1. No bursaries are available for those with 2:2 degrees applying to train in these subjects.

NEW DIRECTIONS

In May 2010 the new Coalition Government came into power, and time and money has been spent reviewing the education system in order to propose and implement changes and improvements. By January 2012, the Government had overseen the creation of 1,300 new academies and 24 free schools. A £2 million scholarship scheme has been launched to help teachers in England develop their skills and deepen their subject knowledge – in December 2011 280 scholarships had been awarded to teachers working in English, mathematics and science, and nearly 400 scholarships to teachers working with children with special educational needs. Other measures taken to improve teaching standards include the selection of 100 outstanding schools to act as teaching centres and a greater degree of influence given to schools over the content of initial teacher training courses. The National Curriculum has been slimmed down to allow a great focus on essential knowledge and skills, bureaucracy has been reduced, and reading and sport have been announced as priorities for schoolchildren.

GET IN THE KNOW

The big players in education are the following
organisations:

- **Department for Education**:
  The Department for Education is responsible for the
  education system and children's services in England.
- **General Teaching Councils**: These are the
  independent professional bodies for teachers – the
  General Teaching Council for England (GTC), the
  General Teaching Council for Wales (GTCW), the
  General Teaching Council for Scotland (GTCS) and the
  General Teaching Council for Northern Ireland (GTCNI).

However, the General Teaching Council for England
ceased to exist after 31 March 2012, and has been
replaced by a new body called the Teaching Agency.

- **Office for Standards in Education, Children's
  Services and Skills (Ofsted)**: Established in 1992
  to improve quality and standards in education and
  childcare through independent inspection and
  regulation in England, from nursery to secondary
  schools.

- **Welsh Assembly Government**: The Assembly
  Government's Department for Children, Education,
  Lifelong Learning and Skills (DCELLS) has
  responsibility for the delivery of education and skills
  policy in Wales.
- **Teaching Agency (TA)**: This agency is part of the
  Department for Education and replaced the Training
  and Development Agency for Schools (TDA) in April
  2012. It is responsible for raising standards in
  education by attracting able and committed people to
  teaching, and ensuring that all routes to qualified
  teacher status (QTS) are of high quality.
- **Estyn**: Estyn is the office of Her Majesty's Chief
  Inspector of Education and Training in Wales. Its aim
  is to raise standards and quality of education and
  training in Wales through inspection and advice
- **Scottish Government Education Department**
  The department of the Scottish Government
  responsible for education in Scotland.

Jargon buster

There is a lot of specialist vocabulary in teaching. We define some of the more common words and phrases you'll come across both here and elsewhere.

AST

Advanced Skills Teacher: a teacher who has passed a national assessment, qualifying them to help develop and support teachers working in their local schools.

ATL

Association of Teachers and Lecturers: a trade union and professional association (**www.atl.org.uk**).

CHALLENGING BEHAVIOUR

Non-judgemental term to cover behaviour from severe problems to straightforward naughtiness.

CONTACT TIME

The time teachers spend with students.

CPD

Continuing Professional Development.

DCELLS

Welsh Assembly government's department for Children, Education, Lifelong Learning and Skills.

DFE

The Department for Education replaced the Department for Children, Schools and Families in May 2010. It is responsible for education and children's services.

DENI

Department of Education in Northern Ireland.

EAL

English as an Additional Language.

EBD

Emotional and Behavioural Difficulties.

ELS

Early literacy support for Year 1 children who need more intensive assistance.

ESTYN

The Office of Her Majesty's Chief Inspector of Education and Training in Wales. Its objectives are to deliver high quality inspection of individual education and training providers, and related services, in Wales; and to provide independent and sound advice, based on inspection evidence, to inform the Welsh Assembly Government in the formulation and evaluation of education and training policy.

FOUNDATION STAGE

For children aged three to the end of reception year.

GTCNI

The General Teaching Council for Northern Ireland: an independent professional and regulatory body for school teachers in Northern Ireland (**www.gtcni.org.uk**).

GTCS

The General Teaching Council for Scotland: an independent professional and regulatory body for school teachers in Scotland (**www.gtcs.org.uk**).

GTCW

The General Teaching Council for Wales: an independent professional and regulatory body for school teachers in Wales (**www.gtcw.org.uk**).

GTP

Graduate Teacher Programme: an employment-based training programme for applicants who already have a degree.

GTTR

Graduate Teacher Training Registry: a central clearing house for postgraduate teacher-training applications (**www.gttr.ac.uk**).

HLTA

Higher Level Teaching Assistant.

HOD

Head of Department.

HOY

Head of Year.

IAPS

Independent Association of Preparatory Schools (**www.iaps.org.uk**).

INDUCTION

A compulsory year-long, on-the-job training period for all newly qualified teachers.

ITT

Initial Teacher Training: involves completion of a recognised teaching qualification.

LAs

Local authorities: local government departments that own school property, monitor their work and provide services (previously known as LEAs – Local Education Authorities).

LSA

Learning Support Assistant: a person who provides classroom-based support.

NAPE

National Association for Primary Education (**www.nape.org.uk**).

NASEN

National Association for Special Educational Needs (**www.nasen.org.uk**).

NASUWT

National Association of Schoolmasters Union of Women Teachers (**www.nasuwt.org.uk**).

NATIONAL CURRICULUM

National guidelines on teaching (**www.education.gov.uk/schools/ teachingandlearning/curriculum**).

NQT

Newly Qualified Teacher: a teacher who has completed their initial teacher training, but who still needs to complete induction.

NUT

National Union of Teachers: a trade union and professional association (**www.teachers.org.uk**).

OFSTED

Office for Standards in Education, Children's Services and Skills in England: an office run by the DfE that organises regular school inspections.

OTT

Overseas Trained Teacher.

PGCE

Professional Graduate or Postgraduate Certificate in Education: a HEI-based teacher training course that includes 18 to 24 weeks spent in a school. The Professional Graduate Certificate in Education is the same academic level as the final year of an honours degree course (H level). The Postgraduate Certificate in Education includes some credits at master's degree level (M level credits) and H level credits.

Many school-based teaching programmes also include the award of a PGCE from a higher education institution.

POS

Programme of study: sets out what needs to be taught in every subject at each Key Stage.

PPA

Planning, Preparation and Assessment: time allocated on the timetable for teachers to devote to these areas.

PRU

Pupil Referral Unit: an LA-maintained unit for students who have been excluded from other schools.

PTR

Pupil-Teacher Ratio.

QTS

Qualified Teacher Status: a qualification gained by trainees on initial teacher training courses or people on employment based training schemes who have demonstrated that they have met the appropriate professional standards. In Scotland qualified teachers are awarded a Teaching Qualification (TQ) rather than QTS.

RECEPTION CLASS

First class at primary school or Year 1 for children between four and five years old.

RTP

Registered Teacher Programme: a two-year on-the-job training programme for those who want to teach and who have already spent at least two years in higher education.

SCITT

School-Centred Initial Teacher Training: a school-based on-the-job teacher training programme in England for graduates. Applicants are employed by a consortium of schools and education providers.

SEN

Special Educational Needs: learning difficulties for which a pupil needs special educational help.

SENCO

Special Educational Needs Co-ordinator: a teacher who is responsible for co-ordinating provision for pupils with special educational needs within a school.

SMT

Senior Management Team: includes the head teacher, deputy head and other senior teachers.

TA

Teaching Assistant.

TA

Teaching Agency: This organisation is part of the Department for Education and promotes careers and training opportunities in the teaching profession (**www.education.gov.uk/get-into-teaching**).

UCAC

Undeb Cenedlaethol Athrawon Cymru (National Union of Teachers in Wales): a Welsh-medium based trade union and professional association (**www.athrawon.com**).

VOICE

Trade union for educational professionals (**www.voicetheunion.org.uk**).

Which area?

With such a range of teaching career paths to choose from, potential teachers are spoilt for choice.

Most people think of unruly teenagers when you mention teaching. However, the situation is far more diverse and complex than that. There are many different disciplines, age groups and specialisms to choose from, varying from a special educational needs co-ordinator in a primary school to a university lecturer in politics. We have explained the ages and Key Stages for you, and have summarised the main areas into which people are recruited to give you a flavour of what you might end up doing as a recent graduate.

AGES AND KEY STAGES

Understanding more about the education system in the different countries will help you to decide which subject(s) and age groups you might want to teach.

A BIT OF BACKGROUND

In England and Wales, compulsory education starts at age five and finishes at age 16. Education is normally split into two tiers for this vast age range, though some local authorities (LAs) run a three-tier system.

- In a **two-tier system**, primary schools either provide for children aged 5 to 11 in one unit or are divided into infant schools (ages 5 to 7) and junior schools (ages 7 to 11). After this, pupils go on to secondary schools where they remain until their compulsory education stops at age 16.
- In a **three-tier system**, pupils leave their first school a little earlier than they would a primary school, at age eight, and then attend a middle school before going on to their secondary school.

The National Curriculum

This was established in 1989 to ensure that pupils in state-sector (maintained) schools received a broad and balanced curriculum that would help schools raise standards of achievement and widen educational opportunities. In England, the curriculum is kept under review by the Qualifications and Curriculum Authority (QCA). In Wales, this responsibility rests with the Curriculum and Assessment Division of the Department for Education, Lifelong Learning and Skills. The Scottish Government is responsible for implementing the Curriculum for Excellence in Scotland. In Northern Ireland the Council for the Curriculum, Examinations and Assessment (CCEA) administers the Northern Ireland Curriculum.

Privately funded independent schools do not have to follow this curriculum if they do not wish to do so.

In January 2011 the Secretary of State for Education announced a review of the National Curriculum in England for primary and secondary schools. The new National Curriculum will be slimmed down to set out only the essential knowledge for children to acquire, giving teachers greater freedom on how to teach this within the context of a wider school curriculum that best meets the needs of their pupils.

In England the National Curriculum is divided into four 'Key Stages', reflecting pupils' age ranges and abilities. Currently the following subjects are taught in England from Key Stages 1 through to 4 (covering ages 5 to 16):

- Art and design
- Citizenship
- Design and technology (DT)
- English
- Geography
- History
- Information and communication technology (ICT)
- Mathematics
- Modern foreign languages (MFL)
- Music
- Personal, social and health education
- Physical education
- Religious education
- Science

A review of the National Curriculum is currently being undertaken by the Department for Education, supported by experts such as teachers, academics and business people. The review will look at what subjects should be compulsory at different ages and what children should learn within these subjects. The new National Curriculum will come into force in stages in maintained schools from September 2013.

In Wales the Foundation Phase replaced Key Stage 1 in 2011/12, superseding the National Curriculum for Key Stage 1. The Foundation Phase is a new approach to learning for children aged 3 to 7, focusing on children learning by doing through play and active involvement. The following subjects must be taught throughout Key Stages 2 to 4: Welsh, English, mathematics, science, and physical education; at Key Stages 2 and 3 music, information and communication technology, design and technology, history, geography, and art and design are compulsory; and modern foreign languages are compulsory at Key Stage 3.

Scottish children attend primary school from age 5 or 6 to age 11 or 12, with non-compulsory nursery for age 3 to 5. Secondary school starts at 12 or 13 finishing at 15 or 16. Scotland's curriculum is non statutory: the Government provides the framework for learning and teaching through its Curriculum for Excellence, which has set out eight areas of learning: expressive arts, health and well-being, languages, mathematics, religious and moral education, sciences, social studies, and technology.

Responsibility for children rests with individual schools and local authorities with the support of national guidelines.

GCSE and A levels

Until very recently, students studied for GCSEs (these are called applied GCSEs) at ages 14 to 16, sometimes followed by A levels at ages 16 to 19. However, the education of 14 to 19-year-olds is increasingly regarded as a single stage, during which they can undertake a range of qualifications such as:

- **Entry-level qualifications**: certificates that can be taken in over 100 subjects, including basic skills, National Curriculum subjects and vocational subjects. These are aimed at students with special educational needs or those who have been out of the education system for some time.
- **GCSEs (General Certificate of Secondary Education)**: the main qualification taken by 14- to 16-year-olds, available in a wide range of academic and applied (work-related) subjects. Many GCSEs can also be taken as short courses. Applied GCSEs, sometimes also called 'vocational' GCSEs, include subjects such as health and social care, and leisure and tourism.
- **Diploma for 14- to 19-year olds**: these are designed to offer a practical, hands-on way of gaining the essential skills employers and universities look for. They are available in 14 subject areas in selected schools and colleges and all include theoretical and practical learning, functional English, maths, ICT, and personal learning and thinking skills.
- **Key skills in communication, application of number and information technology**: separate qualifications that are usually taken alongside other qualifications.
- **NVQs (National Vocational Qualifications)**: work-related and competence-based qualifications.

- **A levels (General Certificate of Education – Advanced level)**: consisting of the AS (the first half of an A level and a self-standing qualification) and A2 (completion of the full A level).
- **AEAs (advanced extension awards)**: designed to stretch talented A level students.
- **VCEs (vocational A levels, also referred to as GCEs in applied subjects)**: an applied, practical approach to A levels. Subjects include business and tourism.
- **Vocationally related qualifications**: usually studied at further education colleges and known by the brand name of the awarding body (eg BTEC).

EARLY YEARS EDUCATION (ENGLAND ONLY)

In summary: encouraging learning through play in children, from birth to five

The work

Professionals in this area work with children to help them learn basic things such as literacy and numeracy through play. Work settings normally include children's centres, nurseries, pre-schools and classes in infant and primary schools. Children are currently entitled to free part-time education in an early years setting from the age of three, but education is not compulsory until after five years of age.

The curriculum for foundation stage pupils has six areas of learning: personal, social and emotional development; communication; language and literacy; mathematical development; knowledge and understanding of the world; physical development; and creative development.

Foundation Phase in Wales

Seven areas of learning have been identified to describe an appropriate curriculum for three to seven year-olds that supports the development of children and their skills. The seven areas of learning are:

- personal and social well being and cultural diversity
- language, literacy and communication skills
- Welsh language development
- knowledge and understanding of the world
- physical development
- creative development
- mathematical development.

The Foundation Phase is not only taught in schools, but also before compulsory school age in other settings.

Skills and qualifications

In the state sector, there must be a qualified teacher in nursery or reception classes who will work alongside other professionals such as nursery nurses. Many of these will gain QTS through a BEd or PGCE, specialising in early years education. A new development, early

years professional (EYP) status, is an alternative graduate-level status aimed mainly at those working in non-school settings. QTS is not compulsory for the private and voluntary sectors.

An ability to stay calm under pressure is essential; nursery classes are notoriously noisy and busy areas! Stamina is also important; the working hours in private nurseries match those of working parents and can involve early starts (7.00am) and late finishes (6.30pm).

The best bits

Working with young children is full of surprises and it can be rewarding to see things through the eyes of a child, as well as to watch how quickly they progress in their language skills and confidence.

ENGLAND ONLY

AGE	STAGE	YEAR	TEST/QUALIFICATION
3 to 4 4 to 5	Foundation	Reception	N/A
5 to 6 6 to 7	Key Stage 1	Years 1 and 2	
7 to 8 8 to 9 9 to 10 10 to 11	Key Stage 2	Years 3, 4, 5 and 6	National tests (SATs) in English and maths at end of Year 6.
11 to 12 12 to 13 13 to 14	Key Stage 3	Years 7, 8 and 9	
14 to 15 15 to 16	Key Stage 4	Years 10 and 11	Some children take GCSEs in Year 10; most children take GCSEs or other national qualifications at the end of Year 11.
16 to 17 17 to 18 18 to 19	Post-compulsory education and/ or training	Year 12 (college, year 1) and Year 13 (college, year 2)	Learning programmes leading to general, vocationally related and occupation qualifications, eg A levels, NVQs, modern apprenticeships.

In Wales there are no statutory tests at the end of Key Stages 1-3. Assessment is by teacher assessment only.

PRIMARY EDUCATION

In summary: providing education for children aged 5 to 11

The work

Primary schools are a child's first experience of formal, compulsory education, and include infant schools for 5 to 7 year-olds and junior schools for 7 to 11 year-olds, or a combination of the two. Many primary schools also offer a foundation year for 4 to 5 year-olds. In Wales, primary schools also cover the Foundation Phase.

Primary school teachers must deliver the subjects stipulated in the national curriculum, particularly focusing on literacy, numeracy and science. They are also responsible for testing at Key Stages 1 and 2. Class sizes on average, contain 26 pupils, depending on the size of the school, and if a class is on the large side, pupils may be split into several groups for different subjects.

Skills and qualifications

Primary school teachers need to have reached qualified teacher status. You will need to have a broad knowledge of various subjects, which is why many primary school teachers choose to take a three- or four-year BEd course as this gives them the necessary skills and knowledge for the classroom.

One of the biggest skills you will need in primary education is multitasking. Even if you are dealing with one child, you need to be constantly alert to what is happening in the rest of the classroom to avoid potential problems.

The best bits

A child can develop in leaps and bounds from the start to the end of a school year and it can feel rewarding and amazing to be part of that process.

SECONDARY EDUCATION

In summary: compulsory education for pupils aged 11 to 16

The work

Children must attend secondary education from 11 to 16 years of age, although many choose to continue until 18. As a secondary school teacher, you could be teaching across this age range, depending on whether or not the school you teach in has a sixth form. Many schools do not have this and post-16 education – A levels and equivalent – are provided in separate sixth-form colleges. This could make a difference to where you choose to teach, as science teachers, for example, must teach all sciences to Key Stage 4 level, and can only specialise in one area in post-16 education.

From 2009, a new slimmed down version of the National Curriculum was implemented in England, with more emphasis on 'key concepts', 'processes' and 'cross-curricular dimensions'. The aim was to offer teachers more flexibility and opportunity for project-based, collaborative work across the curriculum.

Skills and qualifications

To teach in a secondary school you will need to have QTS professional qualifications out of the way. You will also need to enjoy working with teenagers – a notoriously difficult age group!

Essential personal qualities include empathy and sympathy, patience to deal with troublesome students, and energy and enthusiasm to motivate your learners.

Time management skills are vital, as are good organisational skills.

The best bits
In this area of teaching you can often see the difference you have made to a child's life, particularly if they come from a difficult home life. Inspiring someone to carry on with your subject at a higher level can feel rewarding, and teaching a subject you love day in, day out is enjoyable.

FURTHER EDUCATION
In summary: teaching non-compulsory education to 16 to 19 year-olds

The work
While many secondary schools have a sixth form, some, particularly those in urban areas, do not offer this facility and post-16 education is offered in a special sixth-form college. Teaching is similar to that in secondary schools but the student age range is 16 to 19-year-olds studying for A levels, NVQs, and other post-GCSE qualifications, either academic or vocational in nature. Adult learners are also catered for at these colleges.

Teaching normally takes the form of tutorials and lectures and the atmosphere is often less formal than in a school. Behavioural difficulties tend to be less common as students are generally attending out of choice.

Skills and qualifications
To teach in the further education sector including sixth form colleges you need as a minimum a level 3 qualification (eg NVQ/vocational level 3) in the subject you wish to teach (and for some academic subjects, a degree); GCSE or equivalent in English, maths and ICT; and to complete a number of teaching qualifications.

These are:

- The Award in Preparing to Teach in the Lifelong Learning Sector (PTLLS) – a short introductory course
- Level 3 / 4 Certificate in Teaching in the Lifelong Learning Sector (CTLLS) – if you want to qualify as an associate teacher. Associate teachers have fewer responsibilities than full teachers
- Level 5 Diploma in Teaching in the Lifelong Learning Sector (DTLLS) – the minimum qualification if you want to work as a full teacher. This diploma is comparable to the PGCE/Cert Ed in Further Education.

You can study for these qualifications with City & Guilds, Edexcel, OCR and some universities. For more details about qualifications and training providers, go to **www.talent.ac.uk**. The Learning and Skills Improvement Service (LSIS) website, **www.excellencegateway.org.uk**, also has a lot of useful resources.

The best bits
Seeing a student put the theory you have taught them into practice is fantastic and it is generally less stressful teaching students who want to be there rather than those who don't!

HIGHER AND ADULT EDUCATION
In summary: for adults in universities and higher education colleges

The work
Once students have completed secondary or further education, they can move on to higher education in either higher education colleges or universities.

In universities, teaching is usually carried out through tutorials and lectures. Class sizes vary from a huge auditorium of students listening to your lecture to a small group discussion between four or fewer people. In addition to general teaching duties, university lecturers are also expected to carry out research into their chosen subject area and present or write papers.

Adult education lecturers teach in a wide range of areas, from basic education to higher education evening courses. Teaching may be carried out in a community setting, such as a school or hall, through evening classes or by distance learning. You could be teaching a basic skills course, English as a second language (TESL) or a creative writing class.

Skills and qualifications

Many adult education teachers will have taught at secondary level or further education before and a qualification in the subject you want to teach is essential.

To teach at higher education level normally requires a first class or 2:1 undergraduate degree and a master's in your subject. You will also need to have studied at a university with a high grade for research, and hold or be working towards a PhD. You do not need a formal teaching qualification although many higher education institutions offer teacher training as part of continuing professional development.

An ability to communicate effectively is essential, as are research skills, particularly for university lecturers. It is desirable for teachers in adult education to have ICT skills or a willingness to learn them.

The best bits

Becoming an expert in your field is rewarding, especially when you can pass on your knowledge and love of your subject to others.

TEFL/TESOL

In summary: Teaching English as a foreign or second language within the UK

The work

First of all, let's make a quick distinction. TEFL (Teaching English as a Foreign Language) normally involves you going abroad to teach English in another country. TESL (Teaching English as a Second Language), however, means teaching English in the UK to people whose first language is not English. TESOL (Teaching English to Speakers of Other Languages) is the blanket term to cover everything.

NOTE: In Wales the above terms are no longer used – they refer to pupils from non-English-based/non-Welsh-based education systems.

Typical students range from school or university students to refugees and immigrants to professionals who need to learn English for their jobs. Vacancies exist anywhere in the world where people need to learn English and the chance to travel is one of the major attractions of a career in this area of teaching.

TEFL/TESL teachers do not follow a normal working schedule. Often they have to teach at times that fit in with their students' commitments, such as evenings and weekends, and contact hours can range from two to seven hours. Class sizes also vary from small one-on-one sessions to large groups of up to 20 students.

Skills and qualifications

Many people go abroad and teach English privately with no recognised qualification. However, if you want to gain regular work within respected organisations, you will need to gain a recognised qualification, such as the Cambridge certificate known as CELTA (Certificate of English Language Teaching to Adults) and the Trinity TESOL certificate. University degrees, in any subject area, are normally desired by employers.

Personal skills that are essential in these areas include good communication skills, to be able to work with a wide variety of students and ages, and patience to deal with different abilities within the same group.

The best bits

The travel opportunities, particularly for TEFL, are fantastic, as is the chance to meet and work with people from many different cultures.

The
UCAS Guide
to getting into
University
and College

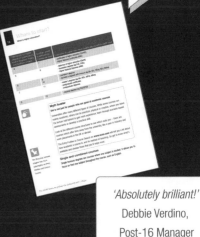

What would 650,000 potential students like to know about UCAS? Everything!

- With rising costs and high competition for places, thorough research and preparation have never been more crucial for future students.

- Relevant throughout the whole year.

- Published by UCAS, a well-known and respected brand with direct access to the most up-to-date information.

- Written in a friendly, step-by-step format, with myth busters, checklists and helpful tips from students and experts at universities and colleges.

'...the most comprehensive guide... completely impartial... offers fabulous tips and advice...'
David Fullerton, Head of Careers

'Absolutely brilliant!'
Debbie Verdino,
Post-16 Manager

Order your copy now...

t +44 (0)1242 544 610

f +44(0)1242 544 806

e publicationservices@ucas.ac.uk

Price: £11.99

The career
for you?

Is teaching for you?

Building a successful career in teaching requires more than a willingness to talk in front of others. To help you decide if this is the right working area for you, we suggest you think about the following three areas:

- What you want from your future work.
- What a teaching degree or postgraduate teaching qualification typically involves.
- Which skills and qualities admissions tutors in this field typically seek in new recruits.

WHAT DO YOU WANT FROM YOUR CAREER?

You may not have an instant answer for this but your current studies, work experience, and even your hobbies can help give you clues about the kind of work you enjoy and the skills you have already started to develop. Start with a blank sheet of paper and note down the answers to the questions at the end of this section to help get you thinking. Be as honest with yourself as you can: don't write what you think will impress your teachers or parents. Write what really matters to you, and you'll start to see a pattern emerging.

WHAT DO TEACHING COURSES INVOLVE?

Unsurprisingly, the skills you'll require as a successful teacher will also be required at various stages of your studies. Therefore, it is important to know what typical teaching courses entail before you apply to be sure it's the kind of work you will enjoy. For example, most university courses will involve theoretical study, which can then be applied and used in the classroom.

WHAT SKILLS WILL YOU NEED?

Despite the many different career options within the teaching profession, the skills set they all require is broadly the same. Key skills required of any potential teacher are:

- **communication skills:** Whether you are spending hours talking to and engaging students in a classroom or lecture hall or in a one-to-one tutorial, you will need to be able to communicate effectively to pass on knowledge in an interesting and informative manner.
- **patience:** Teachers need this in spades! Students learn at different rates according to their own ability, and you need to be able to make allowances for this so that those who are slower to understand do not feel discouraged or stressed.
- **self-confidence:** When dealing with often troubled or unmotivated students, you need to feel confident in yourself and your abilities to show others that they need to follow your guidance and listen to your advice.

- **teamworking:** If you work in any educational institution, you will be teaching alongside colleagues, with the same objectives in common. Effective teamwork among teachers can help turn round a school that is struggling.
- **interpersonal skills:** Since most, if not all, roles in teaching involve working in teams of teachers and dealing with many students of different ages, you need to be comfortable working with, and relating to, other people.
- **empathy and sympathy:** As a teacher you will be meeting people from all walks of life, some of whom could be experiencing potentially traumatic times at home. This could have an impact on their studies and a sensitive listener is often required to ensure their needs are met and heard.
- **written communication:** An ability to make yourself clearly understood in words, whether on a school report, an interactive whiteboard or on report cards, is as essential as the verbal communication skills required in the classroom.
- **organisational skills:** As with most jobs these days, teaching involves juggling various responsibilities and tasks at once, from preparing for classes, to marking homework, to dealing with detentions, to running parent evenings.

A CAREER IN TEACHING?

- When you think of your future, what kind of environment do you see yourself working in, eg in an office, outdoors, 9am to 5pm, relaxed or high-pressured?
- What are your favourite hobbies outside school?
- What is it about them you enjoy, eg performing in front of an audience? Do you enjoy giving information to others who do not know much about your topic of interest?
- What are your favourite subjects in school and what is it about them that you enjoy most, eg working together to put on a play or finding out as much as possible about a subject that really interests you?
- What do you dislike about the other subjects you're studying?
- If you've had any work experience, which aspects have you most enjoyed?

Professional bodies

Professional bodies are responsible for overseeing a particular profession or career area, ensuring that people who work in the area are fully trained and meet ethical guidelines. Professional bodies may be known as institutions, societies and associations. They generally have regulatory roles: they make sure that members of the profession are able to work successfully in their jobs without endangering lives or abusing their position.

Professional bodies are often involved in training and career development, so courses and workplace training may have to follow the body's guidelines. In order to be fully qualified and licensed to work in your profession of choice, you will have to follow the professional training route. In many areas of work, completion of the professional training results in gaining chartered status – and the addition of some extra letters after your name. Other institutions may award other types of certification once certain criteria have been met. Chartered or certified members will usually need to take further courses and training to ensure their skills are kept up to date.

WHAT PROFESSIONAL BODIES ARE THERE?

Not all career areas have professional bodies. Those jobs that require extensive learning and training are likely to have bodies with a regulatory focus. This includes careers such as engineering, law, construction, health and finance. If you want to work in one of these areas, it's important to make sure your degree course is accredited by the professional body – otherwise you may have to undertake further study or training later on.

Other bodies may play more of a supportive role, looking after the interests of people who work in the sector. This includes journalism, management and arts-based careers. Professional bodies may also be learned bodies, providing opportunities for further learning and promoting the development of knowledge in the field.

CAN I JOIN AS A STUDENT?

Many professional bodies offer student membership – sometimes free or for reduced fees. Membership can be extremely valuable as a source of advice, information and resources. You'll have the opportunity to meet other students in the field, as well as experienced professionals. It will also look good on your CV, when you come to apply for jobs.

See below for a selection of professional bodies and associations in teaching and education.

General Teaching Council for England (GTCE)
This organisation ceased to operate on 31 March 2012. Visit **www.gtce.org.uk** for information about the transfer of the GTCE's responsibilities.

General Teaching Council for Northern Ireland (GTCNI)
www.gtcni.org.uk

General Teaching Council for Scotland (GTCNS)
www.gtcs.org.uk

General Teaching Council for Wales (GTCW)
www.gtcw.org.uk

The Higher Education Academy
www.heacademy.ac.uk

Association for the Study of Primary Education (ASPE)
www.aspe-uk.eu

British Association for Early Childhood Education (Early Education)
www.early-education.org.uk

British Association of Teachers of the Deaf (BATOD)
www.batod.org.uk

The College of Teachers
www.collegeofteachers.ac.uk

Institute for Outdoor Learning
www.outdoor-learning.org/

National Association for Able Children in Education (NACE)
www.nace.co.uk

National Association for Primary Education (NAPE)
www.nape.org.uk

National Association for Special Educational Needs (NASEN)
www.nasen.org.uk

National Association of Teachers of Travellers and other Professionals (NATT+)
www.natt.org.uk

Graduate destinations

Teaching and Education
HESA Destination of Leavers of Higher Education Survey

Each year, comprehensive statistics are collected on what graduates are doing six months after they complete their course. The survey is co-ordinated by the Higher Education Statistics Agency (HESA) and provides information about how many graduates move into employment (and what type of career) or further study and how many are believed to be unemployed.

The full results across all subject areas are published by the Higher Education Careers Service Unit (HECSU) and the Association of Graduate Careers Advisory Services (AGCAS) in *What Do Graduates Do?*, which is available from **www.ucasbooks.com**.

	From undergraduate courses	From postgraduate courses
In UK employment	72.0%	83.7%
In overseas employment	0.8%	0.8%
Working and studying	8.0%	5.9%
Studying in the UK for a higher degree	1.1%	0.7%
Studying in the UK for a teaching qualification	5.1%	0.1%
Undertaking other further study or training in the UK	2.4%	0.2%
Undertaking other further study or training overseas	0.0%	0.0%
Not available for employment, study or training	2.4%	1.4%
Assumed to be unemployed	4.3%	3.4%
Other	3.9%	3.8%

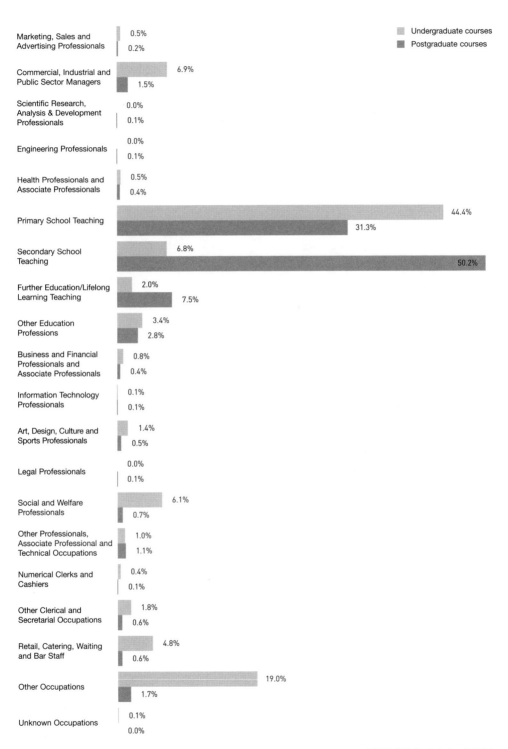

Marketing, Sales and Advertising Professionals — Undergraduate courses 0.5%, Postgraduate courses 0.2%

Commercial, Industrial and Public Sector Managers — 6.9%, 1.5%

Scientific Research, Analysis & Development Professionals — 0.0%, 0.1%

Engineering Professionals — 0.0%, 0.1%

Health Professionals and Associate Professionals — 0.5%, 0.4%

Primary School Teaching — 44.4%, 31.3%

Secondary School Teaching — 6.8%, 50.2%

Further Education/Lifelong Learning Teaching — 2.0%, 7.5%

Other Education Professions — 3.4%, 2.8%

Business and Financial Professionals and Associate Professionals — 0.8%, 0.4%

Information Technology Professionals — 0.1%, 0.1%

Art, Design, Culture and Sports Professionals — 1.4%, 0.5%

Legal Professionals — 0.0%, 0.1%

Social and Welfare Professionals — 6.1%, 0.7%

Other Professionals, Associate Professional and Technical Occupations — 1.0%, 1.1%

Numerical Clerks and Cashiers — 0.4%, 0.1%

Other Clerical and Secretarial Occupations — 1.8%, 0.6%

Retail, Catering, Waiting and Bar Staff — 4.8%, 0.6%

Other Occupations — 19.0%, 1.7%

Unknown Occupations — 0.1%, 0.0%

Legend: ▢ Undergraduate courses ◼ Postgraduate courses

Reproduced with the kind permission of HECSU/AGCAS, *What Do Graduates Do? 2011*.
All data from the HESA Destinations of Leavers from Higher Education Survey 2009/10

Case studies

HEAR IT FROM THE EXPERTS

Still not sure whether you want to work in teaching? Perhaps you don't know if working with younger children is your cup of tea or whether life as a secondary school teacher takes your fancy. Read the following profiles to see where the world of work has taken recent graduates.

Primary school teacher

Northamptonshire County Council

CHARLOTTE JOHNSON

Route into primary teaching:
A level maths and ICT, BTEC Level 3 music performance (2007); BEd primary education, University of Bedfordshire (2011)

WHY PRIMARY TEACHING?

For my Year 11 work experience I spent two weeks in a primary school as a teaching assistant and by the end of the placement I knew I wanted to be a classroom teacher. I have always wanted to work with young children, so primary was the obvious level for me.

HOW DID YOU GET WHERE YOU ARE TODAY?

In addition to my Year 11 work placement I have helped out in my local primary school and have experience as a private tutor.

My four-year teaching degree included placements in five schools, from a small rural village school to a large inner city primary and with a variety of age ranges. By the end of the course I had a good idea of the type of school that would suit me best, and that I preferred to teach Year 2 (six to seven year-olds) upwards, as this was the age group I felt most comfortable with.

In the first year of the course we were introduced to the primary curriculum subjects and in the second year had the chance to select one as a specialist subject. This is particularly useful when applying for jobs, to show you could progress to lead teacher for this subject area.

From January of my final year I started to apply for teaching posts. I applied for 20 jobs, got four interviews and was successful in gaining my current job two weeks before graduation. During the summer I went into the school a few times to meet the other staff before starting my NQT (newly qualified teacher) year in September.

WHAT DOES YOUR JOB INVOLVE?

I teach a class of Year 3 and Year 4 pupils (seven to nine year-olds) in a large town-based school. As I work in a team with other teachers in the same year group we are able to support each other and share ideas. Responsibilities also include playground duty and leading assemblies. I start work at around 8am (school officially starts at 9am) and don't usually leave until 5pm (the school day ends at 3.20pm) and then have preparation work to do at home. As a NQT I get two half days of planning time during each school week (all teachers get at least one half day a week).

Behaviour management is a major part of the job; I have learnt to change my approach and teaching style continually to maintain students' interest. The school has paid for me to go on professional development courses on behaviour management led by experienced teachers. It has been invaluable to get their tips!

WHAT HAS BEEN YOUR BIGGEST CHALLENGE?

Getting this job! Finding my first post was competitive and during the process I learnt how necessary it was to sell myself to employers and to target the personal statement part of my applications to each individual employer.

AND THE BEST BITS?

I love interacting with the children and have some real characters in my class! I love the 'light bulb moment' when something clicks for a child or when I hear them talking enthusiastically in the playground about one of my lessons they have enjoyed – this makes all the hard work worthwhile.

CHARLOTTE'S TOP TIPS

Get lots of class-based work experience before you go to university: make sure it is something you definitely want to do before opting for a teaching degree. Never be afraid to ask for help and advice from more experienced teachers.

English teacher

City of Edinburgh Council

CLAIRE CHALMERS

Route into secondary teaching:

Advanced Highers – English, history, religious moral and philosophical studies (2003); BA English language and literature, University of Oxford (2006); professional graduate diploma in education (PGDE) secondary in English, University of Edinburgh (2009)

WHY TEACHING?

I enjoyed school and learning and wanted a people-based job. A range of work experience in education, youth work and the community helped me consider where I would best be suited and I eventually decided to train to be a teacher. I chose secondary teaching because I could focus on one subject; I am passionate about sharing my love of English and literature.

HOW DID YOU GET WHERE YOU ARE TODAY?

In my sixth year at school I assisted with junior classes and at university I helped on access programme summer schools. I also gained experience at an asylum seeker centre and in a local school. After university I was definitely interested in teaching but not sure if I was confident enough to go straight on to a teaching course as I felt I needed time to develop my interpersonal skills. I did two six-month placements as a volunteer with Project Scotland, in learning development work and youth work. I taught English as a foreign language and went back to my old school to spend some time in the English department.

I studied for a postgraduate diploma in education (PGDE) where the focus was on gaining lots of classroom experience in a supportive environment. The course also included practical workshops on my specialist subject, English, understanding the curriculum, ways to deliver it and then putting this into practice on placement.

WHAT DOES YOUR JOB INVOLVE?

I teach English to 12 to 18 year olds. I teach every year group in the school and enjoy having to adapt how I present my subject to suit each age group. It keeps the job interesting and challenging but does mean lots of planning! It is also fascinating to see young people at different stages in their development.

I teach for about 22 hours a week with one or two free periods each day. The job goes well beyond the standard working week with marking, extra-curricular activities and study support groups to run and the occasional trip or residential week. Time outside the classroom can be one of the most enjoyable parts of the job allowing you to develop your relationships with pupils further. I enjoy working closely with school support staff such as classroom assistants, learning support staff and guidance staff to ensure an integrated approach to student welfare.

WHAT HAS BEEN YOUR BIGGEST CHALLENGE?

It takes time to become a good teacher; I have had to be realistic about what I can achieve and be prepared to keep learning and developing. You need to be both flexible and resilient. Finding a healthy work-life balance is also challenging: it is important to be able to switch off from teaching.

AND THE BEST BITS?

I love working with young people and feel privileged to be in a position where I can help them develop and improve their lives. I like that I can keep on learning and developing as well as helping others to learn.

CLAIRE'S TOP TIPS

Speak to as many teachers and get into as many classrooms as you can to see how the profession works and whether you could fit in. Make the most of your time on teaching placements; this is the best opportunity to try techniques out in a supportive atmosphere. Be prepared to accept feedback and advice and then act on this - it is how you will improve.

Head of design and technology

Leicestershire County Council

DANIEL MARKHAM

Route into secondary teaching:
A levels – product design, maths, PE (2006); BA secondary design and technology education, Nottingham Trent University (2009)

WHY TEACHING?

In the sixth form I was inspired by my design and technology teacher and started thinking about teaching as a career. I decided to do a ski instructor qualification and then taught at the local dry-ski slope. I enjoyed helping people learn and decided on secondary teaching because I like the rapport you can have with older children.

HOW DID YOU GET WHERE YOU ARE TODAY?

My degree covered the full range of design areas from craft skills to graphics. As a result I qualified as a versatile teacher able to apply for a range of teaching jobs. The teaching practice element of the course was particularly valuable, with an excellent support network, tutors from the university visited us on placement and we were also supported by an ITT team mentor from the placement school.

After graduation my first job was to teach GCSE resistant materials at my current school. This led to a position as year house manager in my second year of teaching (a pastoral role where I was responsible for 250 students and eight staff). In my third year I was promoted to my current role of head of faculty. I am now responsible for 1,200 students studying design and technology and 23 staff. It has been a rapid but very satisfying career progression.

WHAT DOES YOUR JOB INVOLVE?

Ashby School is an Upper School with Year 10 to Year 13 pupils (aged 14 to 18). I teach BTEC First Diploma in Construction, GCSE resistant materials and A level product design. This involves teaching every year group and a wide range of abilities, including many children with special educational needs and English as an additional language (EAL).

On a daily basis I teach an average of four lessons with one free period. Like all teachers I get free periods for planning and as a head of faculty I get additional free time for management responsibilities. These include staff management, liaison with parents, work with feeder schools, monitoring assessment across the faculty, checking reports and examination entries and data analysis of results.

I'm in school from 7.30am and leave when everything is done, around 6.30pm. I try not to take any work home.

WHAT HAS BEEN YOUR BIGGEST CHALLENGE?

Engaging all of the students all of the time! I teach children with a range of special educational needs and continually having to show that all students are progressing at an appropriate pace is challenging.

Exam syllabuses change continually so it is difficult to keep up with preparation of new resources. We overcome this by working in a team to divide the extra workload equally. Support is ongoing for all teachers with staff INSET days and training sessions in faculty meetings.

AND THE BEST BITS?

Definitely being thanked by students for the help you have given them – particularly on exam results days. I am ambitious and I would like to work my way up to being a headteacher. I am attracted by the challenge of being responsible for a large cohort of students.

DANIEL'S TOP TIPS

Don't go into teaching unless you are passionate about it – this would be a very stressful job if your heart was not in it! If you want to progress, be proactive in your first few years of teaching and go out of your way to take on additional responsibilities to benefit the school and students – as well as being rewarding this is how you can open up potential management opportunities.

Trainee secondary teacher

JONATHAN WHYBROW

Route into secondary teaching:

AS engineering (2006), A level maths, physics, chemistry, AS further maths (2007); MEng electronic engineering and cybernetics, University of Reading (2011); PGCE secondary science, University of Reading (graduating 2012)

WHY TEACHING?

By the end of my third year at university I had decided that engineering wasn't the right career direction for me and I wanted to use my knowledge of science in a more people-centred job. I tested out an interest in teaching by doing three weeks of work experience in a secondary school, observing lessons. Talking to the staff was very useful as they were very honest about both the perks and downsides of teaching! Four months later I returned to the same school to spend a few more days observing lessons and then decided to apply for a postgraduate certificate in education (PGCE) initial teacher training course.

TELL US ABOUT YOUR PGCE

I am on a PGCE secondary specialising in teaching physics. It is a highly interactive course with students from various ages and backgrounds and a range of experiences working together and supporting each other. There is a steep learning curve and it is intensive with ups and downs (especially going out on school placements) but rapid progress can be made.

The first teaching placement involved observing lessons for two days a week for four weeks before a five-week block of an increasing teaching timetable. I am currently on my second placement which is full-time for 11 weeks in a different and contrasting school. The placements are arranged by the course tutors to give a range of experiences and to fit your own developmental needs and goals.

WHAT DOES YOUR WORK PLACEMENT INVOLVE?

I teach about 12 lessons a week. I prepare for lessons, teach, mark and give feedback to pupils. I have similar responsibilities to a permanent teacher but with a reduced timetable. You are given space to find out about yourself and your teaching style (including making mistakes and learning from them!) but at the same time you are given plenty of support if you ask for it.

I'm at school from 8am to 4pm and then do about four hours' lesson preparation a night, but try to keep my weekends free. I have already become more efficient at planning lessons.

The school provides weekly professional studies sessions for trainee teachers (there are six of us!), covering topics such as report writing, working with parents, pupil assessment and applying for teaching jobs. The support network is very good; every trainee teacher has a mentor at the school and university tutors come into school to observe us and give feedback.

WHAT HAS BEEN THE TOUGHEST CHALLENGE?

Having a presence in the classroom! I have had to work hard at establishing my own teaching style. This can be achieved by getting feedback from other teachers on how you are coming across and reflecting on your own performance. Observing other teachers and seeing what works for them and then trying out these strategies for yourself is also part of the learning process.

AND THE BEST BITS?

Definitely when a lesson goes well, the pupils have enjoyed it and are enthusiastic about what they have learnt. Building up a working relationship with pupils is also enjoyable. It is great to be in the same school with other trainee teachers; we can share experiences and support and encourage each other.

JONATHAN'S TOP TIPS

Contact local schools to shadow teachers to see both whether teaching is for you and to get valuable experience for your teacher training application. On placement learn how to manage your time well – it is important to find a good work-life balance.

Pre-kindergarten teacher in Cambodia

KATY HELEN

Route into early years teaching:

A levels – business studies, IT, biology (2003); BA in primary education with QTS, Birmingham City University (2010)

WHY EARLY YEARS TEACHING?

I wanted a career where I could make a real difference to people's lives – teaching seemed like the natural choice. I decided on early years teaching because I believe it is the most important time of a child's personal, social, emotional and academic life, when foundations can be laid down for the future.

HOW DID YOU GET WHERE YOU ARE TODAY?

I decided to study for a teaching degree, specialising in early years. During the summer of the third year of my course I volunteered as an English teacher at an orphanage in Cambodia. It was through this work that I secured a job at the International School of Siem Reap (ISSR) after graduation.

At ISSR my role was reception teacher and early years co-ordinator. When I first arrived at the school, the nursery and reception 1 classrooms were very formal learning environments. I managed to convince the school of the importance of learning through play, spent a week getting resources together and now each classroom has a play-based area, role play area and home corner. Seeing the children's faces when they saw it for the first time was a very special moment.

After a year I moved to my current job as a pre-kindergarten teacher for a non-governmental organisation. The aims of the school are to offer free education to local children to prepare them for entry to respected institutions in the US and other developed countries. I decided to work for an NGO because I felt I could make a real difference to the lives of children who without the school would most likely not receive an education. They have a real thirst for knowledge and even at the age of four are very appreciative of the opportunity they have been given.

WHAT DOES YOUR JOB INVOLVE?

I teach a class of 30 Cambodian children. When they start at the school they have no English and the school aims to give them a level of comprehension and oral abilities that allows them to access the curriculum. I teach reading language arts (sounds and letters, reading and responding and writing) and maths and work closely with a Khmer teacher on the implementation of Khmer language arts, which is taught daily for one hour.

I have responsibilities for planning, working with the early years and Key Stage 1 team, and organising extra-curricular activities and academic excursions.

WHAT HAS BEEN YOUR BIGGEST CHALLENGE?

Before coming to Cambodia I had limited experience of teaching English as an additional language (EAL). At ISSR the children came from many different countries, including Italy, France, Korea, Vietnam and Cambodia, and with only a basic level of English, so this was a major challenge! While at ISSR I took time to learn about EAL and I was then able to apply and build on this in my current school. My job now includes professional development on working with EAL students.

AND THE BEST BITS?

Being part of a child's life and watching them develop is invaluable. It could be something as simple as a child who has never initiated communication in English before asking me a question in English – it is these moments I treasure.

KATY'S TOP TIPS

Teaching for me is a very rewarding career. If you are somebody who has a natural desire to work with children and make a difference, this is the career for you – but be prepared to work hard.

Entry routes

Routes to qualification

If you want to pursue a career in teaching, you need to decide on the best way to achieve the requisite Qualified Teacher Status (QTS). Read on to find out more.

YOUR OPTIONS

In England, Wales and Northern Ireland, you are legally required to have Qualified Teacher Status (QTS) to teach pupils aged 4 to 16 in state-maintained schools. Teachers working in independent schools do not need to have QTS, but most do. Once awarded, you have QTS for life, whether you stay in teaching or not. To gain QTS, you need to complete a suitable teacher training course, of which there are options to suit everyone.

To teach in Scotland you need to obtain the Teaching Qualification (TQ) by successfully completing an Initial Teacher Education (ITE) course.

INITIAL TEACHER TRAINING (ITT)

Initial teacher training courses aim to get you up to speed quickly so that when you first set foot in the classroom, you will be thoroughly prepared.

ITT involves completion of a recognised teaching qualification such as a PGCE (Professional or Postgraduate Certificate in Education), the most popular route by far, or a BEd (Bachelor of Education). If you gain QTS and are awarded one of the recognised qualifications you will be known as an NQT (Newly Qualified Teacher) until you have finished your induction programme. If you will be undertaking your ITT in England, you will also need to complete skills tests in literacy, numeracy, and information and communication technology (ICT) to qualify for QTS. These tests are normally taken at the end of the ITT period.

If you gain QTS in Wales, Scotland or Northern Ireland, you will not be required to undertake the skills tests in order to take up teaching posts in England.

Initial teacher training courses are normally split between primary or secondary levels, and students train to teach at least two Key Stages. Primary school teachers teach all subjects in the National Curriculum and specialise in a particular area, whereas secondary school teachers train in just one or two subjects.

UNDERGRADUATE OPTIONS

You can train to be a teacher while undertaking a degree, either a Bachelor of Education (BEd) or a Bachelor of Arts (BA) or Bachelor of Science (BSc) with QTS. Course content can vary depending on where you study but you will receive QTS at the end, as well as your degree, no matter what university awards it. A BEd degree tends to be more popular with students who are interested in teaching primary school children but it is just as valid for those who want to become a secondary school teacher. A BA or BSc degree may also include QTS and therefore qualify graduates to teach.

Course duration

Courses normally last three or four years full time or four to six years part time and are available at universities and colleges throughout the UK. If you have undergraduate credits from a previous course of study, you may be able to complete the course in two years instead.

Entry requirements

These vary between courses but a minimum of two A levels or their equivalent is normally essential. Check out the exact requirements with individual course providers. More generally, teachers need to have attained GCSEs at grade C in English and mathematics or equivalent qualifications or have the required knowledge of both subjects to obtain this level of qualification. If you are interested in teaching primary or Key Stages 2 or 3 (ages 7 to 14) you also need to have a GCSE at grade C in a science subject or an equivalent qualification or the knowledge of science required to obtain this level of qualification.

When and how to apply

Applications must be made through UCAS. For courses starting in September or October, you should apply between September and January of the preceding year. You can also defer your entry for a year if you wish.

POSTGRADUATE OPTIONS

If you want to study for a degree in another subject at undergraduate level, such as a modern language, a science or an arts subject, you can still become a teacher, as long as you take a recognised vocational teaching qualification.

PROFESSIONAL GRADUATE/POSTGRADUATE CERTIFICATE IN EDUCATION (PGCE)

PGCEs mainly focus on developing your teaching skills, rather than on the subject you want to teach. Therefore, you are expected to have a thorough understanding of your chosen subject(s) at degree level before you start training.

Course duration

PGCEs normally last for one year on a full-time basis or two years part time and are available at universities and colleges throughout the UK. You can also study for a PGCE through distance learning or in a school by completing a programme of school-centred initial teacher training (SCITT).

Entry requirements

Applicants must have an undergraduate degree or an equivalent recognised qualification. If your degree subject is not closely linked to the subject you want to teach, you could improve your chances of gaining a place on a course by undertaking a pre-training course to increase your knowledge of the subject.

More generally, you need a good educational standard, with at least a GCSE at grade C in English and mathematics (or equivalent qualifications), or you need to have the knowledge of both subjects required to obtain this level of qualification. If you want to teach primary or Key Stages 2 and 3 (ages 7 to 14) you also need to have achieved a GCSE at grade C or an equivalent qualification in a science subject or have the knowledge of science required to obtain this level of qualification.

When and how to apply

Most PGCE applications are made through the Graduate Teacher Training Registry (GTTR), but some ITT providers want you to approach them directly. For Key Stages 2 and 3, and secondary courses, you can apply to up to four different providers, or two providers for primary courses, in order of preference.

You make your GTTR application online at **www.gttr.ac.uk**.

The GTTR accepts applications from early October to the end of June for courses starting in the following September or October. However, be warned that courses in primary teaching, and secondary physical education and history teaching are extremely popular and competition for places is tough. Therefore, if you want to be considered by your first-choice training provider it is best to apply by the end of November in the year prior to starting your training.

SCHOOL-CENTRED INITIAL TEACHER TRAINING (SCITT)

(There are no SCITTs in Wales, Scotland or Northern Ireland)

If you want to study a degree in a non-education-related subject and then do your training in a school environment, then school-centred initial teacher training (SCITT) could be for you. SCITT programmes ensure that you spend more time training in the classroom, putting theory you learn into practice, and giving you the confidence you need to stand up in front of students. SCITT programmes are designed and delivered by groups of neighbouring schools and colleges. Experienced, practising teachers carry out the training and mentor trainee teachers. All SCITT courses lead to Qualified Teacher Status (QTS) and many, though not all, will also give you the Professional or Postgraduate Certificate in Education (PGCE), validated by a higher education institution.

Course duration

SCITT courses last for one academic year and run from September to June. Some do start earlier, such as The National SCITT in Outstanding Primary Schools , which begins in August.

Groups of schools and colleges throughout England run SCITT courses, covering primary, middle years (ages 7 to 14) and the range of secondary subjects. Normally you will be based in one school in the consortium in which you are training, but will probably also undertake teaching practice at other schools within the group.

Entry requirements

As with PGCEs, you will need a UK degree or equivalent, in a subject related to the area you want to teach in school. Pre-training courses are available if you cannot offer your intended subject at a high enough level.

More generally, you will need a good standard of education, including a grade C or higher in GCSE English and mathematics, and a grade C or higher in GCSE science if you want to teach primary or Key Stage 2 and 3 (ages 7 to 14). Equivalent qualifications or the subject knowledge required to obtain this level of qualification are also acceptable.

When and how to apply

Normally you will need to apply through the Graduate Teacher Training Registry (GTTR), although some SCITT providers ask for direct applications; check with the providers. You make your GTTR application online at **www.gttr.ac.uk**. For middle years (ages 7 to 14) and secondary courses you can apply to up to four different providers, or two providers for primary courses in order of preference. Since SCITT courses follow the normal academic year, you need to apply for a place the year before you intend to start your September or October training.

Go to the GTTR website for full details of courses and how to apply.

TEACH FIRST

Teach First is a programme run by an independent charity. It allows top graduates to spend two years working in challenging primary and secondary schools in several regions of England, in order to qualify as a teacher. The scheme is suitable for high-flying graduates who might not have thought of a career in teaching or for those who are not completely sure about having a long-term career in this area. Graduates will achieve QTS at the end of the scheme.

Course duration and location

Teach First lasts for two years and is limited in location to London, the East and West Midlands, Yorkshire and Humber, the North East and the North West.

Entry requirements

You must be a high calibre graduate, with sound academic ability and proof of strong leadership and communication skills. You can apply straight from university or with a number of years' working experience, as long as you have a good first degree.

Entry requirements are very strict and include: a minimum 2:1 classification in your undergraduate degree; 300 UCAS Tariff points (equivalent to BBB at A level); and grade C or above in GCSE (or equivalent) English and mathematics.

Evidence of high levels of competency in areas such as leadership, teamwork, resilience, critical thinking, communication skills, initiative and creativity, as well as respect, humility and empathy are also desirable, if not essential.

Your degree subject is not important, as long as at least 40 per cent of it relates to a National Curriculum subject.

When and how to apply

You must submit an application online through **http://graduates.teachfirst.org.uk**. If you are successful, you will be invited to attend a challenging day-long assessment at a centre in London.

Teach First operates a rolling recruitment process. For further details about the application process and deadlines go to **http://graduates.teachfirst.org.uk**.

Two-year full-time subject conversion PGCE courses

Some ITT providers in England offer PGCE courses lasting two academic years, which provide additional support in certain subjects and professional training.

- The courses are designed to enable graduates in a wide range of disciplines to train to be specialist teachers in the secondary age range, particularly in design and technology, mathematics, modern languages and science.
- The content of your undergraduate degree must include at least one year of full-time higher education study (or equivalent) relevant to the subject specialism chosen for the PGCE course.
- The two-year full-time study period involves intensive study of the subject at higher education level. This study will provide professional training and may also lead to a diploma in the subject concerned.

You must contact the ITT providers direct to obtain full details about these courses. You should also find out if the qualifications you hold are appropriate for the subject conversion course you want to study.

Subject knowledge enhancement courses

Some ITT providers in England run subject knowledge enhancement courses (SKEs) for applicants who need to increase or revise their knowledge of a subject before beginning teacher training. Taking a course will help you to fill the specific gaps in your knowledge, especially where that might be difficult to accomplish on your own.

If a training provider thinks you need to do an SKE course before you begin your postgraduate degree, they will make an offer conditional on your completing a specified course. Not all training providers offer SKEs, so they may refer you to a course run by another institution in the same region. Applications for an SKE are made directly to the course provider.

Mathematics, physics and chemistry make up the majority of SKE courses, but courses are also offered in other subjects including design and technology, information and communications technology, music, religious education and modern languages. Courses vary in length from two weeks to a year, depending on individual needs, and learning may be offered on a full- or part-time basis, and in a variety of settings. Training bursaries may be available to assist with living costs.

TEACHER TRAINING ROUTES IN ENGLAND AND WALES

SCHEME	WHO'S IT FOR?	INFORMATION
Undergraduate degree	School leavers or mature candidates with no degree	• Leads to a BA, BEd or BSc – all with QTS • Most full-time courses last 3 or 4 years • The 2-year course is for those who have already completed a qualification amounting to part of a degree • Traditionally more popular with primary teachers as the extended training period provides more time to learn the full range of national curriculum subjects they have to teach
Professional Graduate/Postgraduate Certificate in Education (PGCE)	Graduates	• Most popular route into teaching • Can be taken through an HE institution or through a SCITT (see below) • Courses usually last one year full time or two years part time • 2-year full-time courses are available in some subjects to those who have completed their degree in a subject other than that in which they are undertaking their degree • There are more flexible routes available, including for individuals with overseas or independent experience
School-centred initial teacher training (SCITT)	For graduates – ideally those with some prior teaching experience	• Training provided by a consortium of schools and education providers in England, who share responsibility for training. There are no SCITTS elsewhere in the UK • All trainees will be awarded QTS, though not all SCITT providers offer a full PGCE

Graduate teacher programme (GTP)	For people who want to change to a teaching career and need to keep earning while they train. Ideally applicants should have prior teaching experience, either in schools or with young people.	• Applicants are employed by a school as an unqualified teacher and undertake on-the-job training to attain QTS.
		They must:
		  • have a UK degree
		  • find a school that will employ them as an unqualified teacher, with a view to completing a Graduate Teacher Programme

Registered teacher programme (RTP)		• Similar to the GTP except that applicants who do not hold a full degree must have successfully completed two years of higher education (eg an HND) and must go on to complete a degree while they train • Places are very limited • Only available in England

For more information on options, contact the Teaching Agency on 0800 389 2500 (0800 085 0971 for Welsh speakers) or visit **www.education.gov.uk/get-into-teaching/teacher-training-options.aspx**.

APPLICATIONS		DURATION		AMOUNT OF TEACHING PRACTICE
WHERE	WHEN BY	FULL-TIME	PART-TIME	
UCAS **www.ucas.com** for applications to undergraduate degree courses	▪ Applications must reach UCAS by 15 January to guarantee consideration. All applications received after 30 June go directly into Clearing	3–4 years	4–6 years	4-year course: 32 weeks 3-year course: 24 weeks
The Graduate Teacher Training Registry (GTTR) **www.gttr.ac.uk** for applications to most Professional Graduate/ Postgraduate Certificate in Education (PGCE) courses. A few course providers recruit direct	▪ Applications accepted by the GTTR from early October for courses that start in September of the following year ▪ Applications for primary courses must reach the GTTR by 1 December to guarantee that they are sent to the first choice ITT provider ▪ For applications to middle years (Key Stages 2/3), secondary and post-compulsory education courses there is no early deadline for receipt at the GTTR to guarantee that applications are sent to the first choice ITT provider. You should apply early because popular courses fill up quickly	1 or 2 years	2 years	Primary: 18 weeks Secondary: 24 weeks (usually in two schools)
Apply through the GTTR (information as above) or direct to a small number of SCITT consortia.	Information for the GTTR as above, if applying directly to a SCITT, check the deadline with the individual course provider	1 year	N/A	School-based for 90% of the time
Through an employment-based initial teacher training provider (EBITT) in England. In Wales employment-based schemes are administered by the Welsh Assembly Government. For details of the GTP in England, call the Teaching Information Line on 0800 389 2500 (or 0800 085 0971 for Welsh speakers).	▪ Year-round applications	12 months (minimum 3 months) 24 months (minimum 12 months)	N/A	School-based

Introduction to induction

All newly qualified teachers (NQTs) must successfully complete a 12-month induction period to qualify legally to teach in state schools in England and Wales. Your induction year will normally begin with your first paid teaching job as long as your employment is long enough to cover the induction period.

You can undertake an induction in nearly all state schools, apart from pupil referral units (PRUs) and those on special measures. You can do your induction in an independent school but it must have an 'appropriate body', such as a local authority or an Independent Schools Council Teacher Induction Panel (ISCTIP) to oversee the induction period. In Wales, your induction can also be undertaken in an FE college, but they must have an 'appropriate body' to oversee the induction period.

WHY DO IT?

The whole purpose of induction is to develop the skills you acquired during training to gain further experience and to meet a number of 'core standards', which are professional standards to help guide your development and career as a teacher. When you have finished your year-long induction period, you should be able to teach confidently and competently in any school. During the year you will have lots of support and feedback when you have your lessons observed and when observing your more experienced colleagues. The school(s) where you do your induction will work with your local authority (LA) to ensure that you receive all the training and help you need and will draw up a personal programme for you with your induction tutor.

WHEN TO DO IT

You are not subject to a strict time limit between getting your teaching qualification and undertaking your induction year but it's normally good to apply for a place soon after your course as everything you have learned will still be fresh in your mind. In Wales, there is no limit on when you have to complete your induction period, but there is a limit on the amount of short-term supply teaching that you can do and that limit is five years from the date you gain your QTS. The flexibility of the programme means you can choose where and when you want to complete the three school terms, even to the point where you can do each term in a different school.

WHAT YOU WILL GET

All newly qualified teachers are entitled to:

- a 10% reduction in their timetable compared to other staff
- a personal induction tutor who will be an experienced teacher
- a programme of support and activities designed especially for them to help them meet their personal aims and standards
- support in compiling their career entry and development profile (CEDP), which acts as a bridge between training and continuing professional development (CPD) after induction
- half-termly observations with both oral and written feedback
- agreed objectives that are reviewed every half term
- a formal assessment meeting and report at the end of each term.

In Wales, teachers who successfully complete their induction period are entitled to a further two years of early professional development (EPD) funding.

THE SUPPORT YOU WILL RECEIVE

No matter how much training and teaching you are given, nothing can completely prepare you for the classroom! However, your induction year will enable you to start developing your own teaching style. NQTs are not left alone to fend for themselves, nor are they expected to know everything under the sun, so don't worry about asking your induction tutor for help as and when you need it. You'll also find that other teachers in your school(s) will be more than happy to help, as will your teaching union and your LA.

Teaching in Scotland and Northern Ireland

Requirements for becoming a teacher in Scotland and Northern Ireland are slightly different from those in England and Wales. The following information should get you started.

SCOTLAND

The Scottish education system

Scotland's education system differs to that in the rest of the UK, as they do not have a National Curriculum or Key Stages. The 'Curriculum for Excellence' (**www.ltscotland.org.uk/curriculumforexcellence**) was introduced in 2009/10, applying to children from age 3 to 18. Its emphasis is on developing 'four capacities', so that each child can be a successful learner, confident individual, responsible citizen and effective contributor.

Getting into teaching in Scotland

If you decide to study in Scotland there are three types of initial teaching education (ITE) on offer:

- **Bachelor of Education (BEd)** – a four-year undergraduate course that qualifies students to become primary teachers.

- **Professional Graduate Diploma in Education (PGDE)** – a one-year full-time postgraduate course that qualifies people who already hold a degree in a related subject to become either primary or secondary school teachers. There are also some opportunities to do part-time or distance learning PGDE courses.

- **Combined (or concurrent) degree** – an undergraduate degree programme that allows students to study a subject and an initial teacher education programme at the same time.

Learning to teach in Scotland

Seven Scottish universities currently offer initial teacher education programmes. All eligible newly qualified teachers (also known as probationer teachers) will be offered a one-year training post in Scotland – this teacher induction scheme is designed to give probationer teachers the best possible start to their career, although it is not necessary to do the scheme to complete the probationary period.

Registration

Registration with the General Teaching Council Scotland (GTCS) is required in order to teach in any local authority nursery, primary, secondary and special school. Most independent schools will also require teachers to be registered. Newly qualified teachers are provisionally registered with the GTCS until they meet the standard for full registration.

If you choose to train as a teacher outside Scotland, you can still apply for registration with the GTCS providing you meet all the eligibility requirements. See **www.gtcs.org.uk** for more information.

Useful contacts

Learning Directorate
The Scottish Government
Victoria Quay
Edinburgh EH6 6QQ
t: 0131 556 8400
e: ceu@scotland.gsi.gov.uk

General Teaching Council for Scotland
Clerwood House
96 Clermiston Road
Edinburgh EH12 6UT
t: 0131 314 6000
e: gtcs@gtcs.org.uk
www.gtcs.org.uk

Education Scotland
The Optima
58 Robertson Street
Glasgow G2 8DU
t: 08700 100 297
e: enquiries@educationscotland.gov.uk
www.educationscotland.gov.uk
www.teachinginscotland.com
www.scotland.gov.uk/topics/education/

NORTHERN IRELAND

The education system in Northern Ireland

In Northern Ireland there are 12 years of compulsory education, beginning at age four, which are divided into five Key Stages. The curriculum is set out in seven areas of learning: languages and literacy; mathematics and numeracy; the arts; the world around us; personal development and mutual understanding; physical education; and religious education.

Getting into teaching in Northern Ireland

In Northern Ireland there are three stages to teacher education: initial, induction and early professional development (EPD). On completion of an initial teacher training course you must obtain eligibility to teach status, which is granted by the Department of Education. You will then participate in a three-year professional development programme consisting of a one-year induction and two years of EPD.

There are five initial teacher training providers in Northern Ireland and two main routes into teaching: the 'concurrent' route, which involves completion of a BEd, and the 'consecutive' route, where you will take a primary or secondary PGCE after your first degree.

Registration

Once you have been granted eligibility to teach by the Department of Education in Northern Ireland (DENI), you must apply to register with the General Teaching Council for Northern Ireland.

Useful contacts

Department for Employment and Learning (DELNI)
Adelaide House
39-49 Adelaide Street
Belfast BT2 8FD
t: 028 9025 7777
e: del@nics.gov.uk
www.delni.org.uk

General Teaching Council for Northern Ireland
3rd Floor Albany House
73-75 Great Victoria Street
Belfast BT2 7AF
t: 028 9033 3390
e: info@gtcni.org.uk
www.gtcni.org.uk

What others say...

What others say...

These are extracts from case studies in previous editions of this book. They give some insights into the experiences and thoughts of people who were once in the same position as you.

DAVID CLARKE - SENIOR LECTURER IN GERMAN

The most challenging part of my job is juggling the different roles of lecturer, research academic and administrator. Doing a PhD in the humanities does not teach you how to teach – I learnt this during my PhD and the year I spent in Mainz. Luckily, there is now an increasing emphasis on encouraging new lecturing staff to work towards gaining a postgraduate certificate in higher education.

With all the different roles I have to perform my job is never dull. I love the fact that research is part of my role: it means I continually get to explore new areas that interest me. It's the ideal job if you never want to stop studying and learning.

If you want to become a lecturer, get as much teaching experience as you can – as an undergraduate you may be able to get involved in your university's school outreach programme, or do some TEFL teaching if you are a linguist. When applying for postgraduate work, if you cannot get support from government funding bodies, remember that many universities offer bursaries, so be prepared to move.

VAL SILVESTER – PRIMARY SCHOOL TEACHER

When I left school, I worked in the financial sector but soon realised my passion lay in teaching. I have always wanted to work with children from disadvantaged backgrounds, to inspire them to achieve the very best that they are capable of and nurture abilities they do not see or believe are there.

I teach Year One children (aged five to six) in a state primary school. The school supports all the areas I am passionate about: a creative curriculum, streaming by ability rather than age and giving opportunities to children from disadvantaged backgrounds. I teach all areas of the national curriculum, including literacy and numeracy on a daily basis, to a class of 26 pupils.

As a new teacher you have to realise that you are still learning and that some lessons will be more successful than others. The organisational skills I developed as a financial adviser have helped me cope with the large amounts of paperwork. I am also building up a bank of teaching resources that I can dip into, to reduce the time I spend on lesson planning.

I finally feel that I am doing something I am passionate about, and I gain tremendous satisfaction from seeing children progress. It is a privilege working with children and the rewards are worth all the hard work.

I would advise anyone considering a career in teaching to spend time in a variety of local schools. Try to find out what type of school you are drawn to and why – this will help when it comes to applying for jobs.

LUKE SARTAIN – TRAINEE SECONDARY TEACHER

The PGCE is quite an intensive course, with most of the year spent on teaching practice. After only three weeks at university I was out on placement in a school for three days a week to observe lessons. I also got up to speed with school policies, such as behaviour management and child protection. After three weeks I was in school full time, teaching whole classes of around 25 pupils.

My first placement involved teaching 11 to 16 year olds at a state comprehensive school. I felt confident to teach whole lessons but if I hadn't it was possible to just lead a part of the lesson and the class teacher would take over. Mostly, I taught Year 9 pupils on a vocational IT course called DiDA, equivalent to three GCSEs. The teaching day was 8.30am to 2.45pm, but I was in from 8am to 4pm. Free periods were spent observing other teachers, lesson planning and completing my PGCE course work.

During my first placement I also had the opportunity to teach some PSHE (personal, social and health education) sessions. I liaised with the PSHE co-ordinator, who suggested topics, and I had to plan how to present them. This was informal and based much more on discussion than normal lessons and I particularly enjoyed engaging pupils who normally don't enjoy school activities.

The PGCE is a big step up from my undergraduate experience; managing and prioritising my workload has been the biggest challenge. One of the most important things I have done is to buy a diary!

If you're interested in secondary teaching, get as much work experience as you can with teenagers. My experience with young people at PGL gave me more confidence when I went into the classroom for the first time. On the school placements, participate in extra-curricular activities, so you can get to know pupils outside of the classroom. This really helps with building relationships and bonding with them.

JOSEPH GARRITY - INFANT SCHOOL TEACHER

Parents can be very demanding; they don't usually have the experience of working as a teacher and can forget that you have other children to look after as well. I have to be diplomatic, maintain good relationships and remember that they only want the best for their child.

It's important to maintain a disciplined class and make sure that the children know the rules from the beginning. Even though I want them to have fun and enjoy themselves, sometimes I feel that I am repeating myself endlessly!

If you want to become a teacher, take your teacher training seriously: if you learn the theory and do your research thoroughly, you will be able to apply it in the classroom. Learn from everyone, whether that's your tutors or teachers in the classroom. Doing a PGCE is very hard work, so it's vital to make sure you have time for yourself and regularly plan some fun activities.

SARAH HOPE - CLASS TEACHER IN AN AUTISTIC SPECTRUM DISORDER UNIT

The anxiety experienced by the children can cause outbursts of frustration and anger, which can be very upsetting. However, each day I work on enabling them to adopt strategies to help them cope appropriately when they are feeling distressed and it's great when we make breakthroughs.

It can also be difficult working with teaching assistants who come from a very different background from me and have certain expectations of how teaching should happen. I need to be sensitive to their backgrounds and former experiences while continuing to teach in a way that is true to my own values.

If you want to enter the teaching profession, follow your interests and always be yourself. Remember your values and what made you decide to go into teaching. Accept help and constructive criticism from other teachers.

JAMES WALDING – FRENCH TEACHER

I teach French at a mixed comprehensive school and am the Duke of Edinburgh's award co-ordinator and student leadership co-ordinator. A big highlight of my role is running trips both in the UK and overseas.

When I first started the job time management was a real challenge – I found it extremely difficult to fit all the planning, lesson preparation and teaching into one day. It is still a hard job with long hours, but the rewards and satisfaction I get from it makes it all worthwhile.

There are lots of perks – not just the holidays! You can really make a difference to a child's life. I enjoy seeing members of my tutor group progress and develop as individuals through their five years of secondary schooling. This culminates in the pleasure of being there on GCSE exam results day to see my students open their results and the handshake I get along with a hug of thanks. I also enjoy bumping into ex-students several years later and finding them happy and successful in a job.

DANIEL HOLMES - PRIMARY SCHOOL TEACHER

The biggest challenge I have faced is managing the huge variety of tasks and interactions I need to balance: you simply have to do it to find out, because everyone's experience is different. But if you can't multi-task, don't become a teacher. The hardest part is probably that you expect more of yourself each year. It's mostly a self-imposed pressure but it doesn't get easier – sorry!

The most important qualities for a primary teacher are patience, humour, clear communication, motivation and commitment. You must believe teaching is worthwhile and have a good sense of why you want to do it. It's not an easy option, so be prepared to work very hard and have great humility about learning from more experienced teachers. Although you may not always feel in the mood, you need to be able to energise yourself to be excited and positive about what you're teaching, as this will be reflected in your pupils' learning and behaviour.

EMMA BENTLEY- EFL TEACHER

Being an EFL teacher requires an element of performance: you need to come across as eager and enthusiastic to keep your students motivated. It's a constant challenge to come up with fresh ideas to enable students to practise the same things without becoming bored. One of the most frustrating elements for me is that teaching English as a foreign language doesn't have as much prestige in other people's eyes as other branches of teaching – some see it as an easy holiday job, which is far from the case!

If you're interested in becoming an EFL teacher, get up to speed on your grammar and syntax – there's nothing more embarrassing than being asked a question about your own language that you can't answer! You also need to get an internationally recognised qualification to make sure that you're employable.

LAURA ASTON – ASSOCIATE LECTURER IN SPORTS SCIENCE

I teach 16 to 18 year olds who are studying for vocational level 3 courses in sport and exercise science, and I also teach A2 PE. Class sizes range from 15 to 23 students. At the moment I teach theory so I spend my day in the classroom but in the future I could also be outside using my level 1 coaching qualifications.

I work independently (and really like this) but if I needed help I could contact my college teaching and learning mentor for advice. I have to do a lot of research, including downloading teaching resources, and be very organised, keeping to deadlines for marking and returning coursework.

At first standing up in front of a large group of 18-year-old students when I was only 22 was very daunting. Meeting a group of students for the first time is challenging as you have to immediately take control of the group and not show you are nervous – this requires confidence.

I love having a positive rapport with students and being thanked for the support I have given them. I particularly enjoy the pastoral side of teaching, such as helping with university applications.

If you are thinking about teaching, get a wide range of teaching experience: different ages, levels and class sizes. This will help determine whether you would enjoy teaching and the variety of skills gained will make you more employable.

www.ucas.com

www.gttr.ac.uk

at the heart of connecting people to higher education

Applicant
journey

SIX EASY STEPS TO UNIVERSITY AND COLLEGE

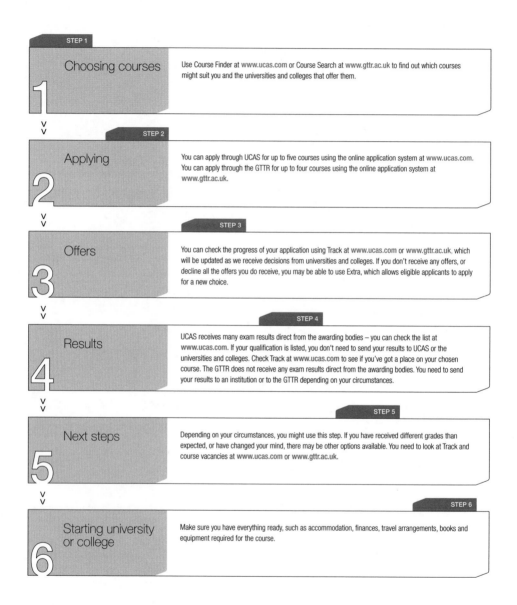

STEP 1

Choosing courses

Use Course Finder at www.ucas.com or Course Search at www.gttr.ac.uk to find out which courses might suit you and the universities and colleges that offer them.

STEP 2

Applying

You can apply through UCAS for up to five courses using the online application system at www.ucas.com. You can apply through the GTTR for up to four courses using the online application system at www.gttr.ac.uk.

STEP 3

Offers

You can check the progress of your application using Track at www.ucas.com or www.gttr.ac.uk, which will be updated as we receive decisions from universities and colleges. If you don't receive any offers, or decline all the offers you do receive, you may be able to use Extra, which allows eligible applicants to apply for a new choice.

STEP 4

Results

UCAS receives many exam results direct from the awarding bodies – you can check the list at www.ucas.com. If your qualification is listed, you don't need to send your results to UCAS or the universities and colleges. Check Track at www.ucas.com to see if you've got a place on your chosen course. The GTTR does not receive any exam results direct from the awarding bodies. You need to send your results to an institution or to the GTTR depending on your circumstances.

STEP 5

Next steps

Depending on your circumstances, you might use this step. If you have received different grades than expected, or have changed your mind, there may be other options available. You need to look at Track and course vacancies at www.ucas.com or www.gttr.ac.uk.

STEP 6

Starting university or college

Make sure you have everything ready, such as accommodation, finances, travel arrangements, books and equipment required for the course.

1 Choosing courses

Step 1 – Planning your application – undergraduate courses

This section will help you decide what course to study and how to choose a university where you'll enjoy living and studying.

Find out about qualifications, degree options, how they'll assess you and coping with the costs of higher education.

ENTRY REQUIREMENTS

WHICH SUBJECTS?

Newsflash – you **don't** have to study teaching at undergraduate level to become a teacher. In fact, the most popular method of training to become a teacher is by studying for a degree in another subject (eg modern languages, science, English, etc) and then taking a year-long PGCE. Undergraduate degrees in teaching are often taken by people who are interested in teaching in primary schools, where the subject knowledge base is broader and less specialised.

WHICH GRADES?

If you are going to be teaching a special subject to a group of students, you will need to be an expert of sorts in that field. Grades vary widely between universities (AAA or AAB is standard for Oxford and Cambridge) and between subject areas. It is important that you look carefully at the admissions requirements of each university you are interested in, either on their website or in their prospectus, to see if your predicted results are high enough.

HOW DO I FIND THE BEST UNDERGRADUATE DEGREE COURSE FOR ME?

For courses on offer, see Course Finder at **www.ucas.com**.

Try to use various sources of information to make your choices for higher education. League tables might be a component of this research, but you should bear in mind that these tables attempt to rank institutions in an overall order, which reflects the interests, preoccupations and decisions of those who have produced and edited them. The ways in which they are compiled vary greatly and you need to look closely at the criteria that have been used. See page 85 for more information about league tables.

REMEMBER

You don't have to study teaching at university to become a teacher, but this book focuses on studying a teaching or education degree at university. You can study a non-education-related degree of your choosing and then take a postgraduate course.

UCAS CARD

At its simplest, the UCAS Card scheme is the start of your UCAS journey. It can save you a packet on the high street with exclusive offers to UCAS Card holders, as well as providing you with hints and tips about finding the best course at the right university or college. If that's not enough you'll also receive these benefits:

- frequent expert help from UCAS, with all the essential information you need on the application process
- free monthly newsletters providing advice, hints, tips and exclusive discounts
- tailored information on the universities and courses you're interested in
- and much more

If you're in Year 12, S5 or equivalent and thinking about higher education for autumn 2013, sign up for your FREE UCAS Card today to receive all these benefits at **www.ucas.com/ucascard**.

V

UCAS

Confused about courses?

Indecisive about institutions?

Stressed about student life?

Unsure about UCAS?

Frowning over finance?

Help is available at
www.ucasbooks.com

Choosing courses

1

Choosing courses

USE COURSE FINDER AT WWW.UCAS.COM OR COURSE SEARCH AT WWW.GTTR.AC.UK TO FIND OUT WHICH COURSES MIGHT SUIT YOU, AND THE UNIVERSITIES AND COLLEGES THAT OFFER THEM.

Use the UCAS and GTTR websites – www.ucas.com and www.gttr.ac.uk have lots of advice on how to find a course. Go to the students' sections of the websites for the best advice or go straight to Course Finder or Course Search to see all the courses available through UCAS or the GTTR. Our maps of the UK at www.ucas.com/students/choosingcourses/choosinguni/map/ and www.gttr.ac.uk/students/beforeyouapply/wheretotrain/map show you where all the institutions that recruit through UCAS and the GTTR are located.

Watch UCAStv – at www.ucas.tv there are videos on *How to choose your course*, *Attending events*, and *Open days* as well as case studies from students talking about their experiences of finding a course at university or college.

Attend UCAS conventions – UCAS conventions are held throughout the UK. Universities and colleges have exhibition stands where their staff offer information about courses and institutions. Details of when the conventions are happening and a convention planner to help you prepare can be found at www.ucas.com/conventions.

Look at university and college websites and prospectuses – universities and colleges have prospectuses and course-specific leaflets on their undergraduate courses. Your school or college library may have copies or go to the university's website to download a copy or ask them to send one to you.

Go to university and college open days – most institutions offer open days to anyone who wants to attend. See the list of universities and colleges on **www.ucas.com** and the UCAS *Open Days* publication (see the Essential Reading chapter) for information on when they are taking place. Aim to visit all of the universities and colleges you are interested in before you apply. It will help with your expectations of university life and make sure the course is the right one for you.

League tables – these can be helpful but bear in mind that they attempt to rank institutions in an overall order reflecting the views of those that produce them. They may not reflect your views and needs. Examples can be found at **www.thecompleteuniversityguide.co.uk**, **www.guardian.co.uk/education/universityguide**, **www.thetimes.co.uk** (subscription service) and **www.thesundaytimes.co.uk** (subscription service). See page 85 for more information about league tables.

Do your research – speak and refer to as many trusted sources as you can find. Talk to someone already doing the job you have in mind. The section on 'Which area?' on pages 26 to 33 will help you identify the different areas of teaching or education you might want to enter.

DECIDING ON YOUR COURSE CHOICES

Through UCAS you can initially apply for up to five undergraduate courses and through the GTTR you can initially apply for up to four postgraduate courses, including no more than two primary teaching courses. How do you find out more information to make an informed decision?

Remember you don't have to make the maximum number of course choices. Only apply for a course if you're completely happy with both the course and the university or college and you would definitely be prepared to accept a place.

How do you narrow down your course choices? First of all, look up course details in this book or on Course Finder at **www.ucas.com** or Course Search at **www.gttr.ac.uk**. This will give you an idea of the full range of courses and topics on offer. You'll quickly be able to eliminate institutions that don't offer the right course, or you can choose a 'hit list' of institutions first, and then see what they have to offer.

Once you've made a short(er) list, look at institutions' websites, and generally find out as much as you can about the course, department and institution. Don't be afraid to contact them to ask for more information, request their prospectus or arrange an open day visit.

Choosing courses

1

Choosing your institution

Different people look for different things from their course, but the checklist below sets out the kinds of factors all prospective students should consider when choosing their institution. Keep this list in mind on open days, when talking to friends about their experiences at various universities and colleges, or while reading prospectuses and websites.

WHAT TO CONSIDER WHEN CHOOSING YOUR TEACHING OR EDUCATION COURSE	
Location	Do you want to stay close to home? Would you prefer to study in a city or at a campus university or college? If you are applying for postgraduate teacher training courses, would you prefer a course at a university or college or a course based in a group of schools?
Course entry requirements	Use Course Finder on the UCAS website, **www.ucas.com** or Course Search on the GTTR website **www.gttr.ac.uk**, to view entry requirements for courses you are interested in. Also, check out the university, college or SCITT consortium website or call up the admissions office. For undergraduate courses some institutions specify grades required, eg AAB, while others specify points required, eg 340. If they ask for points, it means they're using the UCAS Tariff system, which basically awards points to different types and levels of qualification. For example, an A grade at A level = 120 points; a B grade at A level = 100 points. The full Tariff tables are available on pages 123 to 129 and at **www.ucas.com**. For postgraduate teaching courses most training providers will ask for a 2:2 degree or higher and classroom experience.

WHAT TO CONSIDER WHEN CHOOSING YOUR TEACHING OR EDUCATION COURSE (CONT.)	
Links with schools and other employers in the educational sector	Ask the course tutor or department about links with schools and other employers in the educational sector for teaching placements or work experience.
Prospects of obtaining a post in teaching or education	Ask institutions how many of their students find permanent posts in teaching or education each year after completing their course.
Cost	Ask the admissions office about course fees and financial assistance.
Teaching or non-teaching degree	If you want to become a teacher, ensure that your chosen degree course has been approved for the award of Qualified Teacher Status (QTS) in England or Wales or the Teaching Qualification (TQ) in Scotland.
Degree type	How many lectures and tutorials per week, amount of one-to-one work, time spent on school placements, etc?
Coursework (undergraduate degree courses)	Is there another subject that you enjoy that you could study first, that might help give you an edge in employers' eyes?
Course assessment	Can you see yourself writing regular essays and undertaking teaching placements?
Facilities for students	Check out the campus library and computing facilities, and find out if there is a careers adviser dedicated to teaching.
'Fit'	Even if all the above criteria stack up, this one relies on gut feel – go and visit the institution if you can and see if it's 'you'.

Choosing courses

1

League tables

The information that follows has been provided by Dr Bernard Kingston of *The Complete University Guide*.

League tables are worth consulting early in your research and perhaps for confirmation later on. But never rely on them in isolation – always use them alongside other information sources available to you. Universities typically report that over a third of prospective students view league tables as important or very important in making their university choices. They give an insight into quality and are mainly based on data from the universities themselves. Somewhat confusingly, tables published in, say, 2012 are referred to as the 2013 tables because they are aimed at applicants going to university in that following year. The well known ones - *The Complete University Guide*, *The Guardian*, *The Times*, and *The Sunday Times* - rank the institutions and the subjects they teach using input measures (eg entry standards), throughput measures (eg student : staff ratios) and output measures (eg graduate prospects). Some tables are free to access whilst others are behind pay walls. All are interactive and enable users to create their own tables based on the measures important to them.

The universities are provided with their raw data for checking and are regularly consulted on methodology. But ultimately it is the compilers who decide what measures to use and what weights to put on them. They are competitors and rarely consult amongst themselves. So, for example, *The Times* tables differ significantly from *The Sunday Times* ones even though both newspapers belong to the same media proprietor.

Whilst the main university rankings tend to get the headlines, we would stress that the individual subject tables are as least as important, if not more so, when deciding where to study. All universities, regardless of their overall ranking, have some academic departments that rank highly in their subjects. Beware also giving much weight to an institution being a few places higher or lower in the tables – this is likely to be of little significance. This is particularly true in the lower half of the main table where overall scores show considerable bunching.

Most of the measures used to define quality come from hard factual data provided by the Higher Education Statistics Agency (HESA) but some, like student satisfaction and peer assessment, are derived from surveys of subjective impressions where you might wish to query sample size. We give a brief overview of the common measures here but please go to the individual websites for full details.

- **Student satisfaction** is derived from the annual National Student Survey (NSS) and is heavily used by *The Guardian* and *The Sunday Times.*
- **Research assessment** comes from a 2008 exercise (RAE) aimed at defining the quality of a university's research (excluded by *The Guardian*).
- **Entry standards** are based on the full UCAS Tariff scores obtained by new students.
- **Student : staff ratio** gives the number of students per member of academic staff.
- **Expenditure figures** show the costs of academic and student services.
- **Good honours** lists the proportion of graduates gaining a first or upper second honours degree.
- **Completion** indicates the proportion of students who successfully complete their studies.

- **Graduate prospects** usually reports the proportion of graduates who obtain a graduate job – not any job – or continue studying within six months of leaving.
- **Peer assessment** is used only by *The Sunday Times* which asks academics to rate other universities in their subjects.
- **Value added** is used only by *The Guardian* and compares entry standards with good honours.

All four main publishers of UK league tables (see Table 1) also publish university subject tables. *The Complete University Guide* and *The Times* are based on four measures: student satisfaction, research quality, entry standards and graduate destinations. *The Sunday Times* uses student satisfaction, entry standards, graduate destinations, graduate unemployment, good degrees and drop-out rate, while *The Guardian* uses student satisfaction (as three separate measures), entry standards, graduate destinations, student-staff ratio, spend per student and value added. This use of different measures is one reason why the different tables can yield different results (sometimes very different, especially in the case of *The Guardian* which has least in common with the other tables).

League tables compiled by *The Complete University Guide* (**www.thecompleteuniversityguide.co.uk**) and *The Guardian* (**www.guardian.co.uk**) are available in spring, those by *The Times* (**www.thetimes.co.uk**) and *The Sunday Times* (**www.thesundaytimes.co.uk**) in the summer.

Table 1 – measures used by the main publishers of UK league tables

	Universities	Measures	Subjects	Measures
The Complete University Guide	116	9	62	4
The Guardian	119	8	46	8
The Sunday Times	122	8	39	6
The Times	116	8	62	4

THINGS TO WATCH OUT FOR WHEN READING SUBJECT LEAGUE TABLES

- Much of teacher training provision is postgraduate (leading to a PGCE qualification) and some universities only have postgraduate provision. This means entry standards and destinations data may be unavailable. *The Complete University Guide* uses Ofsted inspection scores instead of the National Student Survey as a measure of teaching so that all universities offering teacher training have enough data to be included.
- The tables will include data for all education courses and not just those which are initial teacher training.

WHO PUBLISHES TEACHING AND EDUCATION LEAGUE TABLES?

The Complete University Guide, The Guardian, The Times and *The Sunday Times* all publish education or education studies league tables.

Save with UCAS Card

If you're in Year 12, S5 or equivalent and thinking about higher education, sign up for the **FREE** UCAS Card to receive all these benefits:

- information about courses and unis
- expert advice from UCAS
- exclusive discounts for card holders

UCAS

1

Choosing courses

How will they choose you?

ITT providers receive thousands of applications each year for only a limited number of places. So how can you make your UCAS or GTTR application stand out from the others?

ACADEMIC ABILITY
(ADVICE FOR UNDERGRADUATES)

Most, if not all, degrees are intellectually demanding. Not only will you possibly be learning about the basics of your course for the very first time but you will also be expected to work on them in greater depth than you have ever done before at GCSE and A level (or equivalent). Therefore, in order for admissions tutors to be certain that you have what it takes to cope with the course, you will have to show you have the academic ability to take on new ideas.

SELF-MOTIVATION AND SELF-DISCIPLINE
(ADVICE FOR UNDERGRADUATES)

Studying at university is very different from school and sixth form. In these settings, you will have followed a set course, normally following a study pattern suggested by your teachers. Homework set each night will have ensured that you completed your study regularly and on time.

At university, tutors and lecturers do not have the time to keep tabs on their students in the same way. Whereas at A level your teachers will have helped motivate you to finish your work on time, at university tutors will hand out reading lists and essay titles or problem sheets in advance and will expect you to complete them on time without constant reminders.

This can, understandably, be daunting for some people. Certainly, time management and self-motivation are skills you hone at university but it also helps if your referee can write about any instances where you have shown an ability to work well on your own, as this is how you will be studying throughout your undergraduate course.

DEVOTION TO TEACHING AND EDUCATION

The tutors who select students onto their courses want to see evidence that you have carefully considered what a course in teaching or education will involve and why it appeals to you so much. Only you will know the reasons why you're fascinated by this area and it's your job to convey this enthusiasm to others, initially in the personal statement on your UCAS or GTTR application and then at interview.

DO SOME READING

This is related to the above point. A good way to prove to potential admissions tutors that you have an interest in their field is to find out their specialist academic areas and do some reading on these, potentially from books that they have written. Additionally, contact the relevant department and ask for their first-year reading list, if this is not available online. You do not need to read everything on it but if you choose two or three books that most appeal to you and read them in some depth it does show a commitment to teaching or education and the relevant university's course.

Be warned though: don't think that merely mentioning a few key books will automatically get you through. Admissions tutors will know if you're lying, so unless you can make a few valid points about why you enjoyed their books, don't bother: it could do more harm than good.

WORK EXPERIENCE

How much does it count? Ask any teaching admissions tutor or employer about the importance of work experience on a candidate's application and they'll all agree – classroom or other relevant work experience shows a real, rather than theoretical, interest in the teaching profession or the education sector in general. An absence of work experience suggests questionable commitment to your choice of career, especially if you are specialising so early on in your degree. Most, if not all, admissions tutors for PGCE courses will expect applicants to have had some experience in schools and/or Early Years settings that is relevant to the course they are applying for.

Classroom experience will not only give you a real insight into the work of a teacher, it will also give you valuable examples of the skills you have to offer.

As part of the application process, you'll be asked to write a personal statement setting out why you want to take a teaching or education course. If you want a teaching career, you should comment on your skills, personal qualities and experience that would make you a successful teacher. This is where your classroom experience, or other related experiences, will help you stand out.

WHAT KIND OF WORK EXPERIENCE COUNTS?

If you are still at school or college:

- spending time in a primary school as a comparison with the teaching you are experiencing at secondary level
- volunteering for vacation programmes for younger school children

- spending time helping in holiday camps or youth clubs with younger school children
- helping younger children with reading
- organising activities for younger children
- helping at a local playgroup or nursery.

If you have completed your first degree recently or are considering a career change, all the above activities are relevant and valuable, but you should also try to spend time with children of a range of different ages to see which age group suits you best. It is essential to get experience in a school. There are several ways you can do this:

- get in touch with a school in your area and ask if you can spend a few days helping in any capacity
- the Teaching Agency runs a school experience programme: see **www.education.gov.uk/get-into-teaching/school-experience.aspx** for further information.

Other relevant experience could include:

- training sessions that you have delivered to colleagues at work
- helping with youth clubs
- coaching, eg sports clubs
- any tutoring that you have done at university or within the local community.

If possible, try to keep a brief record of your experiences and what you learnt from them. Take notes about how lessons were structured and the way in which the teacher engaged with the children. This could give you valuable insight and ideas into teaching in practice and something to either write about on your application or talk about at interview.

YOUR PERSONAL STATEMENT

Your personal statement can really enhance your application. It is here that you can show evidence of academic attainment, self-discipline, work experience, and a desire to work in teaching and education. Most institutions place much importance on personal statements as this is where the applicant's voice comes through, so make the most of it and use it to your advantage. Be honest but not overly familiar and give well-reasoned statements. And above all make sure your personal statement is free from mistakes and easy to read. There's nothing more offputting for an admissions tutor than applications and personal statements that have glaring grammatical and spelling mistakes or are difficult to decipher.

As this is such an important part of your application, it's worth drafting it a few times before entering it into your online application. Ask your family, friends or teacher to check it, not only for mistakes but also to see if you're leaving anything out that should be in, or equally if there's anything there that should come out.

Make sure you write your personal statement in an ordinary fashion. Some admissions tutors have stories of personal statements where students have written in spirals or unusual handwriting, which could mean your application stands out for the wrong reasons. Let it be your voice that argues your application, not your unique presentation skills.

For more advice on how to write a personal statement, see pages 109 to 111.

UNDERGRADUATE APPLICATIONS TO
THE UNIVERSITIES OF OXFORD AND
CAMBRIDGE

The University of Oxford and the University of
Cambridge have slightly different application procedures
from other universities and colleges. Neither of these
universities currently offers any undergraduate teaching
courses, but the University of Cambridge does offer
undergraduate education courses. If you are applying
for any of these education courses, UCAS must receive
your application by 15 October. If you live outside the
EU, you will also need to obtain a Cambridge Online
Preliminary Application (COPA) form from the University
of Cambridge and return the completed form to them
by 15 October. Visit the University of Cambridge's
website for detailed information about their application
procedures.

UCAS HIGHER EDUCATION CONVENTIONS

Meet face-to-face with over 100 UK university representatives, attend seminars on How to Apply through UCAS and Financing yourself through university.

For further details visit
www.ucas.com/conventions

Choosing courses

1

The cost of
higher education

The information in this section was up-to-date when this book was published. You should visit the websites mentioned in this section for the very latest information.

THE COST OF STUDYING IN THE UK

As a student, you will usually have to pay for two things: tuition fees for your course, which for most students do not need to be paid for up front, and living costs such as rent, food, books, transport and entertainment. Fees charged vary between courses, between universities and colleges and also according to your normal country of residence, so it's important to check these before you apply. Course fee information is supplied to UCAS by the universities and is displayed in Course Finder at www.ucas.com.

STUDENT LOANS

The purpose of student loans from the Government is to help cover the costs of your tuition fees and basic living costs (rent, bills, food and so on). Two types are available: a tuition fee loan to cover the tuition charges and a maintenance loan to help with accommodation and other living costs. Both types of student loan are available to all students who meet the basic eligibility requirements. Interest will be charged at inflation plus a fixed percentage while you are studying. In addition, many other commercial loans are available to students studying at university or college but the interest rate can vary considerably. Loans to help with living costs will be available for all eligible students, irrespective of family income.

Find out more information from the relevant sites below:

England: Student Finance England –
www.direct.gov.uk/studentfinance
Northern Ireland: Student Finance Northern Ireland –
www.studentfinanceni.co.uk
Scotland: Student Awards Agency for Scotland –
www.saas.gov.uk
Wales: Student Finance Wales –
www.studentfinancewales.co.uk or
www.cyllidmyfyrwyrcymru.co.uk
England and Wales: particularly for postgraduate courses: Teaching Agency – **www.education.gov.uk/ get-into-teaching/funding.aspx**

BURSARIES AND SCHOLARSHIPS

- The National Scholarships Programme gives financial help to students studying in England. The scheme is designed to help students whose families have lower incomes.
- Students from families with lower incomes will be entitled to a non-repayable maintenance grant to help with living costs.
- Many universities and colleges also offer non-repayable scholarships and bursaries to help students cover tuition and living costs whilst studying.
- All eligible part-time undergraduates who study for at least 25% of their time will be able to apply for a loan to cover the costs of their tuition, which means they no longer have to pay up front.

There will be extra support for disabled students and students with child or adult dependants. For more information, visit the country-specific websites listed earlier in this section.

Choosing courses

1

International students

APPLYING TO STUDY IN THE UK

Deciding to go to university or college in the UK is very exciting. You need to think about what course to do, where to study, and how much it will cost. The decisions you make can have a huge effect on your future but UCAS and the GTTR are here to help.

How to apply?

Whatever your age or qualifications, if you want to apply for any of over 35,000 courses listed at 300 universities and colleges on the UCAS website, you must apply through UCAS at **www.ucas.com**. If you are unsure, your school, college, adviser, or local British Council office will be able to help. Further advice and a video guide for international students can be found on the non-UK students' section of the UCAS website at **www.ucas.com/international**.

Students may apply on their own or through their school, college, adviser, or local British Council if this is registered with UCAS to use Apply. If you choose to use an education agent's services, check with the British Council to see if they hold a list of certificated or registered agents in your country. Check also on any charges you may need to pay. UCAS charges only the application fee (page 97) but agents may charge for additional services.

You need to apply through the GTTR at **www.gttr.ac.uk** for the majority of postgraduate teacher training courses at

- most universities, colleges of higher education and school-centred initial teacher training (SCITT) consortia in England
- most universities and colleges of higher education in Wales
- all higher education institutions in Scotland, except the University of the West of Scotland.

Students apply through the GTTR as independent applicants. You cannot apply through a registered centre or use agents' services.

How much will my application cost?
UCAS applications

For 2013 entry, if you choose to apply to more than one course, university or college you need to pay £23 GBP when you apply. If you only apply to one course at one university or college, you pay £12 GBP.

GTTR applications

When you apply for postgraduate teacher training through the GTTR for 2013 entry, you pay £19 GBP regardless of whether you have applied for one or more courses.

WHAT LEVEL OF ENGLISH?

UCAS and the GTTR provide a list of English language qualifications and grades that are acceptable to most UK universities and colleges. However, you are advised to contact the institutions directly as each have their own entry requirement in English. For more information go to
www.ucas.com/students/wheretostart/nonukstudents/englangprof or
www.gttr.ac.uk/students/nonukstudents/englishlanguageproficiency

INTERNATIONAL STUDENT FEES

If you study in the UK, your fee status (whether you pay full-cost fees or a subsidised fee rate) will be decided by the UK university or college you plan to attend. Before you decide which university or college to attend, you need to be absolutely certain that you can pay the full cost of:

- your tuition fees (the amount is set by universities and colleges, so contact them for more information – visit their websites where many list their fees). Fee details will also be included on Course Finder at **www.ucas.com**.
- the everyday living expenses for you and your family for the whole time that you are in the UK, including accommodation, food, gas and electricity bills clothes, travel and leisure activities.
- books and equipment for your course
- travel to and from your country.

You must include everything when you work out how much it will cost. You can get information to help you

do this accurately from the international offices at universities and colleges, UKCISA (UK Council for International Student Affairs) and the British Council. There is a useful website tool to help you manage your money at university – **www.studentcalculator.org.uk.**

Scholarships and bursaries are offered at some universities and colleges and you should contact them for more information. In addition, you should check with your local British Council for additional scholarships available to students from your country who want to study in the UK.

LEGAL DOCUMENTS YOU WILL NEED

As you prepare to study in the UK, it is very important to think about the legal documents you will need to enter the country.

Everyone who comes to study in the UK needs a valid passport, details of which will be collected either in your UCAS or GTTR application or later through Track. If you do not yet have a passport, you should apply for one as soon as possible. People from certain countries also need visas before they come into the UK. They are known as 'visa nationals'. You can check if you require a visa to travel to the UK by visiting the UK Border Agency website and selecting 'Studying in the UK', so, please check the UK Border Agency website at **www.ukba.homeoffice.gov.uk** for the most up-to-date guidance and information about the United Kingdom's visa requirements.

When you apply for your visa you need to make sure you have the following documents:

- A confirmation of acceptance for studies (CAS) number from the university or college where you are going to study. The institution must be on the UKBA Register of Sponsors in order to accept international students.
- A valid passport.
- Evidence that you have enough money to pay for your course and living costs.
- Certificates for all qualifications you have that are relevant to the course you have been accepted for and for any English language qualifications.

You will also have to give your biometric data.

Do check for further information from your local British Embassy or High Commission. Guidance information for international students is also available from UKCISA and from UKBA.

ADDITIONAL RESOURCES

There are a number of organisations that can provide further guidance and information to you as you prepare to study in the UK:

- British Council
  www.britishcouncil.org
- Education UK (British Council website dealing with educational matters)
  www.educationuk.org
- English UK (British Council accredited website listing English language courses in the UK)
  www.englishuk.com
- UK Border Agency (provides information on visa requirements and applications)
  www.ukba.homeoffice.gov.uk
- UKCISA (UK Council for International Student Affairs)
  www.ukcisa.org.uk
- Directgov (the official UK Government website)
  www.direct.gov.uk
- Prepare for Success
  www.prepareforsuccess.org.uk

www.ucas.com

www.gttr.ac.uk

at the heart of connecting people to higher education

Applying

2

Step 2 – Applying

You apply through UCAS or the GTTR using the online application systems, called Apply, at **www.ucas.com** or **www.gttr.ac.uk**. You can apply for a maximum of five choices through UCAS or four choices, including no more than two primary courses, through the GTTR. You don't have to use all your choices if you don't want to. If you apply for fewer than the maximum number of choices, you can add more at a later date if you want to. But be aware of the course application deadlines.

IMPORTANT DATES FOR 2012 ENTRY	
Early June 2012	UCAS Apply opens for 2013 entry registration.
Mid-September 2012	Applications can be sent to UCAS.
Early October 2012	GTTR Apply opens for 2013 entry registration. GTTR applicants can submit their completed applications.
15 October 2012	Application deadline for the receipt at UCAS of applications for all medicine, dentistry, veterinary medicine and veterinary science courses and for all courses at the universities of Oxford and Cambridge.
1 December 2012	Final date for the GTTR to receive applications for primary teaching courses to ensure that they are sent to the first choice training provider for consideration.
15 January 2013	Application deadline for the receipt at UCAS of applications for all courses except those listed above with a 15 October deadline, and some art and design courses with a 24 March deadline.
25 February 2013	UCAS Extra starts (see page 115 for more information about Extra).
14 March 2013	GTTR Extra starts (see page 115 for more information about Extra).
24 March 2013	Application deadline for the receipt at UCAS of applications for art and design courses except those listed on Course Finder at www.ucas.com with a 15 January deadline.
31 March 2013	If you apply through UCAS by 15 January, the universities and colleges should aim to have sent their decisions by this date (but they can take longer).
9 May 2013	If you apply through UCAS by 15 January, universities and colleges need to send their decisions by this date. If they don't, UCAS will make any outstanding choices unsuccessful on their behalf.
30 June 2013	Last date to apply through GTTR Extra. If you send your application to UCAS or the GTTR by this date, we will send it to your chosen institutions. Applications received after this date are entered into UCAS or GTTR Clearing (see page 132 for more information about Clearing).
3 July 2013	Last date to apply through UCAS Extra.
August 2013 (date to be confirmed)	Scottish Qualifications Authority (SQA) results are published.
15 August 2013	GCE and Advanced Diploma results are published (often known as 'A level results day'). Adjustment opens for registration (see page 133 for more information about Adjustment).

DON'T FORGET...

Institutions guarantee to consider your application only if we receive it by the appropriate deadline. Check application deadlines for your courses on Course Finder at www.ucas.com or Course Search at www.gttr.ac.uk.

If you send your application to UCAS or the GTTR after the deadline but before 30 June 2013, institutions will consider you only if they still have places available.

Applying

2

How to apply through UCAS

You apply online at www.ucas.com through Apply – a secure, web-based application service that is designed for all our applicants, whether they are applying through a UCAS-registered centre or as an individual, anywhere in the world. Apply is:

- easy to access – all you need is an internet connection
- easy to use – you don't have to complete your application all in one go: you can save the sections as you complete them and come back to it later
- easy to monitor – once you've applied, you can use Track to check the progress of your application, including any decisions from universities or colleges. You can also reply to your offers using Track

Watch the UCAStv guide to applying through UCAS at www.ucas.tv.

APPLICATION FEE

For 2013 entry the fee for applying through UCAS is £23 for two or more choices and £12 for one choice.

DEFERRED ENTRY

If you want to apply for deferred entry in 2014, perhaps because you want to take a year out between school or college and higher education, you should check that the university or college will accept a deferred entry application. Occasionally, tutors are not happy to accept students who take a gap year, because it interrupts the flow of their learning. If you apply for deferred entry, you must meet the conditions of any offers by 31 August 2013, unless otherwise agreed by the university or college. If you accept a deferred place for 2014 entry and then change your mind, you cannot reapply through UCAS in the 2014 entry cycle unless you withdraw your original application.

INVISIBILITY OF CHOICES

Universities and colleges cannot see details of the other choices on your application until you reply to any offers or you are unsuccessful at all your choices.

You can submit only one UCAS application in each year's application cycle. You may apply through both UCAS and the GTTR (see page 106) in the same application cycle, but if you hold a confirmed place in both systems, you will have to withdraw from one of these places.

APPLYING THROUGH YOUR SCHOOL OR COLLEGE

1 GET SCHOOL OR COLLEGE 'BUZZWORD'

Ask your UCAS application coordinator (may be your sixth form tutor) for your school or college UCAS 'buzzword'. This is a password for the school or college.

2 REGISTER

Go to www.ucas.com/students/apply and click on **Register/Log in to use Apply** and then **register**. After you have entered your registration details, the online system will automatically generate a username for you, but you'll have to come up with a password and answers to security questions.

3 COMPLETE SEVEN SECTIONS

Complete all the sections of the application. To access any section, click on the section name at the left of the screen and follow the instructions. The sections are:

Personal details – contact details, residential status, disability status

Additional information – only UK applicants need to complete this section

Student finance – UK students can share some of their application details with their student finance company. Finance information is provided for other EU and international applicants

Choices – which courses you'd like to apply for

Education – your education and qualification

Employment – for example, work experience, holiday jobs

Statement – see page 109 for personal statement advice

Before you can send your application, you need to go to the **View all details** screen and tick the **section completed** box.

4 PASS TO REFEREE

Once you've completed all the sections, send your application electronically to your referee (normally your form tutor). They'll check it, approve it and add their reference to it, and will then send it to UCAS on your behalf.

USEFUL INFORMATION ABOUT APPLY

- Important details like date of birth and course codes will be checked by Apply. It will alert you if they are not valid.
- We strongly recommend that the personal statement and reference are written in a word-processing package and pasted into Apply.
- If you want, you can enter European characters into certain areas of Apply.
- You can change your application at any time before it is completed and sent to UCAS.
- You can print and preview your application at any time. Before you send it, you need to go to the **View all details** screen and tick the **section completed** box.
- Your school, college or centre can choose different payment methods. For example, they may want us to bill them, or you may be able to pay online by debit or credit card.

NOT APPLYING THROUGH A SCHOOL OR COLLEGE

If you're not currently studying, you'll probably be applying as an independent applicant rather than through a school, college or other UCAS-registered centre. In this case you won't be able to provide a 'buzzword', but we'll ask you a few extra questions to check you are eligible to apply.

If you're not applying through a UCAS-registered centre, the procedure you use for obtaining a reference will depend on whether or not you want your reference to be provided through a registered centre.

For information on the procedures for providing references, visit **www.ucas.com/students/applying/howtoapply/reference.**

APPLICATION CHECKLIST

We want this to run smoothly for you and we also want to process your application as quickly as possible. You can help us to do this by remembering to do the following:

✓ check the closing dates for applications – see page 99

✓ check the student finance information at **www.ucas.com/students/studentfinance/** and course fees information in Course Finder at **www.ucas.com**

✓ start early and allow plenty of time for completing your application – including enough time for your referee to complete the reference section

✓ read the online instructions carefully before you start

✓ consider what each question is actually asking for – use the 'help'

✓ pay special attention to your personal statement (see page 109) and start drafting it early

✓ ask a teacher, parent, friend or careers adviser to review your draft application – particularly the personal statement

✓ if you get stuck, watch our videos on YouTube where we answer your frequently asked questions on completing a UCAS application at **www.youtube.com/ucasonline**

✓ if you have extra information that will not fit on your application, send it direct to your chosen universities or colleges after we have sent you your Welcome letter with your Personal ID – don't send it to us

✓ print a copy of the final version of your application, in case you are asked questions on it at an interview.

Applying

2

Applying through the GTTR

WHAT IS THE GTTR?

The Graduate Teacher Training Registry (GTTR) is an admissions service operated by UCAS. The GTTR processes applications for postgraduate initial teacher training (ITT) and initial teacher education (ITE) courses at:

- most universities, colleges of higher education and school-centred initial teacher training (SCITT) consortia in England
- most universities and colleges of higher education in Wales
- all higher education institutions (HEIs) in Scotland, except the University of the West of Scotland.

Almost all training providers in England and Wales award an academic Professional Graduate or Postgraduate Certificate in Education (PGCE) qualification with the award of Qualified Teacher Status

(QTS). The Professional Graduate Certificate in Education is the same level academically as the final year of an honours degree course (H level). The Postgraduate Certificate in Education contains some credits at master's degree level (M level credits) and H level credits. The number of M level credits in postgraduate awards varies significantly from one training provider to another. Some providers will give you the opportunity to study for the additional M level credits required to obtain a full master's level qualification after you have completed your PGCE course.

Course provision in England and Wales also differs from one training provider to another. Some providers only offer professional graduate or postgraduate courses and others offer courses at both levels.

Some institutions' profiles listed from page 147 state whether their courses are offered at professional graduate level, postgraduate level or both. Before you apply, you should contact training providers where you want to study to find out whether or not the level of their course provision meets your requirements.

HEIs in Scotland award an academic Professional Graduate Diploma of Education (PGDE) qualification at level 9 or 10 in the Scottish Credit and Qualifications Framework (SCQF) together with the Teaching Qualification (TQ).

Level 9 is academically equivalent to ordinary degree level and level 10 is academically equivalent to honours degree level. If you are applying to HEIs in Scotland, you may want to confirm whether their courses are offered at level 9 or 10.

All the GTTR member institutions with profiles in this book have received full accreditation as teacher training providers from the Teaching Agency (TA) or the Higher Education Funding Council for Wales (HEFCW) or provide ITE courses approved by the Scottish Executive Education Department (SEED).

ONLINE APPLICATION SERVICE

You apply online through the GTTR website **www.gttr.ac.uk** from early October for courses that mostly start in September the following year. For 2013 entry the application fee is £19, for up to four choices of course. The online application system provides detailed screens and help text to guide you through the application process.

You may apply for up to four courses, including no more than two primary courses. You list your chosen training providers in the order in which you wish them to consider you. Applications to primary courses must be received at the GTTR by 1 December to ensure that they are sent to the first choice training provider. There is no closing date for applications to middle years, secondary or post-compulsory education courses to ensure that they are sent to the first choice training provider, but you should apply early because popular courses fill up quickly.

The GTTR sends your completed application online to one training provider at a time in your order of preference, but only if these training providers still have vacancies on your chosen courses. You will be told whenever a training provider makes a decision about your application. If you accept a place, you cannot be considered by other training providers in that application cycle.

If you do not obtain a place on any of your initial choices or you decline any places offered, you can add more choices with vacancies to your application. From October to mid-March of the following year you can add up to four new choices, including no more than two courses for primary teaching. From mid-March to the end of June you can use the Extra process to apply for one further course at a time. For more information about the Extra process, see page 117.
From 1 July you apply for further courses using the GTTR Clearing system. See page 132 for information about Clearing.

The GTTR will process all applications received by 30 June and send them to training providers with vacancies. If the GTTR receives your application after this date, it will be entered directly into the GTTR Clearing system. In Clearing you contact training providers direct to discuss your application.

The online Track service allows you to follow the progress of your application. You can view your personal details, the choices you have made, and the training providers' decisions. You can also use the Track service to update some of your personal details and to reply to your offers.

The service is usually available 24 hours a day, seven days a week.

You can submit only one GTTR application in each year's application cycle. You may apply through both the GTTR and UCAS (see page 102) in the same application cycle, but if you hold a confirmed place in both systems, you will have to withdraw from one of these places.

FURTHER INFORMATION

For further information about the GTTR and the application process visit, **www.gttr.ac.uk**. The website should provide the information you need, but if you still have queries, you can call the GTTR Customer Service Unit. The contact details are on the website.

If you live outside the UK, you can get more help and advice about UK higher education from British Council offices, which have information about the GTTR application process and reference copies of prospectuses for UK universities and colleges.

The GTTR cannot give international students advice about sources of finance or the qualifications that they will need.

Do not travel to the UK unless you are sure that you have a confirmed place on a course at a UK university or college and you have met any financial conditions.

Applying

2

The personal statement

Next to choosing your courses, this section of your application will be the most time-consuming. It is of immense importance as many colleges and universities rely solely on the information in the UCAS application, rather than interviews and admissions tests. The personal statement can be the deciding factor in whether or not they offer you a place. If you are applying through the GTTR or through UCAS to an institution that interviews, your personal statement could be the deciding factor in whether you get called for interview.

Keep a copy of your personal statement – if you are called for interview, you will almost certainly be asked questions based on it.

Tutors will look carefully at your exam results, actual and predicted, your referee's reference and your own personal statement. Remember, they are looking for reasons to offer you a place – try to give them every opportunity to do so!

A SALES DOCUMENT

The personal statement is your opportunity to sell yourself, so do so. The university or college admissions tutor wants to get a rounded picture of you to decide whether you will make an interesting member of the university or college, both academically and socially. They want to know more about you than the subjects you are studying at school or have studied at school and in higher education.

HOW TO START

There are resources on www.ucas.com and www.gttr.ac.uk to help you. At www.ucas.com you'll find several tools to help you write a good personal statement.

- Personal statement timeline, to help you do all your research and plan your statement over several drafts and checks.
- Personal statement mind map, which gives you reminders and hints on preparation, content and presentation, with extra hints for mature and international applicants.
- Personal statement worksheet, which gets you to start writing by asking relevant questions so that you include everything you need. You can also check your work against a list of dos and don'ts .

On the GTTR website there is a link to the 'application form assistant' in the Teaching Agency's section of the Department for Education's website which helps you to compile a personal statement by answering five questions.

Include things like hobbies, and try to link the skills you have gained to the type of course you are applying for. Describe your career plans and goals. Have you belonged to sports teams or orchestras or held positions of responsibility in the community? Try to give evidence of your ability to undertake higher level study successfully by showing your commitment and maturity. If you left full-time education a while ago, talk about the work you have done and the skills you have gained or how you have juggled bringing up a family with other activities – that is solid evidence of time management skills. Whoever you are, make sure you explain what appeals to you about the course you are applying for.

For teacher training courses you should show how the knowledge acquired through your degree, other education and work experience is relevant to the primary school curriculum or the secondary school curriculum subject(s) that you want to teach.

Try to observe lessons and help out in the classroom at a local school before you apply. In your personal statement you can then describe what you've gained from this experience and how it has increased your motivation to become a teacher and developed your appreciation of what is required to be an effective teacher. Include details of the type of school where you gained your experience and give the age range of the students with whom you worked. For more about work experience, see pages 90-91.

Visit www.ucas.tv to view the video to help guide you through the process and address the most common fears and concerns about writing a personal statement.

WHAT ADMISSIONS TUTORS LOOK FOR	WHAT TO TELL THEM
• Your reasons for wanting to take this subject in general and this particular course. • Your communication skills – not only what you say but how you say it. Your grammar and spelling must be perfect. • Relevant experience – practical things you've done that are related to your choice of course. • Evidence of your teamworking ability, leadership capability, independence. • Evidence of your skills, for example: IT skills, empathy and people skills, debating and public speaking, research and analysis. • Other activities that show your dedication and ability to apply yourself and maintain your motivation.	• Why you want to do this subject – how you know it is the subject for you. • What experience you already have in this field – for example work experience, school projects, hobbies, voluntary work. • The skills and qualities you have as a person that would make you a good student, for example anything that shows your dedication, communication ability, academic achievement, initiative. • Examples that show you can knuckle down and apply yourself, for example running a marathon or your Extended Project. • If you're taking a gap year, why you've chosen this and (if possible) what you're going to do during it. • About your other interests and activities away from studying – to show you're a rounded person. (But remember that it is mainly your suitability for the particular course that they're looking to judge.)

Applying

Non-academic requirements for teaching courses

FITNESS TO TEACH

It is a statutory requirement that all students should be medically fit before starting a programme that leads to the award of QTS in England or Wales or a TQ in Scotland. Training providers are required to satisfy themselves, on the basis of a health questionnaire returned to the training provider's medical adviser, that you are fit to train to teach. Where the medical adviser considers that further assessment is necessary before a decision can be reached, a medical examination will be arranged in consultation with you. This is only likely to be required in exceptional cases. You may be required to pay for this examination. Questionnaires, and any further details, will be issued by the training providers to those applicants who have been offered a conditional or firm place.

Training providers have a duty to make reasonable adjustments with regard to students with disabilities. You are encouraged to declare any disabilities on your application to allow training providers to take account of these needs. Additional funding may be available.

Further information can be found on the following websites

- **www.direct.gov.uk/studentfinance** if you live in England
- **www.saas.gov.uk** if you live in Scotland
- **www.studentfinancewales.co.uk** if you live in Wales
- **www.studentfinanceni.co.uk** if you live in Northern Ireland.

WORKING WITH CHILDREN – DECLARATION OF CRIMINAL CONVICTIONS

If you are applying for teaching programmes, you will be required to disclose any previous criminal convictions, cautions or bindovers irrespective of when they occurred and to agree to an enhanced criminal record check through the Criminal Records Bureau (CRB) or the Scottish Criminal Record Office Disclosure Service.

The training provider(s) where you have accepted a place will notify you of the procedures to be followed and will issue you with the forms you will need to complete so that your check can be made.

The Criminal Records Bureau (CRB) was set up to provide access to criminal record information for pre-employment vetting. This service is designed to improve protection for vulnerable groups, such as children, the disabled and the elderly. For people seeking to work with children, an 'enhanced disclosure' of criminal records will offer training providers and employers information held by the police, the Department of Health and the Department for Education. The Scottish Criminal Record Office Disclosure Service offers a similar service in Scotland.

For more information on the CRB and enhanced disclosures, call 0870 90 90 811 or visit **www.direct.gov.uk/crb**. To find out more about the Scottish Criminal Record Office Disclosure Service, visit **www.disclosurescotland.co.uk**, call 0870 609 6006 or email info@disclosurescotland.co.uk.

PROTECTING VULNERABLE GROUPS (PVG) SCHEME IN SCOTLAND

If you are starting a teacher training programme in Scotland, you will need to join the PVG scheme. This scheme enables training providers in Scotland to identify potential trainee teachers who are barred from working with children, young people or vulnerable adults. For more information about the PVG scheme, visit **www.scotland.gov.uk**.

REGISTRATION WITH THE GENERAL TEACHING COUNCILS (GTCs)

In previous years if you had a place on a teacher training programme in England, you had to register provisionally with the General Teaching Council for England (GTCE) before you started your course. From 1 April 2012 the GTCE ceased to operate and many of its responsibilities were transferred to the Teaching Agency, which is a new executive agency of the Department for Education. There is currently no requirement to register with the Teaching Agency.

If you are doing your teacher training in Scotland, Wales or Northern Ireland, you currently need to register with the General Teaching Councils in these countries only after you have completed your training programme. The General Teaching Councils for Wales, Scotland and Northern Ireland will continue to operate after 31 March 2012.

Offers

3

Step 3 – Offers

Once we have sent your UCAS application to your chosen universities and colleges, they will each consider it independently and tell us whether or not they can offer you a place. If you have applied through the GTTR, we send your application to one institution at a time in your order of preference. If the institution considering your application cannot make you an offer or you turn down their offer, we send your application to your next highest choice with vacancies.

Some universities and colleges will take longer to make decisions than others. You may be asked to attend an interview, sit an additional test or provide a piece of work such as an essay before a decision can be made.

TEACHING COURSES

Institutions must interview all applicants for undergraduate and postgraduate teaching courses leading to Qualified Teacher Status (QTS) or the Teaching Qualification (TQ) in Scotland before they can offer places.

EDUCATION COURSES

If you are applying for undergraduate education courses, you may be called for interview as part of the selection process. Many universities (particularly the more popular ones, running competitive courses) use interviews as part of their selection process. Universities will want to find out why you want to study your chosen course at their institution, and they want to judge whether the course is suitable for you and your future career plans. Interviews also give you an opportunity to visit the university and ask any questions you may have about the course or their institution.

INTERVIEWS

If you are called for interview, the key areas they are likely to cover will be:

- evidence of your academic ability
- your capacity to study hard
- your commitment to a teaching career, best shown by classroom experience
- your awareness of current issues in the news that relate to teaching or the education sector in general: for example, Every Child Matters in England or the Foundation Phase in Wales and the shortage of teachers in certain subjects
- your interpersonal skills and ability to get on with children of different ages.

A lot of the interview will be based on information supplied on your application – especially your personal statement; see pages 107 and 109 for tips about how to write a personal statement.

Each time a university or college makes a decision about your application we record it and let you know. You can check the progress of your application using Track at www.ucas.com or www.gttr.ac.uk. This is our secure online service which gives you access to your application using the same username and password you used when you applied. You can use it to find out if you have been invited for interview or need to provide an additional piece of work, as well as check to see if you have received any offers.

TYPES OF OFFER

Institutions can make two types of offer: conditional or unconditional.

Conditional offer

A conditional offer means the institution will offer you a place if you meet certain conditions – usually based on exam results. The conditions may be based on Tariff points (for example, 300 points from three A levels), or specify certain grades in named subjects (for example, A in chemistry, B in biology, C in physics). If you are applying through the GTTR, you may be asked to obtain a certain degree classification, such as a 2:2 or 2:1.

Unconditional offer

If you've met all the academic requirements for the course and the institution wants to accept you, they will make you an unconditional offer. If you accept this you'll have a definite place.

However, for both types of offer, there might be other requirements to meet before you can start the course. All offers of places on teacher training courses will be subject to satisfactory health and criminal record checks and students who are not resident in the UK or EU may have to meet certain financial conditions.

REPLYING TO OFFERS THROUGH UCAS

When you have received decisions for all your choices, you must decide which offers you want to accept. You will be given a deadline in Track by which you have to make your replies. Before replying, get advice from family, friends or advisers, but remember that you're the one taking the course so it's your decision.

Firm acceptance

- Your firm acceptance is your first choice - this is your preferred choice out of all the offers you have received. You can only have one firm acceptance.
- If you accept an unconditional offer, you are entering a contract that you will attend the course, so you must decline any other offers.
- If you accept a conditional offer, you are entering a contract that you will attend the course at that university or college if you meet the conditions of the offer. You can accept another offer as an insurance choice.

Insurance acceptance

- If your firm acceptance is a conditional offer, you can accept another offer as an insurance choice. Your insurance choice can be conditional or unconditional and acts as a back-up, so if you don't meet the conditions for your firm choice but meet the conditions for your insurance, you will be committed to the insurance choice. You can only have one insurance choice.
- The conditions for your insurance choice would usually be lower than your firm choice.
- You don't have to accept an insurance choice if you don't want one. You need to be certain that it's an offer you would be happy to accept.

For more information watch our video guides How to use Track, Making sense of your offers, and How to reply to your offers at **www.ucas.tv**.

WHAT IF YOU HAVE NO OFFERS?

If you have used all five choices on your application and either received no offers, or decided to turn down any offers you have received, you may be eligible to apply for another choice through Extra. Find out more about Extra on page 117.

If you are not eligible for Extra, in the summer you can contact universities and colleges with vacancies in Clearing. See page 132 for more information.

REPLYING TO OFFERS THROUGH THE GTTR

The GTTR sends your application to one institution at a time for consideration, starting with the first choice or highest choice with vacancies in your order of preference. If you receive a conditional or unconditional offer and you accept it, you cannot be considered by any other institutions you may have listed on your application.

If you decline the offer, the GTTR will send your application to your next highest choice of institution with vacancies. If they cannot send your application to another institution, you will have the opportunity to make new choices or apply for further courses in Extra or Clearing depending on the stage of the application cycle. For information about Extra and Clearing, see pages 117 and 132.

You accept and decline offers online using Track at **www.gttr.ac.uk**.

```
┌─────────────────────────────────┐
│        Offers                   │
│  ╔╗                             │
│  ╚╝                             │
│  ╔╝                             │
└─────────────────────────────────┘
```

Extra

Extra allows you to make additional choices, one at a time without having to wait for Clearing in July. It is completely optional, and is designed to encourage you to continue researching and choosing courses if you need to. You can search for courses available through Extra on Course Finder, at **www.ucas.com**. All courses with vacancies on the GTTR website **www.gttr.ac.uk** should be available through Extra.

The UCAS Extra service is available to eligible applicants from 25 February to early July 2013 through Track at **www.ucas.com**. GTTR Extra is available to eligible applicants from mid-March to the end of June 2013 through Track at **www.gttr.ac.uk**.

WHO IS ELIGIBLE?

You will be eligible for Extra in the UCAS application system if you have already made five choices and:

- you have had unsuccessful or withdrawal decisions from all five of your choices
- you have cancelled your outstanding choices and hold no offers
- you have received decisions from all five choices and have declined all offers made to you.

You will be eligible for Extra in the GTTR application system if, after mid-March, your application has been sent to all your choices with vacancies and you have been unsuccessful or declined any offers received. In the GTTR application system you do not need to have made the maximum number of four choices before you are eligible for Extra.

HOW DOES IT WORK?

We contact you and explain what to do if you are eligible for Extra. If you are eligible you should:

- see a special Extra button on your Track screen
- check on UCAS Course Finder or GTTR Course Search for courses that are available through Extra. You need to tick the 'Available in extra' box in the Study options section when looking for courses on UCAS Course Finder. On GTTR Course Search all courses with vacancies should be available through Extra.
- choose a course that you would like to apply for and enter the details on your Track screen.

When you have chosen a course, the institution will be able to see your application and consider you for a place.

WHAT HAPPENS NEXT?

We give institutions a maximum of 21 days to consider your Extra application. During this time, you cannot be considered by another institution. If you have not heard after 21 days, you can apply to a different institution if you wish, but it is a good idea to ring the one currently considering you before doing so. If you are made an offer, you can choose whether or not to accept it.

If you accept any offer, conditional or unconditional, you will not be able to take any further part in Extra.

If you are currently studying for examinations, any offer that you receive is likely to be an offer conditional on exam grades. If you already have your examination results, it is possible that an institution may make an unconditional offer. If you accept an unconditional offer, you will be placed. If you decide to decline the offer or the institution decides they cannot make you an offer, you will be given another opportunity to use Extra, time permitting. You Extra button on Track will be reactivated.

Once you have accepted an offer in Extra, you are committed to it in the same way as you would be with an offer through the main UCAS or GTTR systems. Conditional offers made through Extra will be treated in the same way as other conditional offers, when your examination results become available.

If your results do not meet the conditions and the institution decides that they cannot confirm your Extra offer, you will automatically become eligible for Clearing if it is too late for you to be considered by another institution in Extra.

If you are unsuccessful, decline an offer, or do not receive an offer, or 21 days have elapsed since choosing a course through Extra, you can use Extra to apply for another course, time permitting.

ADVICE

Do the same careful research and seek guidance on your choice of institution and course in Extra as you did for your initial choices. If you applied through UCAS to high-demand courses and institutions in your original application and were unsuccessful, you could consider related or alternative subjects or perhaps apply for the subject you want in combination with another. Your teachers or careers advisers or the universities and colleges themselves can provide useful guidance. If you applied through the GTTR for competitive primary teaching courses and were unsuccessful, you could consider training to teach in secondary schools as an alternative.

UCAS Course Finder and the Entry Profiles for courses on GTTR Course Search are other important sources of information. Be flexible, that is the key to success. But you are the only one who knows how flexible you are prepared to be. Remember that even if you decide to take a degree course other than teaching, you can take the postgraduate route into the profession after you have finished your degree.

Visit **www.ucas.tv** to watch the video guide on how to use UCAS Extra.

Connect with us...

 www.facebook.com/ucasonline

 www.twitter.com/ucas_online

 www.youtube.com/ucasonline

Offers

3

The Tariff

Finding out what qualifications are needed for different higher education courses can be very confusing.

The UCAS Tariff is the system for allocating points to qualifications used for entry to higher education. Universities and colleges can use the UCAS Tariff to make comparisons between applicants with different qualifications. Tariff points are often used in entry requirements, although other factors are often taken into account. Information on Course Finder at **www.ucas.com** provides a fuller picture of what admissions tutors are seeking.

The tables on the following pages show the qualifications covered by the UCAS Tariff. There may have been changes to these tables since this book was printed. You should visit **www.ucas.com** to view the most up-to-date tables.

FURTHER INFORMATION?

Although Tariff points can be accumulated in a variety of ways, not all of these will necessarily be acceptable for entry to a particular higher education course. The achievement of a points score therefore does not give an automatic entitlement to entry, and many other factors are taken into account in the admissions process.

Course Finder facility at **www.ucas.com** is the best source of reference to find out what qualifications are acceptable for entry to specific courses. Updates to the Tariff, including details on how new qualifications are added, can be found at **www.ucas.com/students/ucas_tariff/**.

HOW DOES THE TARIFF WORK?

- Students can collect Tariff points from a range of different qualifications, eg GCE A level with BTEC Nationals.
- There is no ceiling to the number of points that can be accumulated.
- There is no double counting. Certain qualifications within the Tariff build on qualifications in the same subject. In these cases only the qualification with the higher Tariff score will be counted. This principle applies to:
  - GCE Advanced Subsidiary level and GCE Advanced level
  - Scottish Highers and Advanced Highers
  - Speech, drama and music awards at grades 6, 7 and 8.
- Tariff points for the Advanced Diploma come from the Progression Diploma score plus the relevant Additional and Specialist Learning (ASL) Tariff points. Please see the appropriate qualification in the Tariff tables to calculate the ASL score.
- The Extended Project Tariff points are included within the Tariff points for Progression and Advanced Diplomas. Extended Project points represented in the Tariff only count when the qualification is taken outside of these Diplomas.
- Where the Tariff tables refer to specific awarding organisations, only qualifications from these awarding organisations attract Tariff points. Qualifications with a similar title, but from a different qualification awarding organisation do not attract Tariff points.

HOW DO UNIVERSITIES AND COLLEGES USE THE TARIFF?

The Tariff provides a facility to help universities and colleges when expressing entrance requirements and when making conditional offers. Entry requirements and conditional offers expressed as Tariff points will often require a minimum level of achievement in a specified subject (for example, '300 points to include grade A at A level chemistry', or '260 points including SQA Higher grade B in mathematics').

Use of the Tariff may also vary from department to department at any one institution, and may in some cases be dependent on the programme being offered.

In July 2010, UCAS announced plans to review the qualifications information provided to universities and colleges. You can read more about the review at www.ucas.com/qireview.

WHAT QUALIFICATIONS ARE INCLUDED IN THE TARIFF?

The following qualifications are included in the UCAS Tariff. See the number on the qualification title to find the relevant section of the Tariff table.

1   AAT NVQ Level 3 in Accounting
2   AAT Level 3 Diploma in Accounting (QCF)
3   Advanced Diploma
4   Advanced Extension Awards
5   Advanced Placement Programme (US and Canada)
6   Arts Award (Gold)
7   ASDAN Community Volunteering qualification
8   Asset Languages Advanced Stage
9   British Horse Society (Stage 3 Horse Knowledge & Care, Stage 3 Riding and Preliminary Teacher's Certificate)
10 BTEC Awards (NQF)
11 BTEC Certificates and Extended Certificates (NQF)
12 BTEC Diplomas (NQF)
13 BTEC National in Early Years (NQF)
14 BTEC Nationals (NQF)
15 BTEC QCF Qualifications (Suite known as Nationals)
16 BTEC Specialist Qualifications (QCF)
17 CACHE Award, Certificate and Diploma in Child Care and Education
18 CACHE Level 3 Extended Diploma for the Children and Young People's Workforce (QCF)
19 Cambridge ESOL Examinations
20 Cambridge Pre-U
21 Certificate of Personal Effectiveness (COPE)
22 CISI Introduction to Securities and Investment
23 City & Guilds Land Based Services Level 3 Qualifications
24 Graded Dance and Vocational Graded Dance
25 Diploma in Fashion Retail
26 Diploma in Foundation Studies (Art & Design; Art, Design & Media)
27 EDI Level 3 Certificate in Accounting, Certificate in Accounting (IAS)
28 Essential Skills (Northern Ireland)
29 Essential Skills Wales
30 Extended Project (stand alone)
31 Free-standing Mathematics
32 Functional skills
33 GCE (AS, AS Double Award, A level, A level Double Award and A level (with additional AS))
34 Hong Kong Diploma of Secondary Education (from 2012 entry onwards)
35 ifs School of Finance (Certificate and Diploma in Financial Studies)
36 iMedia (OCR level Certificate/Diploma for iMedia Professionals)
37 International Baccalaureate (IB) Diploma
38 International Baccalaureate (IB) Certificate
39 Irish Leaving Certificate (Higher and Ordinary levels)
40 IT Professionals (iPRO) (Certificate and Diploma)
41 Key Skills (Levels 2, 3 and 4)
42 Music examinations (grades 6, 7 and 8)
43 OCR Level 3 Certificate in Mathematics for Engineering
44 OCR Level 3 Certificate for Young Enterprise
45 OCR Nationals (National Certificate, National Diploma and National Extended Diploma)
46 Principal Learning Wales
47 Progression Diploma
48 Rockschool Music Practitioners Qualifications
49 Scottish Qualifications
50 Speech and Drama examinations (grades 6, 7 and 8 and Performance Studies)
51 Sports Leaders UK
52 Welsh Baccalaureate Advanced Diploma (Core)

Updates on the Tariff, including details on the incorporation of any new qualifications, are posted on www.ucas.com.

UCAS TARIFF TABLES

1

AAT NVQ LEVEL 3 IN ACCOUNTING	
GRADE	TARIFF POINTS
PASS	160

2

AAT LEVEL 3 DIPLOMA IN ACCOUNTING	
GRADE	TARIFF POINTS
PASS	160

3

ADVANCED DIPLOMA

Advanced Diploma = Progression Diploma plus Additional & Specialist Learning (ASL). Please see the appropriate qualification to calculate the ASL score. Please see the Progression Diploma (Table 47) for Tariff scores

4

ADVANCED EXTENSION AWARDS	
GRADE	TARIFF POINTS
DISTINCTION	40
MERIT	20

Points for Advanced Extension Awards are over and above those gained from the A level grade

5

ADVANCED PLACEMENT PROGRAMME (US & CANADA)	
GRADE	TARIFF POINTS
Group A	
5	120
4	90
3	60
Group B	
5	50
4	35
3	20

Details of the subjects covered by each group can be found at www.ucas.com/students/ucas_tariff/tarifftables

6

ARTS AWARD (GOLD)	
GRADE	TARIFF POINTS
PASS	35

7

ASDAN COMMUNITY VOLUNTEERING QUALIFICATION	
GRADE	TARIFF POINTS
CERTIFICATE	50
AWARD	30

8

ASSET LANGUAGES ADVANCED STAGE			
GRADE	TARIFF POINTS	GRADE	TARIFF POINTS
Speaking		Listening	
GRADE 12	28	GRADE 12	25
GRADE 11	20	GRADE 11	18
GRADE 10	12	GRADE 10	11
Reading		Writing	
GRADE 12	25	GRADE 12	25
GRADE 11	18	GRADE 11	18
GRADE 10	11	GRADE 10	11

9

BRITISH HORSE SOCIETY	
GRADE	TARIFF POINTS
Stage 3 Horse Knowledge & Care	
PASS	35
Stage 3 Riding	
PASS	35
Preliminary Teacher's Certificate	
PASS	35

Awarded by Equestrian Qualifications (GB) Ltd (EQL)

10

BTEC AWARDS (NQF) (EXCLUDING BTEC NATIONAL QUALIFICATIONS)			
GRADE	TARIFF POINTS		
	Group A	Group B	Group C
DISTINCTION	20	30	40
MERIT	13	20	26
PASS	7	10	13

Details of the subjects covered by each group can be found at www.ucas.com/students/ucas_tariff/tarifftables

11

BTEC CERTIFICATES AND EXTENDED CERTIFICATES (NQF) (EXCLUDING BTEC NATIONAL QUALIFICATIONS)					
GRADE	TARIFF POINTS				
	Group A	Group B	Group C	Group D	Extended Certificates
DISTINCTION	40	60	80	100	60
MERIT	26	40	52	65	40
PASS	13	20	26	35	20

Details of the subjects covered by each group can be found at www.ucas.com/students/ucas_tariff/tarifftables

12

BTEC DIPLOMAS (NQF) (EXCLUDING BTEC NATIONAL QUALIFICATIONS)			
GRADE	TARIFF POINTS		
	Group A	Group B	Group C
DISTINCTION	80	100	120
MERIT	52	65	80
PASS	26	35	40

Details of the subjects covered by each group can be found at www.ucas.com/students/ucas_tariff/tarifftables

UCAS TARIFF TABLES

13

BTEC NATIONAL IN EARLY YEARS (NQF)

GRADE	TARIFF POINTS	GRADE	TARIFF POINTS	GRADE	TARIFF POINTS
Theory				Practical	
Diploma		Certificate		D	120
DDD	320	DD	200	M	80
DDM	280	DM	160	P	40
DMM	240	MM	120		
MMM	220	MP	80		
MMP	160	PP	40		
MPP	120				
PPP	80				

Points apply to the following qualifications only: BTEC National Diploma in Early Years (100/1279/5); BTEC National Certificate in Early Years (100/1280/1)

14

BTEC NATIONALS (NQF)

GRADE	TARIFF POINTS	GRADE	TARIFF POINTS	GRADE	TARIFF POINTS
Diploma		Certificate		Award	
DDD	360	DD	240	D	120
DDM	320	DM	200	M	80
DMM	280	MM	160	P	40
MMM	240	MP	120		
MMP	200	PP	80		
MPP	160				
PPP	120				

15

BTEC QUALIFICATIONS (QCF)
(SUITE OF QUALIFICATIONS KNOWN AS NATIONALS)

EXTENDED DIPLOMA	DIPLOMA	90 CREDIT DIPLOMA	SUBSIDIARY DIPLOMA	CERTIFICATE	TARIFF POINTS
D*D*D*					420
D*D*D					400
D*DD					380
DDD					360
DDM					320
DMM	D*D*				280
	D*D				260
MMM	DD				240
		D*D*			210
MMP	DM	D*D			200
		DD			180
MPP	MM	DM			160
			D*		140
PPP	MP	MM	D		120
		MP			100
	PP		M		80
				D*	70
		PP		D	60
			P	M	40
				P	20

16

BTEC SPECIALIST (QCF)

GRADE	TARIFF POINTS		
	Diploma	Certificate	Award
DISTINCTION	120	60	20
MERIT	80	40	13
PASS	40	20	7

17

CACHE LEVEL 3 AWARD, CERTIFICATE AND DIPLOMA IN CHILD CARE & EDUCATION

AWARD		CERTIFICATE		DIPLOMA	
GRADE	TARIFF POINTS	GRADE	TARIFF POINTS	GRADE	TARIFF POINTS
A	30	A	110	A	360
B	25	B	90	B	300
C	20	C	70	C	240
D	15	D	55	D	180
E	10	E	35	E	120

18

CACHE LEVEL 3 EXTENDED DIPLOMA FOR THE CHILDREN AND YOUNG PEOPLE'S WORKFORCE (QCF)

GRADE	TARIFF POINTS
A*	420
A	340
B	290
C	240
D	140
E	80

19

CAMBRIDGE ESOL EXAMINATIONS

GRADE	TARIFF POINTS
Certificate of Proficiency in English	
A	140
B	110
C	70
Certificate in Advanced English	
A	70

20

CAMBRIDGE PRE-U

GRADE	TARIFF POINTS	GRADE	TARIFF POINTS	GRADE	TARIFF POINTS
Principal Subject		Global Perspectives and Research		Short Course	
D1	TBC	D1	TBC	D1	TBC
D2	145	D2	140	D2	TBC
D3	130	D3	126	D3	60
M1	115	M1	112	M1	53
M2	101	M2	98	M2	46
M3	87	M3	84	M3	39
P1	73	P1	70	P1	32
P2	59	P2	56	P2	26
P3	46	P3	42	P3	20

21

CERTIFICATE OF PERSONAL EFFECTIVENESS (COPE)

GRADE	TARIFF POINTS
PASS	70

Points are awarded for the Certificate of Personal Effectiveness (CoPE) awarded by ASDAN and CCEA

22

CISI INTRODUCTION TO SECURITIES AND INVESTMENT

GRADE	TARIFF POINTS
PASS WITH DISTINCTION	60
PASS WITH MERIT	40
PASS	20

23

CITY AND GUILDS LAND BASED SERVICES LEVEL 3 QUALIFICATIONS

GRADE	TARIFF POINTS			
	EXTENDED DIPLOMA	DIPLOMA	SUBSIDIARY DIPLOMA	CERTIFICATE
DISTINCTION*	420	280	140	70
DISTINCTION	360	240	120	60
MERIT	240	160	80	40
PASS	120	80	40	20

24

GRADED DANCE AND VOCATIONAL GRADED DANCE

GRADE	TARIFF POINTS	GRADE	TARIFF POINTS	GRADE	TARIFF POINTS
Graded Dance					
Grade 8		Grade 7		Grade 6	
DISTINCTION	65	DISTINCTION	55	DISTINCTION	40
MERIT	55	MERIT	45	MERIT	35
PASS	45	PASS	35	PASS	30
Vocational Graded Dance					
Advanced Foundation		Intermediate			
DISTINCTION	70	DISTINCTION	65		
MERIT	55	MERIT	50		
PASS	45	PASS	40		

25

DIPLOMA IN FASHION RETAIL

GRADE	TARIFF POINTS
DISTINCTION	160
MERIT	120
PASS	80

Applies to the NQF and QCF versions of the qualifications awarded by ABC Awards

UCAS TARIFF TABLES

26

DIPLOMA IN FOUNDATION STUDIES (ART & DESIGN AND ART, DESIGN & MEDIA)

GRADE	TARIFF POINTS
DISTINCTION	285
MERIT	225
PASS	165

Awarded by ABC, Edexcel, UAL and WJEC

27

EDI LEVEL 3 CERTIFICATE IN ACCOUNTING, CERTIFICATE IN ACCOUNTING (IAS)

GRADE	TARIFF POINTS
DISTINCTION	120
MERIT	90
PASS	70

28

ESSENTIAL SKILLS (NORTHERN IRELAND)

GRADE	TARIFF POINTS
LEVEL 2	10

Only allocated at level 2 if studied as part of a wider composite qualification such as 14-19 Diploma or Welsh Baccalaureate

29

ESSENTIAL SKILLS WALES

GRADE	TARIFF POINTS
LEVEL 4	30
LEVEL 3	20
LEVEL 2	10

Only allocated at level 2 if studied as part of a wider composite qualification such as 14-19 Diploma or Welsh Baccalaureate

30

EXTENDED PROJECT (STAND ALONE)

GRADE	TARIFF POINTS
A*	70
A	60
B	50
C	40
D	30
E	20

Points for the Extended Project cannot be counted if taken as part of Progression/Advanced Diploma

31

FREE-STANDING MATHEMATICS

GRADE	TARIFF POINTS
A	20
B	17
C	13
D	10
E	7

Covers free-standing Mathematics - Additional Maths, Using and Applying Statistics, Working with Algebraic and Graphical Techniques, Modelling with Calculus

32

FUNCTIONAL SKILLS

GRADE	TARIFF POINTS
LEVEL 2	10

Only allocated if studied as part of a wider composite qualification such as 14-19 Diploma or Welsh Baccalaureate

33

GCE AND VCE

GRADE	TARIFF POINTS	GRADE	TARIFF POINTS	GRADE	TARIFF POINTS	GRADE	TARIFF POINTS	GRADE	TARIFF POINTS
GCE & AVCE Double Award		GCE A level with additional AS (9 units)		GCE A level & AVCE		GCE AS Double Award		GCE AS & AS VCE	
A*A*	280	A*A	200	A*	140	AA	120	A	60
A*A	260	AA	180	A	120	AB	110	B	50
AA	240	AB	170	B	100	BB	100	C	40
AB	220	BB	150	C	80	BC	90	D	30
BB	200	BC	140	D	60	CC	80	E	20
BC	180	CC	120	E	40	CD	70		
CC	160	CD	110			DD	60		
CD	140	DD	90			DE	50		
DD	120	DE	80			EE	40		
DE	100	EE	60						
EE	80								

34

HONG KONG DIPLOMA OF SECONDARY EDUCATION

GRADE	TARIFF POINTS	GRADE	TARIFF POINTS	GRADE	TARIFF POINTS
All subjects except mathematics		Mathematics compulsory component		Mathematics optional components	
5**	No value	5**	No value	5**	No value
5*	130	5*	60	5*	70
5	120	5	45	5	60
4	80	4	35	4	50
3	40	3	25	3	40

No value for 5** pending receipt of candidate evidence (post 2012)

35

IFS SCHOOL OF FINANCE (NQF & QCF)			
GRADE	TARIFF POINTS	GRADE	TARIFF POINTS
Certificate in Financial Studies (CeFS)		Diploma in Financial Studies (DipFS)	
A	60	A	120
B	50	B	100
C	40	C	80
D	30	D	60
E	20	E	40

Applicants with the ifs Diploma cannot also count points allocated to the ifs Certificate. Completion of both qualifications will result in a maximum of 120 UCAS Tariff points

36

LEVEL 3 CERTIFICATE / DIPLOMA FOR iMEDIA USERS (iMEDIA)	
GRADE	TARIFF POINTS
DIPLOMA	66
CERTIFICATE	40

Awarded by OCR

37

INTERNATIONAL BACCALAUREATE (IB) DIPLOMA			
GRADE	TARIFF POINTS	GRADE	TARIFF POINTS
45	720	34	479
44	698	33	457
43	676	32	435
42	654	31	413
41	632	30	392
40	611	29	370
39	589	28	348
38	567	27	326
37	545	26	304
36	523	25	282
35	501	24	260

38

INTERNATIONAL BACCALAUREATE (IB) CERTIFICATE					
GRADE	TARIFF POINTS	GRADE	TARIFF POINTS	GRADE	TARIFF POINTS
Higher Level		Standard Level		Core	
7	130	7	70	3	120
6	110	6	59	2	80
5	80	5	43	1	40
4	50	4	27	0	10
3	20	3	11		

39

IRISH LEAVING CERTIFICATE			
GRADE	TARIFF POINTS	GRADE	TARIFF POINTS
Higher		Ordinary	
A1	90	A1	39
A2	77	A2	26
B1	71	B1	20
B2	64	B2	14
B3	58	B3	7
C1	52		
C2	45		
C3	39		
D1	33		
D2	26		
D3	20		

40

IT PROFESSIONALS (iPRO)	
GRADE	TARIFF POINTS
DIPLOMA	100
CERTIFICATE	80

Awarded by OCR

41

KEY SKILLS	
GRADE	TARIFF POINTS
LEVEL 4	30
LEVEL 3	20
LEVEL 2	10

Only allocated at level 2 if studied as part of a wider composite qualification such as 14-19 Diploma or Welsh Baccalaureate

UCAS TARIFF TABLES

42

MUSIC EXAMINATIONS					
GRADE	TARIFF POINTS	GRADE	TARIFF POINTS	GRADE	TARIFF POINTS
Practical					
Grade 8		Grade 7		Grade 6	
DISTINCTION	75	DISTINCTION	60	DISTINCTION	45
MERIT	70	MERIT	55	MERIT	40
PASS	55	PASS	40	PASS	25
Theory					
Grade 8		Grade 7		Grade 6	
DISTINCTION	30	DISTINCTION	20	DISTINCTION	15
MERIT	25	MERIT	15	MERIT	10
PASS	20	PASS	10	PASS	5

Points shown are for the ABRSM, LCMM/University of West London, Rockschool and Trinity Guildhall/Trinity College London Advanced Level music examinations

43

OCR LEVEL 3 CERTIFICATE IN MATHEMATICS FOR ENGINEERING	
GRADE	TARIFF POINTS
A*	TBC
A	90
B	75
C	60
D	45
E	30

44

OCR LEVEL 3 CERTIFICATE FOR YOUNG ENTERPRISE	
GRADE	TARIFF POINTS
DISTINCTION	40
MERIT	30
PASS	20

45

OCR NATIONALS							
GRADE	TARIFF POINTS	GRADE	TARIFF POINTS	GRADE	TARIFF POINTS	GRADE	TARIFF POINTS
National Extended Diploma		National Diploma		National Certificate			
D1	360	D	240	D	120		
D2/M1	320	M1	200	M	80		
M2	280	M2/P1	160	P	40		
M3	240	P2	120				
P1	200	P3	80				
P2	160						
P3	120						

46

PRINCIPAL LEARNING WALES	
GRADE	TARIFF POINTS
A*	210
A	180
B	150
C	120
D	90
E	60

47

PROGRESSION DIPLOMA	
GRADE	TARIFF POINTS
A*	350
A	300
B	250
C	200
D	150
E	100

Advanced Diploma = Progression Diploma plus Additional & Specialist Learning (ASL). Please see the appropriate qualification to calculate the ASL score

48

GRADE	ROCKSCHOOL MUSIC PRACTITIONERS QUALIFICATIONS				
	TARIFF POINTS				
	Extended Diploma	Diploma	Subsidiary Diploma	Extended Certificate	Certificate
DISTINCTION	240	180	120	60	30
MERIT	160	120	80	40	20
PASS	80	60	40	20	10

49

SCOTTISH QUALIFICATIONS							
GRADE	TARIFF POINTS	GRADE	TARIFF POINTS	GRADE	TARIFF POINTS	GROUP	TARIFF POINTS
Advanced Higher		Higher		Scottish Interdisciplinary Project		Scottish National Certificates	
A	130	A	80	A	65	C	125
B	110	B	65	B	55	B	100
C	90	C	50	C	45	A	75
D	72	D	36				
Ungraded Higher		NPA PC Passport					
PASS	45	PASS	45				
		Core Skills					
		HIGHER	20				

Details of the subjects covered by each Scottish National Certificate can be found at www.ucas.com/students/ucas_tariff/tarifftables

50

SPEECH AND DRAMA EXAMINATIONS							
GRADE	TARIFF POINTS	GRADE	TARIFF POINTS	GRADE	TARIFF POINTS	GRADE	TARIFF POINTS
PCertLAM		Grade 8		Grade 7		Grade 6	
DISTINCTION	90	DISTINCTION	65	DISTINCTION	55	DISTINCTION	40
MERIT	80	MERIT	60	MERIT	50	MERIT	35
PASS	60	PASS	45	PASS	35	PASS	20

Details of the Speech and Drama Qualifications covered by the Tariff can be found at www.ucas.com/students/ucas_tariff/tarifftables

51

SPORTS LEADERS UK	
GRADE	TARIFF POINTS
PASS	30

These points are awarded to Higher Sports Leader Award and Level 3 Certificate in Higher Sports Leadership (QCF)

52

WELSH BACCALAUREATE ADVANCED DIPLOMA (CORE)	
GRADE	TARIFF POINTS
PASS	120

These points are awarded only when a candidate achieves the Welsh Baccalaureate Advanced Diploma

Results

4

Step 4 – Results

UCAS APPLICATIONS

You should arrange your holidays so that you are at home when your exam results are published because, if there are any issues to discuss, admissions tutors will want to speak to you in person.

We receive many exam results direct from the exam boards – check the list at **www.ucas.com**. If your qualification is listed, we send your results to the universities and colleges that you have accepted as your firm and insurance choices. If your qualification is not listed, you must send your exam results to the universities and colleges where you are holding offers.

After you have received your exam results check Track to find out if you have a place on your chosen course.

If you have met all the conditions for your firm choice, the university or college will confirm that you have a place. Occasionally, they may still confirm you have a place even if you have not quite met all the offer conditions; or they may offer you a place on a similar course.

If you have not met the conditions of your firm choice and the university or college has not confirmed your place, but you have met all the conditions of your insurance offer, your insurance university or college will confirm that you have a place.

When a university or college tells us that you have a place, we send you confirmation by letter.

RE-MARKED EXAMS

If you ask for any of your exams to be re-marked, you must tell the universities and colleges where you're holding offers. If a university or college cannot confirm your place based on the initial results, you should ask them if they would be able to reconsider their decision after the re-mark. They are under no obligation to reconsider their position even if your re-mark results in higher grades. Don't forget that re-marks may also result in lower grades.

The exam boards tell us about any re-marks that result in grade changes. We then send the revised grades to the universities and colleges where you're holding offers. As soon as you know about any grade changes, you should also tell these universities and colleges.

'CASHING IN' A LEVEL RESULTS'

If you have taken A levels, your school or college must certificate or 'cash in' all your unit scores before the exam board can award final grades. If when you collect your A level results you have to add up your unit scores to find out your final grades, this means your school or college has not 'cashed in' your results.

We only receive cashed in results from the exam boards, so if your school or college has not cashed in your results, you must ask them to send a 'cash in' request to the exam board. You also need to tell the universities and colleges where you're holding offers that there'll be a delay in receiving your results and call our Customer Service Unit to find out when your results have been received.

When we receive your 'cashed in' results from the exam board we send them straight away to the universities and colleges where you're holding offers.

WHAT IF YOU DON'T HAVE A PLACE?

If you have not met the conditions of either your firm or insurance choice, and your chosen universities or colleges have not confirmed your place, you are eligible for Clearing. In Clearing you can apply for any courses that still have vacancies, but remember that admissions tutors will be reading your original personal statement.

Clearing operates from mid-July to late September 2013. See page 132 for information about Clearing.

BETTER RESULTS THAN EXPECTED?

If you obtain exam results that meet and exceed the conditions of the offer for your firm choice, you can for a short period use a process called Adjustment to look for an alternative place, whilst still keeping your original firm choice. See page 133 for information about Adjustment.

GTTR APPLICATIONS

The GTTR does not receive examination results from the exam boards. You need to send your examination results to any institution that considers you or to the institution where you have accepted a conditional offer.

If you have met all the conditions of your offer, the institution will confirm that you have a place. They may still confirm that you have a place even if you have not quite met all the offer conditions. The GTTR then sends you a letter to confirm your place.

If the institution where you are holding a conditional offer confirms that you do not have a place, the GTTR will send your application to your next choice with vacancies. If there are no other course choices with vacancies on your application, you will be able to make more choices or apply for further courses in Extra or Clearing depending on the stage of the application cycle.

Next steps

5

Step 5 – Next steps

You might find yourself with different exam results than you were expecting, or you may change your mind about what you want to do. If so, there may be other options open to you.

CLEARING

UCAS and GTTR Clearing are services that help people without a place to find suitable course vacancies. UCAS Clearing runs from mid-July until the end of September, but most people use it after the exam results are published in August. GTTR Clearing runs from early July to late September and applicants become eligible to use the service if, after the end of June, they have not accepted a place and there are no other institutions listed on their application where they can be considered.

In UCAS Clearing, you could consider related or alternative subjects or perhaps combining your original choice of subject with another. Your teachers or careers adviser, or the universities and colleges themselves, can provide useful guidance.

In GTTR Clearing, if you applied for popular primary teaching courses, you could consider secondary teacher training as an alternative.

UCAS course vacancies are listed at **www.ucas.com** and in the national media following the publication of exam results in August. **Once you have your exam results**, if you're in Clearing you need to look at the vacancy listings and then contact any university or college you are interested in.

GTTR course vacancies are listed at **www.gttr.ac.uk** and if you become eligible to use GTTR Clearing you will receive a Clearing Passport that explains fully what you need to do.

Talk to the institutions; don't be afraid to call them. Make sure you have your Personal ID and Clearing Number ready and prepare notes on what you will say to them about:

- why you want to study the course
- why you want to study at their university or college

- any relevant employment or activities you have done that relate to the course
- your grades.

Accepting an offer - you can contact as many universities and colleges as you like through Clearing, and you may informally be offered more than one place. If this happens, you will need to decide which offer you want to accept. If you're offered a place for which you want to be formally considered, you

- apply for the course in Track if you've applied through UCAS
- send your paper Clearing passport to the institution if you've applied through the GTTR.

The institution will then let you know if they are accepting you.

ADJUSTMENT FOR UCAS APPLICANTS

If you apply through UCAS ,receive better results than expected, and meet and exceed the conditions of your conditional firm choice, you have the opportunity to reconsider what and where you want to study. This process is called Adjustment.

Adjustment runs from A level results day on 15 August 2013 until the end of August. Your individual Adjustment period starts on A level results day or when your conditional firm choice changes to unconditional firm, whichever is the later. You then have a maximum of five calendar days to register and secure an alternative course, if you decide you want to do this. If you want to try to find an alternative course you must register in Track to use Adjustment, so universities and colleges can view your application.

There are no vacancy listings for Adjustment, so you'll need to talk to the institutions. When you contact a university or college make it clear that you are applying through Adjustment, not Clearing. If they want to consider you they will ask for your Personal ID, so they can view your application.

If you don't find an alternative place then you remain accepted at your original firm choice.

Adjustment is entirely optional; remember that nothing really beats the careful research you carried out to find the right courses before you made your UCAS application. Talk to a careers adviser at your school, college or local careers office, as they can help you decide if registering to use Adjustment is right for you.

More information about Adjustment and Clearing is available at www.ucas.com. You can also view UCAStv video guides on how to use Adjustment and Clearing at www.ucas.tv.

IF YOU ARE STILL WITHOUT A PLACE TO STUDY

If you haven't found a suitable place, or changed your mind about what you want to do, there are lots of other options. Ask for advice from your school, college or careers office. Here are some suggestions you might want to consider:

- studying a part-time course (there's a part-time course search at www.ucas.com from July until September)
- studying a foundation degree
- re-sit your exams
- getting some work experience
- studying in another country
- reapplying next year to university or college through UCAS
- taking a gap year
- doing an apprenticeship (you'll find a vacancy search on the National Apprenticeship Service (NAS) website at **www.apprenticeships.org.uk**)
- finding a job
- starting a business.

More advice and links to other organisations can be found on the UCAS website at www.ucas.com/students/nextsteps/advice or at www.gttr.ac.uk/afteryouapply/otheroptions on the GTTR website.

> 6 | Starting university or college

Step 6 – Starting university or college

Congratulations! Now that you have confirmed your place at university or college you will need to finalise your plans on how to get there, where to live and how to finance it. Make lists of things to do with deadlines and start contacting people whose help you can call on. Will you travel independently or can your parents or relatives help with transport? If you are keeping a car at uni, have you checked out parking facilities and told your insurance company?

Make sure you have everything organised, including travel arrangements, essential documents and paperwork, books and equipment required for the course. The university will send you joining information – contact the Admissions Office or the Students' Union if you have questions about anything to do with starting your course.

Freshers' week will help you settle in and make friends, but don't forget you are there to study. You may find the teaching methods rather alien at first, but remember there are plenty of sources of help, including your tutors, other students or student mentors and the Students' Union.

Where to live - unless you are planning to live at home, your university or college will usually provide you with guidance on how to find somewhere to live. The earlier you contact them the better your chance of finding a suitable range of options, from hall to private landlords. Find out what facilities are available at the different types of accommodation and check whether it fits within your budget. Check also what you need to bring with you and what is supplied. Don't leave it all to the last minute – especially things like arranging a bank account, checking what proof of identity you might need, gathering together a few essentials like a mug

and supplies of coffee, insurance cover,
TV licence etc.

Student finance - you will need to budget for living
costs, accommodation, travel and books (and tuition
fees if you are paying them up front). Learn about
budgeting by visiting **www.ucas.com** where you will
find further links to useful resources to help you
manage your money. Remember that if you do get into
financial difficulties the welfare office at the university
will help you change tack and manage better in future,
but it is always better to live within your means from the
outset. If you need help, find it before the situation gets
stressful.

Useful contacts

CONNECTING WITH UCAS

You can follow UCAS on Twitter at www.twitter.com/ucas_online, and ask a question or see what others are asking on Facebook at www.facebook.com/ucasonline. You can also watch videos of UCAS advisers answering frequently asked questions on YouTube at www.youtube.com/ucasonline.

There are many UCAStv video guides to help with your journey into higher education, such as *How to choose your courses*, *Attending events*, *Open days* and *How to apply*. These can all be viewed at www.ucas.tv or in the relevant section of www.ucas.com.

If you need to speak to UCAS, please contact the Customer Service Unit on 0871 468 0 468 or 0044 871 468 0 468 from outside the UK. Calls from BT landlines within the UK will cost no more than 9p per minute. The cost of calls from mobiles and other networks may vary.

If you have hearing difficulties, you can call the Text Relay service on 18001 0871 468 0 468 (outside the UK 0044 151 494 1260). Calls are charged at normal rates.

CONNECTING WITH THE GTTR

You can find full information about the GTTR and the application process at www.gttr.ac.uk.

If you need to speak to the GTTR, please contact the Customer Service Unit on 0871 468 0 469 or 0044 871 468 0 469 from outside the UK. Calls from BT landlines within the UK will cost no more than 9p per minute. The cost of calls from mobiles and other networks may vary.

If you have hearing difficulties, you can call the Text Relay service on 18001 0871 468 0 469 (outside the UK 0044 151 494 1260). Calls are charged at normal rates.

TEACHING

For information about other routes into teaching and the teaching profession, call the Teaching Agency (TA) Teaching Information Line on 0800 389 2500, or 0800 085 0971 for Welsh speakers or visit **www.education.gov.uk/get-into-teaching.**

CAREERS ADVICE

The Directgov Careers Helpline for Young People is for you if you live in England, are aged 13 to 19 and want advice on getting to where you want to be in life.

Careers advisers can give you information, advice and practical help with all sorts of things, like choosing subjects at school or mapping out your future career options. They can help you with anything that might be affecting you at school, college, work or in your personal or family life.

Contact a careers adviser at **www.direct.gov.uk/en/youngpeople/index.htm**.

Skills Development Scotland provides a starting point for anyone looking for careers information, advice or guidance. **www.myworldofwork.co.uk**.

Careers Wales – Wales' national all-age careers guidance service. **www.careerswales.com** or **www.gyrfacymru.com**.

Northern Ireland Careers Service website for the new, all-age careers guidance service in Northern Ireland. **www.nidirect.gov.uk/careers**.

If you're not sure what job you want or you need help to decide which course to do, give learndirect a call on 0800 101 901 or visit **www.learndirect.co.uk**.

GENERAL HIGHER EDUCATION ADVICE

National Union of Students (NUS) is the national voice of students, helping them to campaign, get cheap student discounts and provide advice on living student life to the full - **www.nus.org.uk**.

STUDENTS WITH DISABILITIES

If you have a disability or specific learning difficulty, you are strongly encouraged to make early direct contact with individual institutions before submitting your application. Most universities and colleges have disability coordinators or advisers. You can find their contact details and further advice on the Disability Rights UK website - **www.disabilityalliance.org**.

There is financial help for students with disabilities, known as Disabled Students' Allowances (DSAs). More information is available on the Directgov website at **www.direct.gov.uk/disabledstudents**.

YEAR OUT

For useful information on taking a year out, see **www.gap-year.com**.

The Year Out Group website is packed with information and guidance for young people and their parents and advisers. **www.yearoutgroup.org**.

Essential reading

UCAS has brought together the best books and resources you need to make the important decisions regarding entry to higher education. With guidance on choosing courses, finding the right institution, information about student finance, admissions tests, gap years and lots more, you can find the most trusted guides at **www.ucasbooks.com**.

The publications listed on the following pages and many others are available through **www.ucasbooks.com** or from UCAS Publication Services unless otherwise stated.

UCAS PUBLICATION SERVICES

UCAS Publication Services

PO Box 130, Cheltenham, Gloucestershire GL52 3ZF

f: 01242 544 806

e: publicationservices@ucas.ac.uk

// **www.ucasbooks.com**

ENTIRE RESEARCH AND APPLICATION PROCESS EXPLAINED

The UCAS Guide to getting into University and College

This guide contains advice and up-to-date information about the entire research and application process, and brings together the expertise of UCAS staff, along with insights and tips from well known universities including Oxford and Cambridge, and students who are involved with or have experienced the process first-hand.

The book clearly sets out the information you need in an easy-to-read format, with myth busters, tips from students, checklists and much more; this book will be a companion for applicants throughout their entire journey into higher education.

Published by UCAS

Price £11.99

Publication date January 2011

NEED HELP COMPLETING YOUR APPLICATION?

How to Complete your UCAS Application 2013
A must for anyone applying through UCAS. Contains advice on the preparation needed, a step-by-step guide to filling out the UCAS application, information on the UCAS process and useful tips for completing the personal statement.
Published by Trotman
Price £12.99
Publication date May 2012

Insider's Guide to Applying to University
Full of honest insights, this is a thorough guide to the application process. It reveals advice from careers advisers and current students, guidance on making sense of university information and choosing courses. Also includes tips for the personal statement, interviews, admissions tests, UCAS Extra and Clearing.
Published by Trotman
Price £12.99
Publication date June 2011

How to Write a Winning UCAS Personal Statement
The personal statement is your chance to stand out from the crowd. Based on information from admissions tutors, this book will help you sell yourself. It includes specific guidance for over 30 popular subjects, common mistakes to avoid, information on what admissions tutors look for, and much more.
Published by Trotman
Price £12.99
Publication date March 2010

CHOOSING COURSES

Progression Series 2013 entry
The 'UCAS Guide to getting into…' titles are designed to help you access good quality, useful information on some of the most competitive subject areas. The books cover advice on applying through UCAS, routes to qualifications, course details, job prospects, case studies and career advice.

New for 2013: information on the pros and cons of league tables and how to read them.

The UCAS Guide to getting into…
Art and Design
Economics, Finance and Accountancy
Engineering and Mathematics
Journalism, Broadcasting, Media Production and
 Performing Arts
Law
Medicine, Dentistry and Optometry
Nursing, Healthcare and Social Work
Psychology
Sports Science and Physiotherapy
Teaching and Education
Published by UCAS
Price £15.99 each
Publication date June 2012

UCAS Parent Guide
Free of charge.
Order online at www.ucas.com/parents.
Publication date February 2012

Open Days 2012

Attending open days, taster courses and higher education conventions is an important part of the application process. This publication makes planning attendance at these events quick and easy.

Published annually by UCAS.

Price £3.50

Publication date January 2012

Heap 2013: University Degree Course Offers

An independent, reliable guide to selecting university degree courses in the UK.

The guide lists degree courses available at universities and colleges throughout the UK and the grades, UCAS points or equivalent that you need to achieve to get on to each course listed.

Published by Trotman

Price £32.99

Publication date May 2012

ESSENTIAL READING

Choosing Your Degree Course & University

With so many universities and courses to choose from, it is not an easy decision for students embarking on their journey to higher education. This guide will offer expert guidance on the questions students need to ask when considering the opportunities available.

Published by Trotman

Price £24.99

Publication date April 2012

Degree Course Descriptions

Providing details of the nature of degree courses, the descriptions in this book are written by heads of departments and senior lecturers at major universities. Each description contains an overview of the course area, details of course structures, career opportunities and more.

Published by COA

Price £12.99

Publication date September 2011

CHOOSING WHERE TO STUDY

The Virgin Guide to British Universities

An insider's guide to choosing a university or college. Written by students and using independent statistics, this guide evaluates what you get from a higher education institution.

Published by Virgin

Price £15.99

Publication date May 2011

Times Good University Guide 2013

How do you find the best university for the subject you wish to study? You need a guide that evaluates the quality of what is available, giving facts, figures and comparative assessments of universities. The rankings provide hard data, analysed, interpreted and presented by a team of experts.

Published by Harper Collins

Price £16.99

Publication date June 2012

A Parent's Guide to Graduate Jobs

A must-have guide for any parent who is worried about their child's job prospects when they graduate.

In this guide, the graduate careers guru, Paul Redmond, advises parents how to help their son or daughter:

- increase their employability
- boost their earning potential
- acquire essential work skills
- use their own contacts to get them ahead
- gain the right work experience.

Published by Trotman
Price £12.99
Publication date January 2012

Which Uni?

One person's perfect uni might be hell for someone else. Picking the right one will give you the best chance of future happiness, academic success and brighter job prospects. This guide is packed with tables from a variety of sources, rating universities on everything from the quality of teaching to the make-up of the student population and much more.
Published by Trotman
Price £14.99
Publication date September 2011

Getting into the UK's Best Universities and Courses

This book is for those who set their goals high and dream of studying on a highly regarded course at a good university. It provides information on selecting the best courses for a subject, the application and personal statement, interviews, results day, timescales for applications and much more.
Published by Trotman
Price £12.99
Publication date June 2011

FINANCIAL INFORMATION

Student Finance - e-book

All students need to know about tuition fees, loans, grants, bursaries and much more. Covering all forms of income and expenditure, this comprehensive guide is produced in association with UCAS and offers great value for money.
Published by Constable Robinson
Price £4.99
Publication date May 2012

CAREERS PLANNING

A-Z of Careers and Jobs

It is vital to be well informed about career decisions and this guide will help you make the right choice. It provides full details of the wide range of opportunities on the market, the personal qualities and skills needed for each job, entry qualifications and training, realistic salary expectations and useful contact details.
Published by Kogan Page
Price £16.99
Publication date March 2012

The Careers Directory

An indispensable resource for anyone seeking careers information, covering over 350 careers. It presents up-to-date information in an innovative double-page format. Ideal for students in years 10 to 13 who are considering their futures and for other careers professionals.
Published by COA
Price £14.99
Publication date September 2011

Careers with a Science Degree

Over 100 jobs and areas of work for graduates of biological, chemical and physical sciences are described in this guide.

Whether you have yet to choose your degree subject and want to know where the various choices could lead, or are struggling for ideas about what to do with your science degree, this book will guide and inspire you. The title includes: nature of the work and potential employers, qualifications required for entry, including personal qualities and skills; training routes and opportunities for career development and postgraduate study options.
Published by Lifetime Publishing
Price £12.99
Publication date September 2010

Careers with an Arts and Humanities Degree

Covers careers and graduate opportunities related to these degrees.

The book describes over 100 jobs and areas of work suitable for graduates from a range of disciplines including: English and modern languages, history and geography, music and the fine arts. The guide highlights: graduate opportunities, training routes, postgraduate study options and entry requirements.
Published by Lifetime Publishing
Price £12.99
Publication date September 2010

'Getting into...' guides

Clear and concise guides to help applicants secure places. They include qualifications required, advice on applying, tests, interviews and case studies. The guides give an honest view and discuss current issues and careers.

Getting into Oxford and Cambridge
Publication date April 2011
Getting into Veterinary School
Publication date February 2011
Published by Trotman
Price £12.99 each

DEFERRING ENTRY

Gap Years: The Essential Guide

The essential book for all young people planning a gap year before continuing with their education. This up-to-date guide provides essential information on specialist gap year programmes, as well as the vast range of jobs and voluntary opportunities available to young people around the world.
Published by Crimson Publishing
Price £9.99
Publication date April 2012

Gap Year Guidebook 2012

This thorough and easy-to-use guide contains everything you need to know before taking a gap year. It includes real-life traveller tips, hundreds of contact details, realistic advice on everything from preparing, learning and working abroad, coping with coming home and much more.
Published by John Catt Education
Price £14.99
Publication date November 2011

Summer Jobs Worldwide 2012
This unique and specialist guide contains over
40,000 jobs for all ages. No other book includes
such a variety and wealth of summer work
opportunities in Britain and aboard. Anything from
horse trainer in Iceland, to a guide for nature walks
in Peru, to a yoga centre helper in Greece, to an
animal keeper for London Zoo, can be found.
Published by Crimson Publishing
Price £14.99
Publication date November 2011

Please note all publications incur a postage and packing
charge. All information was correct at the time of
printing.

For a full list of publications, please visit
www.ucasbooks.com.

UCAS HIGHER EDUCATION CONVENTIONS

Meet face-to-face with over 100 UK university representatives, attend seminars on How to Apply through UCAS and Financing yourself through university.

For further details visit
www.ucas.com/conventions

Institution profiles

Institution profiles

Keen to apply for courses? This section provides institution profiles for most universities, colleges and school-centred initial teacher training consortia in England, Scotland and Wales that offer undergraduate and/or postgraduate courses in teacher training, education or both. Each profile typically includes:

- the institution's contact details
- general information about the institution
- an outline of the courses offered with entry requirements.

You will need to visit the institutions' websites or read their prospectuses for detailed information about their courses.

The profiles in this section appear in institution code alphabetical order.

Planned changes to government funding of teacher training from 2013 onwards may result in significant changes to the course provision described in the institution profiles. This disclaimer advises readers that details in the profiles may have changed since this book was published and that they should contact institutions for the latest information about course provision.

University of Aberdeen

Institution code: A20

Student Recruitment and Admissions Service
King's College
Aberdeen AB24 3FX
t: **01224 272090/91**
f: **01224 272576**
e: **sras@abdn.ac.uk**
// **www.abdn.ac.uk/sras**

GENERAL INFORMATION

Founded in 1495, the University of Aberdeen is one of the UK's most internationally distinguished universities, with a superb reputation going back many centuries.

Education is taught at the King's College Campus in a building that boasts state-of-the-art facilities.

The Professional Graduate Diploma in Education (PGDE) is offered in either Primary, Primary Gaelic or the following Secondary subjects: biology, business studies, chemistry, drama, economics (second subject only), English, French*, Gaelic, German*, geography, history, home economics, mathematics, modern studies, physics and religious and moral education.

* Spanish offered as a subsidiary subject.

Entry requirements for the PGDE programme:
Successful applicants must meet the requirements as set by the *Memorandum on Entry Requirements to Courses of Initial Teacher Education in Scotland* produced by the Scottish Government. The current version of the memorandum is dated 2009.

Applicants must be familiar with using information and communications technology (ICT) in order to realise how it can be used for learning and teaching.

Top-up courses are allowed, however graduates will only be allowed a maximum of 20 credits and they must be obtained before entering the PGDE.

All applicants must have by the date of entry:

- a degree validated by a higher education institution in the UK or a degree of an equivalent standard from outside the UK. For PGDE Secondary, the degree should normally contain 80 SCQF credit points relevant to the teaching qualification or qualifications to be studied. Forty of the credit points must have been studied at SCQF level 8 or above
- SCE Higher grade award in English/ESOL at grade C or above or equivalent. Full details can be obtained from the University of Aberdeen.

PGDE Primary applicants also require SCE Standard grade (credit level) award in mathematics at grade 1 or 2 or equivalent. Full details can be obtained from the University of Aberdeen.

PGDE Primary Gaelic applicants, in addition to the above, must be fluent Scottish Gaelic speakers and will train to become teachers in the Scottish Gaelic medium. The following are **not accepted** as a mathematics qualification at the University of Aberdeen: Core Maths 4, Standard grade 3 or below, GCSE grade C or below, CSE grade 1, O level grade 3, O level grade C.

The university will consult UK NARIC (The National Academic Recognition Information Centre for the United Kingdom), to determine whether or not qualifications achieved outside the UK meet the entry requirements detailed above.

Application route: Apply through GTTR.

School of Education and Lifelong Learning
P5
Penglais Campus
Aberystwyth SY23 3UX
Head of school: Dr Malcom Thomas
t: **01970 621580**
f: **01970 622258**
e: **learning@aber.ac.uk**
// **www.aber.ac.uk/sell**

GENERAL INFORMATION

At Aberystwyth, we can offer you

- an attractive, congenial and friendly environment
- an ideal base for sailing, mountain walking and other pursuits on the west coast of Wales
- a school which prides itself on taking a personal interest in both the welfare and the professional development of its students
- a long tradition of courses of education and training for prospective teachers but is very much in touch with recent and current trends in education
- a close partnership with training schools, established over many years and located in most parts of Wales, giving a wide range of experiences for our students
- a range of features which make the Aberystwyth PGCE course distinctive, including an option subject in addition to your specialist subject and additional training in French for MFL trainees of German and Spanish
- an arts centre, with a full and varied programme of concerts, films, theatre performances and art exhibitions
- access to the National Library of Wales.

ACADEMIC AWARDS

Bachelor degrees
BA Joint Honours Education
Length of course: 3 years
Entry requirements: 280 UCAS points or equivalent.
Course content/structure: This scheme explores ways in which children learn. It includes issues which are central to an understanding of educational systems.

BA Childhood Studies
Length of course: 3 years full-time, may be studied on a part-time basis
Entry requirements: 240 UCAS points or equivalent.
Course content/structure: This course will give you the opportunity to delve into the factors which influence 'childhood' and how these can affect later development. The course will draw upon a variety of disciplines, including sociology, psychology and educational studies in order to help you to understand the childhood years.

Certificates
PGCE Secondary (age 11-16 and 11-18)
Length of course: 1 year full-time
Entry requirements: Relevant first degree, with at least 50% relevance to the subject to be taught; GCSE English and mathematics at grade C or equivalent. We also run equivalence tests for those who do not already have these qualifications.

Secondary subjects taught:
biology, chemistry (all sciences include balanced science, drama, English, French, geography, German (including additional training in Key Stage 3 French), history, information and communication technology (ICT), physics, Spanish (including additional training in Key Stage 3 French) and Welsh.

The course prepares students to teach the main subject at KS3 and KS4 and to achieve QTS. 11 weeks are allocated to the university-based course and 25 weeks are spent on school experience at partnership schools. All subjects can be taken in Welsh or English.
Application route: Apply through the GTTR.

North and Mid-Wales Centre of Teacher Education
Initial teacher training courses provided by the centre include the above PGCE courses and those delivered by our partner university, Bangor University in Primary education and these additional secondary subjects: music, art, mathematics, outdoor activities, PE and RE.

Anglia Ruskin University

Institution code: A60

Cambridge Campus
East Road, Cambridge CB1 1PT

Chelmsford Campus
Bishop Hall Lane
Chelmsford CM1 1SQ
t: **0845 271 3333**
e: **answers@anglia.ac.uk**
// **www.anglia.ac.uk**

GENERAL INFORMATION

The Faculty of Education offers a range of undergraduate taught courses at our campuses at Cambridge, Chelmsford and University Centre Peterborough. Whether you want to train as a teacher, develop your skills as an educational professional or are interested in Early Years education, we offer the course for you. We pride ourselves on having developed programmes which produce high quality and professionally committed teachers. We also work closely with local authorities, schools and teaching assistants to provide up-to-date training. Anglia Ruskin University is committed to widening access to all courses and welcomes applications from people of all backgrounds and ages.

ACADEMIC AWARDS

Educational studies courses
- BA (Hons) Early Childhood Studies
- BA (Hons) Early Years Professional Practice
- BA (Hons) Education and Childhood Studies
- BA (Hons) Education Studies
- BA (Hons) Learning Through Technology (online only)

Initial teacher education at Chelmsford
- BA (Hons) Primary Initial Teacher Education
- BA (Hons) Primary Initial Teacher Education with Early Years
- BA (Hons) Primary Initial Teacher Education with Modern Languages
- PGCE Primary
- PGCE Secondary; (Art and Design/English/ICT/Mathematics/Modern Languages/Science, Biology, Chemistry, Physics)
- Language Extension Courses (French, German, Spanish)
- Subject Knowledge Enhancement Course in Secondary Mathematics (14 Units)

Initial teacher education at University Centre Peterborough
- PGCE Primary

Continuing and professional studies at Chelmsford
- BA (Hons) Education
- Diploma in Teaching English (Literacy) in the Lifelong Learning Sector (DTLLS)
- Diploma in Teaching English to Speakers of Other Languages (ESOL) in the Lifelong Learning Sector (DTLLS)
- Diploma in Teaching Mathematics (Numeracy) in the Lifelong Learning Sector (DTLLS)
- Diploma in Teaching in the Lifelong Learning Sector (DTLLS)
- Diploma in Teaching English (Literacy CPD) in the Lifelong Learning Sector
- Diploma in Teaching Mathematics (Numeracy CPD) in the Lifelong Learning Sector
- Diploma in Teaching English (ESOL CPD) in the Lifelong Learning Sector

Bangor University
College of Education & Lifelong Learning
Normal Site
Holyhead Road
Bangor
Gwynedd LL57 2PZ
t: 01248 383082
f: 01248 383092
e: education@bangor.ac.uk
// www.bangor.ac.uk/education

Aberystwyth University and Bangor University work collaboratively as the North and Mid Wales Centre of Teacher Education

GENERAL INFORMATION

Bangor University was established in 1884 and has always put great emphasis on maintaining excellence. Over half of the departments at Bangor have received an 'excellent' rating for the quality for teaching. Situated close to the rugged mountains of Snowdonia and with the sea on our doorstep, Bangor must be one of the most attractive study locations in the UK. We pride ourselves on our friendly and caring atmosphere and have recently been rated by the Times Higher Education Supplement as the top university in the UK for the help and support provided for students. Education was rated top out of 58 HEIs across the UK for student's overall satisfaction on the Initial Teacher Training courses. (National Student Survey 2010)

The North and Mid-Wales Centre of Teacher Education is a centre of excellence in initial teacher education and training. The centre is a partnership between Aberystwyth and Bangor universities. It offers a unique and vibrant experience for those wishing to pursue a career in teaching. The centre provides the best possible start for trainee teachers in primary and secondary teaching.

The North and Mid Wales Teacher Training Partnerships are well established and partnership schools across north and mid-Wales provide a supported learning environment for student teachers.

ACADEMIC AWARDS

Our undergraduate programmes include:

FdA Early Childhood and Learning Support Studies
BA (single or joint Hons) Childhood Studies
BA Hons (QTS) Primary Education
BSc (QTS) Design and Technology in Secondary Education
BSc Product Design

All courses are also available through the medium of Welsh.

Our postgraduate programmes include:

PGCE Primary (3-7) (7-11) -1 year full-time
PGCE Secondary (11-18) (11-16) - 1 year full-time (Art & design, mathematics, music, outdoor activities, physical education, religious education, science, Welsh)
Education Studies MA (Full-time)
Education Studies MA (Part-time)
Education Studies MA (Part-time) taught in Singapore
Education Doctorate Programme (EdD) (Full-time & Part-time)
Education (PhD/MPhil) (Full-time & Part-time)

Initial Teacher Education Office
Department of Education
University of Bath
Bath BA2 7AY
t: 01225 386225
f: 01225 386113
e: pgce@bath.ac.uk
// www.bath.ac.uk/education/pgce

GENERAL INFORMATION

The initial teacher education programmes promote the highest standards of teaching in a welcoming and dynamic environment. The department also enjoys a close and effective partnership with a wide range of urban and rural schools where you will be supported to develop the skills to establish your own identity as a successful teacher. Our trainee teachers have an excellent record of employment on completion of the course.

The university has an active equal opportunities policy and applications are particularly welcome from graduates from minority ethnic backgrounds and those with disabilities. Whether you are a new graduate or an applicant who already has a range of different experiences and is seeking a career change, if you are passionate about your subject and committed to making a positive difference to the lives of young people, then we welcome your application.

ACADEMIC AWARDS

We offer both the Professional Graduate Certificate in Education (honours level) and the Postgraduate Certificate in Education (master's level). The latter will enable you to gain credit towards a master's degree in education and we place a strong emphasis on continuing professional development (CPD) within the department.

PGCE Secondary (11-18) - 1 year full-time
Subjects offered: English, history, information technology, mathematics, modern foreign languages, physical education and science (with specialisms in biology, chemistry and physics).

PGCE Middle Years (7-14) - 1 year full-time
Subjects offered: English and science.

Entry requirements: Applicants should possess a degree awarded by a British university or other approved university, or degree equivalent qualifications. The degree studies and educational background must be relevant to the subject the candidate wishes to teach.

Applicants should also possess GCSE grade C or above in English language and mathematics (or their accepted equivalents). Applicants for Middle Years courses also need GCSE science grade C or above.

Any offer is conditional upon satisfactory receipt of an enhanced disclosure from the CRB and medical clearance.

OTHER INFORMATION

Applicants are encouraged to visit our website **www.bath.ac.uk/education/pgce** to find out more about the specific subject programmes. As well as the individual subject courses, all trainees follow our Education and Professional Studies Programme which examines the wider professional role of the teacher.

Enquiries: For further details and bursary information, please contact the Initial Teacher Education Office on pgce@bath.ac.uk or call 01225 386225 and we will be happy to advise you.

Application route: Apply through the GTTR.

Bath Spa University

Institution code: B20

Newton St Loe
Bath BA2 9BN
t: 01225 875 875
e: enquiries@bathspa.ac.uk
// www.bathspa.ac.uk

GENERAL INFORMATION

Bath Spa University has had a national reputation in education and teacher training for many years. Our programmes will enable you to explore the nature, aims, values and functions of education in a rapidly changing world, preparing you for a career as a teacher or a wide range of careers in education or related settings.

ACADEMIC AWARDS

Undergraduate programmes
BA/BSc (Hons) Education leading to PGCE Primary and Early Years
The specialised awards in Education Studies are ideal if you intend to qualify as a primary school teacher. They are known as '3+1' courses: a three year honours degree followed by one year of teacher training. You may take this programme as either a single or combined award, and both an Early Years and International Education route are available.

Other education degrees - Early Years (Foundation Degree); Education Studies for Teaching Assistants (Foundation Degree); BA (Hons) Education Studies.

Application route: Apply through UCAS.

PGCE programmes
The university has a long tradition of initial teacher education (ITE) dating back over 60 years. Created as Bath Teacher Training College in 1947, the university is now the largest provider of initial teacher education in the area. Each year we recruit a diverse group of around 500 prospective teachers to our wide range of programmes in initial teacher education, leading to the award of either the Postgraduate or Professional Graduate Certificate in Education, both with Qualified Teacher Status (QTS).

The ITE programme prepares new teachers to work in the 21st century education system, and draws upon research, best practice and the use of new technologies to inform its curriculum.

Primary and Early Years - There are three routes to choose from; 5-11 age phase (full-time); 3-7 age phase (full-time); 3-7 age phase (part-time over 20 months).

Secondary - One year full-time programmes that will qualify you to teach your specialist subject in Key Stage 3 and Key Stage 4, with opportunities to undertake post-16 enhancement work, enabling you to teach up to A level. Subjects include art & design, design & technology, English, ICT, maths, modern languages, music, PE, RE and science.

Subject Knowledge Enhancement Courses - Designed for graduates to develop subject knowledge where their undergraduate degree is not fully relevant to the subject chosen. Subjects include maths, physics, science, design & technology, ICT and modern languages.

Application route: Apply through the GTTR.

University of Bedfordshire

Institution code: B22

Polhill Avenue
Bedford MK41 9EA
t: 01234 793279
// www.beds.ac.uk

GENERAL INFORMATION

The University of Bedfordshire is situated on two main campuses at Luton and Bedford. The Faculty of Education Sport & Tourism is based primarily at the Bedford Campus and has a long tradition of training in primary and secondary education.

ACADEMIC AWARDS

BEd (Hons) Primary - 4 years full-time

Main subjects offered: All students will take the following four strands across the course:

- English, science and mathematics
- Learning & teaching: a curriculum strand
- Perspectives, values, principles and beliefs in education
- Individual training plan

Entry requirements: Five passes at GCSE (A-C grade) including English language, mathematics and science. 280 points - with 240 coming from A2 level or equivalent or BTEC ND merit merit overall. For further information about other acceptable qualifications please contact the Admissions team.

Work experience: Evidence of work undertaken in a UK mainstream primary school context. A minimum of five days in Key Stage 1 and five days in Key Stage 2. Assessment Only and Overseas Trained Teachers QTS routes are available to experienced teachers.

BA (Hons) Physical Education (leading to the award of QTS Secondary) - 4 years full-time

Main subjects offered: a full range of practical activities and theoretical topics with appropriate application to teaching.

Entry requirements: Five passes at GCSE (A-C grade) including English language and mathematics. 260 to 320 points based upon a minimum of two A levels or equivalent or BTEC ND distinction distinction merit overall.

Work experience: Evidence of engagement with children in a coaching/leadership/teaching context, eg volunteering or assisting with classes or extra-curricular activities.

PGCE Primary - 1 year full-time, offered at postgraduate (60 credits at master's level) or professional level

Main subjects offered: All students will take the following three strands

- Perspectives, values, principles and beliefs of education
- Professional development profile
- Learning & teaching: the curriculum

with either Primary modern languages and community languages or extended professional practice.

Entry requirements: GCSE grade C or above in English language, mathematics and science. A minimum of a lower second class honours degree - any subject considered.

Work experience: Evidence of recent work undertaken in a mainstream primary school context, a minimum of five days in Key Stage 1 and five days in Key Stage 2.

PGCE Primary in Early Years - 1 year full-time, offered at postgraduate (60 credits at master's level) or professional level
Main subjects offered: All students will take

- Perspectives, values, principles and beliefs
- Professional development profile
- Learning & teaching: the curriculum

with Early Years practice.

Entry requirements: GCSE grade C or above in English language, mathematics and science. A minimum of a lower second class honours degree any subject considered.

Work experience: Evidence of recent work undertaken in a mainstream primary school context, a minimum of five days in an Early Years setting and five days in Key Stage 1.

PGCE Key Stage 2/3 - 1 year full-time, offered at postgraduate (60 credits at master's level) or professional level.
Main subjects offered:
- English
- Mathematics
- Science

Entry requirements: GCSE grade C or above (or equivalent) in English language, mathematics and science. Second class honours degree or above, at least 50% of which must be in the relevant National Curriculum subject of English, mathematics or science.

Work experience: Evidence of recent work undertaken in a UK mainstream school(s) preferably KS2 and KS3.

PGCE Secondary - 1 year full-time, offered at postgraduate (60 credits at master's level) or professional level.
Main subjects offered:
- Dance
- English
- Mathematics
- Modern languages
- Physical education
- Science with biology
- Science with chemistry
- Science with physics

Entry requirements: GCSE grade C or above (or equivalent) in English and mathematics. Normally second class honours degree or above, at least 50% of which must be in the National Curriculum subject to be studied. To study PE or dance a 2:1 degree is required.

Work experience: Evidence of recent work undertaken in a UK mainstream secondary school.

PGCE Secondary (14-19, Applied Vocational subjects) - 1 year full-time offered at postgraduate (60 credits at master's level) or professional level.
Main subject offered: ICT

University of Bedfordshire

continued

Entry requirements: GCSE grade C or above (or equivalent) in English and mathematics. Normally second class honours degree, at least 50% of which must be in the subject to be studied.

Work experience: Evidence of work-based experience (commercial and/or industrial) in related fields. Recent experience of working with young people in an educational setting, preferably a mainstream secondary school or FE college.

OTHER INFORMATION

Entry route: UG/FT/4 years, PG/FT/1 year

Intended Intake:
- UG Primary - 94
- UG Physical education - 27
- PG Primary - 93 + PG Early Years - 24
- PG Secondary - 92.

Application route: UG apply through UCAS, PG apply through the GTTR.

Enquiries: Please address all enquiries to Admissions at the Bedford Campus.

t: 01234 793279 or
e: admission@beds.ac.uk

Faculty of Education, Law and Social Sciences
City North Campus
Perry Barr, Birmingham, B42 2SU
t: 0121 331 5595
// www.bcu.ac.uk/education

GENERAL INFORMATION

Local interests/activities

Birmingham is a vibrant, cosmopolitan and multicultural city which has the UK's largest student population outside London, with an impressive 70,000 full-time students at three universities and two university colleges.

Birmingham is one of the best places in the country to be a student, with all the attractions of a major city, including some of the best bars, clubs and nightlife around. There's a thriving cultural life with a world-class music, entertainment and arts scene.

Accommodation

At Birmingham City University, we are proud of the varied accommodation that we have to offer. Included in the portfolio are traditional halls of residence, some of which provide specially equipped en-suite rooms and accommodation set in attractive grounds. There are rooms designated for students with special needs, including facilities for carers, and a number of flats for postgraduates and students with babies.

When applying for accommodation you are guaranteed a room in halls of residence for your first year of study providing that you have accepted an offer on a full-time course at the university, that you do not live in Birmingham and apply by the start of the autumn term. If you do live in Birmingham and meet the other criteria, we will make an offer of accommodation subject to availability.

Students' union

All students at Birmingham City University receive free automatic membership of the student's union, which offers a wide variety of student-friendly services, including sporting, social and special interest activities.

ACADEMIC AWARDS

For intending teachers, there is a three-year full-time BA (Hons) Primary Education with QTS course which prepares students to work in primary schools. We also offer PGCE programmes for graduates wishing to become teachers in an Early Years, Primary or Secondary setting or in the Post-Compulsory Education and Training sector. Each of our PGCE courses is offered at both professional graduate and postgraduate level.

In addition to training teachers, the faculty runs courses for those who wish to work with young children in a range of early years settings. We offer a full-time Foundation Degree in Early Years and two programmes in BA (Hons) Early Childhood Education Studies - either as a one-year full-time top-up degree or a three-year full-time degree. Successful completion of the BA (Hons) Early Childhood Education Studies degree can provide an appropriate qualification for entry to the PGCE Primary and Early Years route into teaching, providing all other Teaching Agency requirements for initial teacher training are met. We also offer a BA (Hons) Children and Integrated Professional Care course which is suitable for those interested in working in children's services as part of an integrated professional team.

Birmingham City University

Main courses offered:

FdA Early Years

BA (Hons) Primary Education with QTS

BA (Hons) Early Childhood Education Studies

BA (Hons) Early Childhood Education Studies (Top-up)

BA (Hons) Children and Integrated Professional Care

PGCE Primary and Early Years

PGCE Secondary: Art and design, drama, design and technology (food and textiles), mathematics, music, science with chemistry, science with physics

PGCE Post-Compulsory Education and Training

Entry requirements:

FdA Early Years: You should be over 18 years of age (for insurance purposes) and able to demonstrate an appropriate level of literacy and numeracy. We expect you to have one or more of the following: a BTEC National Certificate/Diploma or Higher National Certificate in Early Years; a CACHE Diploma in Nursery Nursing/Early Years; an NVQ Level 3 in Early Years or Teaching Assistants; an Advanced Modern Apprenticeship in Early Years.

Advanced Diplomas and Progression Diplomas are acceptable as all or part of the required Tariff points. Places will only be offered on the programme after applicants have attended an introductory workshop and obtain an enhanced CRB check.

BA (Hons) Primary Education with QTS: Five GCSEs at grade C and above (or equivalent) including English language, mathematics and a science subject. A minimum of 300 UCAS Tariff points, including a minimum of two A levels (excluding general studies

and key skills) or an equivalent. Please note that grades at AS level cannot contribute towards the 300 points.

For Access candidates we accept Access to Teaching only at Pass, including 40 level 3 credits at merit or higher. Experience of working with children in a state primary school and/or early years setting. Advanced Diplomas and Progression Diplomas are acceptable as all or part of the required Tariff points.

BA (Hons) Early Childhood Education Studies (3 year, full-time): At least 4 GSCEs at grade C or above or equivalent which must include English language or mathematics. A GSCE in science is desirable. Plus 240 UCAS Tariff points made up of two A levels or equivalent which may include general studies. Key skills are not accepted as part of the points. Remaining points can be made up with a maximum of two AS levels in different subjects or a CACHE Diploma in Child Care and Education; or a BTEC Extended Diploma/BTEC National Diploma or a BTEC National Certificate / Diploma in a relevant subject. Applicants with NVQ Level 3 in a related subject or recent Access to Higher Education course qualifications will also be considered.

For Access candidates we require a minimum of 18 Level 3 Access credits at merit or higher. The remaining credits can be passess. Advanced Diplomas and Progression Diplomas are acceptable as all or part of the required UCAS Tariff points. Successful candidates will be required to obtain an enhanced CRB check.

BA (Hons) Early Childhood Education Studies - top-up (one year full-time): Successful completion of a Foundation Degree in Early Years or equivalent (commendation or merit profile). Students with alternative level 5 qualifications, in a related field will be considered on an individual basis. Candidates must have a GCSE minimum grade C or equivalent in English language and mathematics. GCSE science is also desirable.

BA (Hons) Children and Integrated Professional Care: At least 4 GCSEs at grade C or above or equivalent which must include English language and mathematics. GCSE science is also desirable. You also need 240 UCAS Tariff points made up of a minimum of 2 A levels or equivalent. This may include General Studies. Remaining points can be made up with a maximum of 2 AS levels in different subjects. Key skills is not accepted as part of the points. We also accept BTEC Extended Diploma/ National Diploma and BTEC Diploma / BTEC National Certificate in a relevant subject or a CACHE Diploma in Child Care and Education. For Access candidates we require a minimum of 18 (Level 3) Access credits to be achieved at merit or higher. The remaining credits can be passes. Advanced Diplomas and Progression Diplomas are acceptable as all or part of the required Tariff points. Preference will be given to health, society and development.

PGCE Primary and Early Years: GCSE grade C or above (or its equivalent) in English language, mathematics and a science subject. You are expected to have attained a bachelor's honours degree, upper second class or above from a UK higher education institution or a recognised equivalent in a subject that provides the necessary foundation for work as a primary teacher. It is desirable for applicants to have spent time in British state primary schools before submitting an application. You will also need to have a successful enhanced CRB check.

PGCE Secondary: GCSE English language and mathematics at grade C or above (or equivalent). Candidates must possess a degree in a subject which has direct application to teaching their chosen specialism in the secondary schools of England and Wales. This should be a minimum of second class but upper second class and first class are preferred.

PGCE Post-Compulsory Education and Training (PCET): GSCE English language and mathematics at grade C or above, or an equivalent. We do not accept level 2 in numeracy or literacy as an equivalent. You should also possess a degree or equivalent. If you intend to pursue a career in Skills for Life then you will also need a Level 5 qualification in ESOL, literacy or numeracy.

Equivalence tests: Candidates who do not already have GCSEs in English language and mathematics, or their equivalent, and are not registered to take them should visit **www.equivalencytesting.com**.

PGCE courses: All the above PGCE courses are offered at both professional graduate level (level 6) and postgraduate level (level 7).

Initial teacher training: Applicants must also meet Teaching Agency requirements for initial teacher training, which means being medically fit and completing successfully an enhanced disclosure via the Criminal Records Bureau (CRB).

Application routes: FdA Early Years, BA (Hons) Primary Education with QTS, both BA (Hons) Early Childhood Education Studies and the BA (Hons) Children and Integrated Professional Care programmes - apply through UCAS. Applications to all the PGCE programmes must be made through the GTTR.

Billericay Educational Consortium

Institution code: B28

Billericay Educational Consortium SCITT
c/o Sunnymede Junior School
The Meadoway
Billericay
Essex CM11 2HL
t: **01277 622358**
f: **07092 878130**
e: **info@billericayscitt.com**
//: **www.billericayscitt.com**

GENERAL INFORMATION

We offer an exciting and substantial one-year Primary teacher training course, consisting of practical experience in schools around Billericay supported by academic lectures and professional tutorials. There are weekly subject and professional study sessions.

Continuous assessment leads to Professional Graduate Certificate in Education and recommendation for QTS. Trainees spend three days most weeks in their base school and two days attending lectures. Trainees are allocated a trained and experienced mentor in their base school who is responsible for helping them to develop their subject knowledge and classroom management skills, and also to monitor and support their overall professional development. Trainees will spend a period of six weeks in the spring term at a school in the alternative Key Stage to gain valuable experience.

ACADEMIC AWARDS

PGCE Primary (5-11) - 1 year full-time

Entry requirements:

- Entry qualifications: GCSE grade C or above in English language, mathematics and science. Minimum of two, preferably three, A levels at grade C or above.
- Minimum 2.1 honours degree from a UK university (in exceptional cases a 2.2 degree will be considered if supported by evidence of other strong academic and personal qualities).
- Work experience: minimum of two weeks' experience of working with primary school children.
- Tasks undertaken at interview: presentation, reflective writing, mental arithmetic and problem solving tests, grammar and spelling test, comprehension task and classroom task concluding with a formal interview.

OTHER INFORMATION

Entry route: PG/FT/1 year

Awards: Postgraduate Certificate in Education QTS

Intended intake: 60

Application route: Apply through the GTTR

Best House
Samuel Whitbread Community College
Shefford Road
Clifton SG17 5QS
t: 01462 817 445
f: 01462 815 577
e: office@bedsscitt.org.uk
// www.bedsscitt.org.uk

GENERAL INFORMATION

We are a thriving and successful school-based teacher training provider, which operates through a network of middle and upper schools in the Bedfordshire area.

We offer trainees the opportunity to work alongside and learn from experienced teachers in a 'real' school environment.

We welcome applicants from all backgrounds and age ranges and offer a one-to-one mentoring system.

ACADEMIC AWARD

Our PGCE courses are offered at the Professional Graduate level.

PGCE Secondary (11+) - 1 year full-time
Main subjects offered:
- Art
- English
- Geography
- History
- Mathematics
- Science

GTP Secondary - 1 year full-time
Main subjects offered:
- Design technology
- Drama
- Food technology
- ICT
- Music
- Psychology
- RE
- Sociology

Entry requirements: GCSE grade C or above in English language and mathematics; relevant degree of class 2:2 or above.

OTHER INFORMATION

Entry route: PG/FT/1 year

Awards: Professional Graduate Certificate in Education (PGCE) leading to QTS and Graduate Teacher Programme (GTP)

Intended intake: 25 PGCE/13 GTP

Application route: PGCE courses - apply through the GTTR. GTP programme - apply on our website.

Enquiries: Please address all postal enquiries to Jane Archer.

University of Birmingham

Institution code: B32

Edgbaston Park Road
Edgbaston
Birmingham B15 2TT
t: 0121 414 4866
e: admissions@bham.ac.uk

GENERAL INFORMATION

The University of Birmingham is located on an expansive green and leafy campus at Edgbaston, 2.5 miles from the city centre. It is just off the A38, with buses offering easy access to the city centre, and trains between University station (on campus) and New Street station. The university was founded in 1828 and was granted a charter in 1900. You can find out more about the university and its facilities by visiting the following webpages:

Guild of Students
www.guildofstudents.com

University Sport Birmingham
www.sport.bham.ac.uk

The Barber Institute of Fine Arts
www.barber.org.uk

ACADEMIC AWARDS

PGDipED (QTS) Secondary
- English
- French (alone or with Spanish or German)
- Geography
- German (alone or with Spanish or French)
- History
- History with citizenship
- Mathematics
- Mathematics (two-year route)
- Physical education
- Physics with maths
- Religious education
- Science: biology

- Science: chemistry
- Science: physics
- Spanish with French

Entry requirements: A degree in a relevant subject is required. GCSE passes (or equivalent) at grade C or above are required in English language and mathematics on application. For the mathematics two-year route you will need a minimum of A level mathematics plus your degree.

Application route: Apply through the GTTR.

PGDipED (PGCE Advanced) Primary Early Years (3-7)
General Primary (5-11)
Entry requirements: A good honours degree, normally upper second or better, is required. Some National Curriculum content within the degree is desirable but not essential. GCSE passes (or equivalent) at grade C or above are required in English language, mathematics and science on application. Candidates must have a minimum of five days' classroom experience in a mainstream primary school on application.
Application route: Apply through the GTTR.

Initial teacher training at the University of Birmingham is a Postgraduate Diploma in Primary or Secondary Education offered at master's level with 120 credits.

OTHER INFORMATION

Contact (Primary): Amerjit Kaur
t: 0121 415 8366
Contact (Secondary): Judy Dandy
t: 0121 414 4859
//: www.education.bham.ac.uk

School of Childhood and Education
UCB
Summer Row
Birmingham B3 1JB
t: Course Enquiries - 0121 693 5959
e: marketing@ucb.ac.uk
t: Admissions Enquiries - 0121 604 1040
e: admissions@ucb.ac.uk
// www.ucb.ac.uk

GENERAL INFORMATION

The training provider is situated in the School
of Childhood and Education at University College
Birmingham (UCB), which is accredited by the
University of Birmingham. It is located in Birmingham
city centre. The School of Childhood and Education
has approaching 700 students studying Early
Years/Early Childhood Studies at undergraduate level.
To meet the requirements of these students, the
college has many specialist resources, including a
dedicated ICT suite. Over the years, close links have
been developed with local schools and other Early
Years providers, to train students to work within the
sector.

Accommodation

The main halls of residence complex, The Maltings,
is situated just 10 minutes' walk from the college. The
Maltings offers high quality, safe and affordable
accommodation for 832 students. These self-catering
halls consist of recently-built study bedrooms, all but
18 are en suite. A large sports hall with a fitness suite,
a purpose-built social club, two laundries and a shop
are also on site. Limited resident car parking is
available.

Another 247 student bedrooms are available
in Cambrian Hall situated across the road from the
college.

Student Services Unit

The Student Services Unit provides a range
of services: financial advice and assistance, careers
advice, student welfare services, counselling services
and a college nurse. The Learning and Skills
Development Centre offers individual support and a
series of subject-related workshops.

Leisure

The Spa Fitness Club includes a fully equipped
gym, dance studio, sauna, steam room, jacuzzi, spa
pool and solarium. Students are automatically
members of the Guild of Students, which promotes a
number of sports clubs and societies, together with
organising weekly social activities and annual events.

Local interest/activities

Birmingham is now one of the most progressive,
lively and dynamic cities in the UK. There are excellent
shopping facilities, exemplified by the
newly-developed Bullring Centre. Interests in sport,
theatre, music, food and other leisure activities are all
well provided for in Birmingham.

The countryside of Worcestershire, Warwickshire
and Staffordshire is within a few miles of Birmingham
city centre.

ACADEMIC AWARD

PGCE Early Years - 1 year full-time
Intended intake: 63

A postgraduate programme in Early Years is
offered, which carries QTS. The programme has been
validated as a PGCE in Early Years, and is awarded by
the University of Birmingham. It contains three
modules studied at master's level. The programme
covers the Foundation Stage and Key Stage 1,
enabling graduates to teach children between the
ages of three and seven.

This is a specialist Early Years programme, focusing on three themes:

- information communication technology (ICT)
- working with children with learning difficulties and/or disabilities (LDD).
- working with children who use English as an additional language (EAL).

Entry requirements:
- Degree - An in-depth knowledge of children in the age range of 3-7 years is required. This will normally be evidenced by an honours degree (at 2.2 or above) in Early Years/Early Childhood Studies. Degrees in disciplines such as psycology, sociology, English, mathematics, dance, drama, performing arts and sports will also be considered together with substantial experience of working in an Early Years setting.
- GCSE - For admission to the programme, passes are required in English language, mathematics and science grade C or above.

Application route: Apply through GTTR.

FdA Early Childhood Studies - 2 years full-time
Intended intake: 25

This programme is particularly relevant to those who wish to pursue a career, or enhance their qualifications in relation to children. There is scope to work within child-related organisations in the state, voluntary and commercial sectors within fields such as education, welfare, leisure and advocacy. Also, the FdA can lead to the final stages of the BA (Hons) degree programme.

Entry requirements:
140 UCAS Tariff points to include at least 100 UCAS Tariff points from one A level or equivalent for the FdA programme. For admission to the programme, students require English GCSE grade C or above, or an equivalent

Application route: Apply through UCAS.

BA Early Childhood Studies with Practitioner Status - 3 years full time
Intended intake: n/a

The programme is particularly relevant to those who wish to pursue a career, or enhance their qualifications in relation to children. There is scope to work within child-related organisations in the state, voluntary and commercial sectors within fields such as education, welfare, leisure and advocacy. Students who wish to teach will be able to apply to the PGCE (Early Years) at the college from this degree programme.

Those completing the three-year programme with a satisfactory placement report in each setting will also achieve Professional Practise status, which enables them to work in Early Years settings as a qualified member of staff.

Entry requirements:
240 UCAS Tariff points to include at least 200 UCAS Tariff points from two A levels or equivalent for the BA programme. For admission to the programme, students require English GCSE grade C or above, or an equivalent.

Application route: Apply through UCAS.

Woodview Education Centre
Woodview Drive
Lee Bank B15 2HU
t: 0121 464 4608
f: 0121 464 4609
e: admin@bptp.bham.org.uk,
// www.bptp.bham.org.uk

GENERAL INFORMATION

The partnership offers a full-time one year Primary (5-11) course leading to the award of QTS and the academic qualification of a Postgraduate Certificate in Education at master's level validated by Birmingham City University. The course typically recruits just 28 trainees each year and BPTP prides itself on the level and depth of support this enables it to provide for all trainees.

BPTP was formed 12 years ago by a partnership of local primary schools, committed to providing Birmingham schools with highly skilled primary teachers capable of making a positive difference to children's lives. The partnership has now expanded to include over 20 schools all based in Birmingham giving trainees a wide experience of this large multicultural and socially diverse city. Training is centred around the vitally important and extensive time spent in these partnership schools. For two days each week trainees will work alongside experienced teachers and mentors in one of two schools in either a Key Stage 1 or a Key Stage 2 placement. Each term trainees undertake an extended block practice in one of those same schools.

This school experience is integrated with a comprehensive centre-based course of professional academic study enabling trainees to reflect on best practice and make sense of the complexities of the classroom. The course has high expectations and requires trainees to submit a series of master's level assignments. The centre is spacious and centrally located allowing easy access to all areas of Birmingham and the West Midlands. Trainees are provided with a full range of teaching resources, including ICT equipment and, through our collaborative partnership with Birmingham City University, trainees also have access to full library and student union facilities.

Our partnership schools are proud of the training offered and nearly half our trainees find themselves working within the partnership. Our reputation is built on the quality of our trainees and has resulted in very high levels of employment for each of our cohorts both within Birmingham and beyond. Our 2009 Ofsted report was highly favourable awarding an overall grade of 'Good' and judging four categories to be 'Outstanding'.

Entry requirements:
- A good degree (2:2 or above is preferred).
- Evidence of passes at GCSE, grade C or above, in English language, mathematics and science.
- Appropriate personal and intellectual qualities to be a teacher.
- Meet the standards of physical and mental fitness to teach.
- A desire and the personality to be a performer.
- Knowledge that teaching primary children is really what you want to do.
- An understanding that all children have an entitlement to be helped to access the curriculum.

Admissions systems are currently under review: please contact BPTP for details of how to apply.

Bishop Grosseteste University College Lincoln

Institution code: B38

Lincoln LN1 3DY
t: **01522 583658**
f: **01522 530243**
e: **admissions@bishopg.ac.uk**
// **www.bishopg.ac.uk**

GENERAL INFORMATION

Bishop Grosseteste University College Lincoln (BG) is an independent university college offering you the quality of a university experience with the community feel of a smaller university college. We have been offering higher education for over 150 years so we have a great deal of experience to draw upon.

Local Interest
As the Lonely Planet Guide points out, Lincoln is a 'must see' British city, an 'under-visited delight' which successfully combines old medieval past with vibrant modern present.

We are located in the uphill part of Lincoln. This area contains the historic Castle Square overlooked by the majestic cathedral (3rd largest in Britain), and the quaint boutique-packed area of the Bailgate; well worth the tough walk up Steep Hill. Up here you can immerse yourself in the history of Lincolnshire through visits to The Collection and Usher Gallery (both part way up the hill) and to the Museum of Lincolnshire Life - as well as the castle and cathedral. Down the hill and in the middle of the city is the busy high street where the needs of almost all shopaholics are met. There are plenty of shops both well-known and unknown, numerous cafes, juice bars and coffee shops where you can rest your feet.

The campus occupies a single, attractive and compact site which incorporates purpose-built teaching accommodation, a well-stocked library with computer suites, theatre and performing arts studio, music suite and a human performance laboratory. Also on site are the three main halls of residence, the students' union building, chapel and a sport and fitness centre with a sports field.

Accommodation
We have a full-time Accommodation Officer on site who will help you find accommodation, on or off campus for the duration of your studies. For further information about our facilities, please visit **www.bishopg.ac.uk/accommodation**

Students' union
The students' union has its own building in the middle of the campus which houses a bar, function room and a shop and is very active, providing both social and academic support for all students.

ACADEMIC AWARDS

Foundation Degrees in:
Applied Studies (Learning Support)
Applied Studies (Early Childhood)
Applied Studies (Children and Youth Work)

Progression route degrees:
BA (Hons) Applied Studies in Education
BA (Hons) Applied Studies (Early Childhood)
BA (Hons) Applied Studies (Children and Youth Work)
BA (Hons) Primary Teaching Studies with QTS

Entry requirements for the courses listed above are outlined on our website. If you would like further information, please do not hesitate to contact our Admissions team on **admissions@bishopg.ac.uk**

Joint and major/minor undergraduate degrees in:
Education Studies and/with Applied Drama
Education Studies and/with English
Education Studies and/with History
Education Studies and/with Mathematics
Education Studies and/with Music
Education Studies and/with Psychology
Education Studies and/with Special Educational Needs and Inclusion
Education Studies and/with Sport
Education Studies and/with Theology and Ethics
Education Studies and/with Visual Arts
Education Studies with Heritage Studies

Early Childhood Studies and/with Mathematics
Early Childhood Studies and/with Music
Early Childhood Studies and/with Theology and Ethics
Early Childhood Studies and/with Visual Arts
Early Childhood Studies with Psychology

Entry requirements for the courses above vary depending on the individual subject. Up-to-date detailed and further information can be found on our website. However, normally a minimum of 220 UCAS Tariff points are required, 80 of which need to be subject-related. If you wish to become a teacher, you will need to undertake further study on a PGCE or Graduate Teacher Programme course. BG's own PGCE programmes are particularly popular.

BA (Hons) Primary Education with recommendation for QTS - 3 years full-time
Entry requirements:
- All applicants are expected to have a range of GCSEs, including English language, mathematics, and a science at grade C or above (or equivalent qualifications).
- Typically 220 UCAS Tariff points, 80 of which preferably should be in English or mathematics. (However, we will also consider art, drama, geography, history, music, religious studies, science, PE, ICT or DT and modern languages. The remaining 80 should be from a single qualification in any subject excluding general studies.

We welcome students with a range of qualifications and a breadth of experience, so you might have A levels, Advanced or Progression Diploma, Access Programme, BTEC National etc. Please contact Admissions to discuss your individual circumstances.

PGCE Primary - full-time and flexible routes (both professional and postgraduate levels)
Entry requirements:
- GCSEs (or equivalent) at grade C or above including English language, mathematics and a science subject. These must be achieved before an application is submitted.
- Honours degree at a 2.2 classification or above (or equivalent qualifications). Minimum of 10 days' experience normally in a state-funded primary school within the two years prior to submission of an application.

PGCE Secondary - full-time route only (both professional and postgraduate levels)
Main subjects offered:
- English with drama
- Mathematics
- Music
- Religious education
- Science with Biology
- Science with Chemistry
- Science with Physics

Entry requirements:
- GCSEs (or equivalent) at grade C or above including English language and mathematics. These must be achieved before an application is submitted.
- Honours degree (obtained or predicted at least 2.2 class). More than 50% of your degree content should be in a relevant subject. Minimum of five days' experience in a mainstream comprehensive school within the two years prior to submission of an application.

Application route: Undergraduate apply through UCAS, PGCE apply through the GTTR.

Blackburn College

Institution code: B40

Feilden Street
Blackburn BB2 1LH
t: **01254 292594**
e: **he-admissions@blackburn.ac.uk**
// **www.blackburn.ac.uk**

GENERAL INFORMATION

Blackburn College has a long history of excellent education and training in Blackburn, Lancashire. Close to Preston and Manchester - as well as the much greener Ribble Valley and Lake District, there are over 15,000 students of all ages, backgrounds and interests.

September 2009 marked the opening of the new state-of-the-art University Centre. We are the region's purpose-built and dedicated resource for delivering education degree-level courses accredited by institutions such as Lancaster University and University of Central Lancashire (UCLan), all on the college's safe town-centre campus.

This year we are celebrating that over one in ten of our graduates leave with a first class honours degree, that our graduates earn on average £25,000 just six months after graduating (National Student Survey) and that we have a £2,013 plus finance offer for full-time students to support you.

SCHOOL OF EDUCATION AND PROFESSIONAL STUDIES

- Purpose-built state-of-the-art facilities and accommodation.
- Small class sizes and dedicated teaching staff.
- A fantastic selection of courses available.
- Degrees accredited by Lancaster University and University of Central Lancashire (UCLan).
- Full-time and part-time courses available.

A range of degrees, professional qualifications and further education courses are available.

ACADEMIC AWARDS

Degrees
BA (Hons) Education Studies

Foundation Degree - Teaching and Learning Support (Primary)

Professional qualifications
Preparing to Teach in the Life-long Learning Sector
Certificate to Teach in the Life-long Learning Sector
Diploma to Teach in the Life-long Learning Sector (leading to a Postgraduate Certificate in Education (PGCE) or a Certificate in Education)

Further education
Certificate in English Language Teaching to Adults (CELTA)

Entry requirements
Minimum entry qualifications apply and are course specific. You can see the website and current prospectus for more details - or go in and meet the team. Blackburn College like you to see where you will be studying and talk to them about your needs. They are present at northern-based UCAS fairs and have frequent open days.

Application route
Full-time applications must be made through UCAS. Part-time applications and PGCE applications can be made directly to the University Centre.

The University of Bolton

Institution code: B44

Admissions
Bolton BL3 5AB
t: 01204 903903
f: 01204 903809
e: admissions@bolton.ac.uk

GENERAL INFORMATION

The University of Bolton offers two teacher training courses, the Professional Graduate Diploma in Education (PGDE) and the Professional Diploma in Education (PDE).We have provided postgraduate schemes for the training of tutors in the post-16 education sector for more than 50 years. The Education Department's ultimate purpose is to enhance the quality of education and training for post-compulsory learners.

We seek to achieve this by stimulating and supporting the professional development of those who shape, provide, manage and monitor the learning experiences of learners in this sector.

ACADEMIC AWARDS

We aim to provide initial teacher training which prepares course members for a career as a tutor in further, higher or adult education. Placements extend across the range of the Learning and Skills Sector. Our programmes seek to develop practical professional competence and underpinning knowledge, together with reflective strategies needed for effective teaching and support of learning in a range of curriculum areas including:

- Maths, science and ICT
- Language and communication
- Skills for life: literacy, numeracy and ESOL
- Health and childhood studies
- Art and design
- Business and legal studies
- Lifelong learning

These programmes are unique in the region in that tutors have subject specialisms which reflect many of these curriculum areas. Tutors are able to combine expertise in teacher education with knowledge of subject-specific demands.

Content

There are two phases which can be completed in one year of full-time or two year part-time study.

Course members participating in part-time programmes can be either pre-service (new to teaching) or in-service (in teaching).

Entry requirements: Course members may have relevant employment experience and, in addition, possess either a degree (for entry to the PGDE) or an appropriate advanced qualification (for entry to the PDE).

Applicants for the in-service programme must have appropriate teaching class contact hours in the postcompulsory sector.

Course members will also be expected to evidence level 2 literacy and numeracy skills by the end of the programme.

Application route: Apply direct to university.

Enquiries Team
t: **+44 (0)1202 961916**
e: **askBUenquiries@bournemouth.ac.uk**
// **www.bournemouth.ac.uk/askBU**

GENERAL INFORMATION

At Bournemouth University (BU) we aim to deliver an outstanding and personalised student experience. We do this by providing excellent teaching facilities, professional practice work placements and real life consultancy projects. BU is in a great location and offers a stimulating and rewarding learning environment.

ACADEMIC AWARDS: UNDERGRADUATE

FDA Early Years (part-time)
Delivered at Bournemouth and Poole College, Weymouth College and University Centre Yeovil.

The FdA in Early Years provides practitioners with the opportunity to obtain a recognised qualification in Early Years care and education. Students should either be in either part-time or full-time employmnent to study this qualification.

The course meets the requirements for an Early Years Sector-Endorsed Foundation degree.

BA (Hons) Early Years Care & Education (top-up) (part-time and full-time)
Delivered at BU.

This course provides a route to an honours qualification for students who have successfully completed a foundation degree in Early Years. It enables students to reflect critically upon their roles as early years educators and equips them with the knowledge, understanding and skills to develop their practice further.

Entry requirements: Visit our website for details
www.bournemouth.ac.uk/courses

How to apply: Visit www.ucas.com

OTHER COURSES OFFERED

PGCert Education Practice (part-time)
The aim of this course is to provide those who are teaching and supporting learning in a post-compulsory education environment with the knowledge and skills to develop and enhance their practice as educators. For participants who wish to gain the NMC Teacher Standard, the programme aims to prepare them to teach in both academic and practice settings. The programme seeks to support their development as critical reflective practitioners and prepare them to engage fully with the new and significant demands of a rapidly changing educational environment. It will produce students who are capable of initiating and embedding innovative pedagogic practice, which is appropriate to the context and discipline in which they work. The programme will also foster respect for learners and a commitment to continuing professional development.

MA Creative & Media Education (online with residential elements)
This innovative master's course is designed specifically for teachers and college lecturers. Students will learn the intellectual tools and techniques to explore and develop their own teaching practice. They will develop to be critical, knowledgeable and responsible leaders of creative and media education, capable of initiating, developing and embedding new understandings and techniques in the classroom.

For more information on all our courses, visit
www.bournemouth.ac.uk/courses

Open days
For BU open days, please see
www.bournemouth.ac.uk/opendays or call
+44 (0)1202 961916

Bournemouth, Poole and Dorset East SCITT

Institution code: B52

Bournemouth Learning Centre
Ensbury Avenue
Bournemouth BH10 4HG
t: **01202 451992**
f: **01202 451979**
// **www.bpdescitt.org.uk**

GENERAL INFORMATION

Bournemouth, Poole and Dorset East offers a school-centred initial teacher training (SCITT) course for trainee teachers wishing to teach in secondary schools. The programme is full-time over one academic year, and is aimed at postgraduates. On successful completion, trainees are awarded Qualified Teacher Status (QTS), together with a PGCE (Professional or Postgraduate Certificate in Education), validated by the University of Bath.

The Bournemouth, Poole and Dorset area provides a picturesque and lively environment, with a wide variety of educational provision, including single-sex, mixed-gender, selective, comprehensive and middle schools. There is considerable opportunity for successful trainees to contribute to shortage subjects in the area, where increased consolidation and stability are looked for.

Subjects offered:
- Design and technology
- Mathematics
- Modern foreign languages
- Science (biology)
- Science (chemistry)
- Science (physics).

Training

Training is based in two complementary schools, supported by central training at the Bournemouth Learning Centre. During the 37-week course, trainees will spend the majority of their time (30 weeks) in school. All schools have experience of working in ITT and work closely with the local authority and with SCITT staff as part of the scheme. The autumn term will be spent in the first school, commencing with lesson observations and building gradually to a 50% teaching commitment by Christmas. Trainees spend the spring and summer terms in the second school, which provides a contrast to their main school. By the summer, trainees will teach up to 70% of a full timetable across the full age and ability range.

Entry requirements: An honours degree, at 2:2 or above suitable for the subject specialism or equivalent degree-level knowledge of the subject to teach the relevant age range. GCSE or equivalent in english language and mathematics at grade C or above.

Application route: Apply through the GTTR.

Bradford College

Institution code: B60

Bradford School of Teaching, Health & Care
Great Horton Road
Bradford BD7 1AY
t: 01274 433333
f: 01274 433241
// www.bradfordcollege.ac.uk

GENERAL INFORMATION

Bradford College is an associate college of Leeds Metropolitan University. Students receive their degrees and postgraduate awards from the university.

The college prides itself on the quality of the courses and educational facilities that it offers. The School of Teaching, Health & Care is located on the college's McMillan Campus. It has the full range of courses to meet the training needs of teachers, youth workers, social and health workers and those working with very young children in a variety of settings.

Local Information
The campus is situated in the middle of Bradford, which offers easy access to the city's unique attractions and facilities. There is easy access to beautiful countryside, including the Dales and the Lake District.

Students' union
The Bradford campus students' union acts as a democratic channel and voice between the college and students.

Accommodation
There is self-catering accommodation for students within a few minutes' walk of the campus.

ACADEMIC AWARDS

UCAS
- BA (Hons) Primary Education with Qualified Teacher Status
- BA (Hons) Education Studies
- BEd (Hons) Stage 3 Top-up with QTS
- BEd (Hons) Stage 3 Top-up without QTS
- Foundation Degree in Supporting & Managing Learning in Education

GTTR
- PGCE Primary with French leading to QTS
- PGCE Primary
- PGCE (Secondary) citizenship
- PGCE (Secondary) chemistry
- PGCE (Secondary) design and technology (food)
- PGCE (Secondary) Information communication technology
- PGCE (Secondary) mathematics
- PGCE (Secondary) physics
- PGCE (Secondary) science
- PGCE (Secondary) science at Key Stage 2/3
- PGCE (Secondary) vocational subjects : Applied business
- PGCE (Secondary) vocational subjects : Applied ICT
- PGCE (Secondary) vocational subjects : Health & social care
- PGCE (Secondary) vocational subjects : Leisure & tourism

The international dimension of the school's work is very strong and offers opportunities for students to study in many countries in western and central Europe as well as in several parts of the USA, Africa and China.

The school also supports those who wish to follow employment-based and flexible routes into the teaching profession through the Bradford and Northern Employment-based Teacher Training Scheme (B-NETT).

Academic and professional counselling is offered in order to ensure that appropriate study can be secured from the school's portfolio of courses.

BA (Hons) Primary Education with QTS
Entry requirements:
- Normally two passes at A level at grade C and B or above, or an equivalent BTEC National or GNVQ Advanced/Advanced VCE (full award) or completion of an accredited Access course.
- GCSE level passes at grade C or above in English, mathematics and science (grade B preferred in English).

Application route: Apply through UCAS.

BA (Hons) Education Studies
Entry requirements:
- Five GCE passes, including a GCSE in English language and 180 UCAS Points including at least one A level at A2 or BTEC National Diploma, with at least one merit or successful completion of an accredited Access course or equivalent qualification with merit.

Application route: Apply through UCAS.

BEd (Hons) Stage 3 Top-up with QTS
Entry requirements:
- 240 HE credit points, normally with 120 credit points at level 5/Intermediate.
- GCSE level passes at grade C or above in English, mathematics and science or equivalent (grade B preferred in English).

Application route: Apply through UCAS

BEd (Hons) Stage 3 Top-up without QTS
Entry requirements:
- 240 HE credit points, normally with 120 credit points at level 5/Intermediate.
- GCSE level pass at grade C or equivalent in English (grade B preferred).

Application route: Apply through UCAS.

Foundation Degree in Supporting and Managing Learning in Education
Three subjects at GCSE level grade C or above, including English. A minimum of 120 UCAS points together with appropriate A level or equivalent qualifications in childcare and/or education, or the successful completion of an accredited Access Course.

PGCE Primary
Entry requirements: Applicants must have a good honours degree validated by a British university or an equivalent qualification. GCSE mathematics, English language and science at grade C or above (or equivalent)(grade B preferred in English). All candidates are required to have recent and relevant experience in a primary school or other equivalent educational setting.

Application route: Apply through the GTTR.

PGCE Secondary
Entry requirements:
- Applicants must have a subject related honours degree validated by a British university or an equivalent qualification.
- You are invited to discuss the appropriateness of your degree prior to application.
- For science and mathematics there are enhancement courses for those who require additional subject knowledge.
- All applicants must hold a GCSE pass at grade C or above in both English language and mathematics (grade B preferred in English). Experience in a secondary school is desirable.
- Applications are particularly welcomed from members of ethnic minority communities and mature candidates.

Application route: Apply through the GTTR.

University of Brighton

Institution code: B72

School of Education
Checkland Building
Falmer BN1 9PH
t: **01273 643386**
f: **01273 643555**
e: **deped@brighton.ac.uk**
// **www.brighton.ac.uk/education**

GENERAL INFORMATION

Brighton is one of the largest teacher education providers in the country. It has an excellent national reputation and one of the strongest Teaching Quality Assessment and Ofsted Inspection records in the UK. Education courses are delivered at Falmer, near Brighton, and Hastings. Physical education and dance courses are at Eastbourne.

Undergraduate Awards - BA (Hons)

Intended intake: 152 primary, 90 secondary

- BA (Hons) with QTS Primary - either Foundation/Key Stage 1 Education (3-7) or Key Stage 1/Key Stage 2 Education (5-11) - 3 or 4 years full-time
- BA (Hons) with QTS Key Stage 2/Key Stage 3 Education (7-14) specialising in English and mathematics - 3 or 4 years full-time
- BA (Hons) with QTS Secondary Physical Education (11-16) - Eastbourne campus - 4 years full-time
- Two-year BA Hons Secondary Education (11-16) specialising in chemistry, design & technology or mathematics (shortened route for applicants with at least 120 CATS points in a relevant subject area.)

Application route: Apply through UCAS.

Postgraduate Awards - Postgraduate Certificate in Education (PGCE)

Intended intake: 174 primary, 198 secondary

- Primary (3-7) - 1 year full-time
- Primary (5-11) - 1 year full-time
- Secondary (11-16) - art & design, biology, chemistry, dance*, design & technology, English, geography, information and communications technology, mathematics, modern foreign languages, physical education*, physics, physics with mathematics, religious studies (1 year full-time or 16 months part-time. *PE and dance at Eastbourne Campus.)

Application route: Apply through the GTTR.

Entry requirements:

- All applicants - GCSE grade C (or equivalent) in English language and mathematics. A science subject will be required for those applying to teach primary or Key Stage 2/3. Some recent experience of working with children, preferably in a school setting. All suitable applicants are interviewed before being offered a place and offers are subject to satisfactory Criminal Records Bureau Enhanced Disclosure and health checks.
- For undergraduate courses: Typically BBB-ABB, depending on course or successful completion of a QAA recognised Access course which, for secondary and KS2/3 courses, includes a relevant subject area.
- For postgraduate courses: normally a good honours degree or equivalent which, for secondary courses should be in an area relevant to subject specialism. Pre-PGCE subject knowledge enhancement courses in chemistry, design & technology, information and communications technology, mathematics and physics are available for graduates of other disciplines who are keen to teach any of these subjects in secondary schools.

City of Bristol College

Institution code: B77

City of Bristol College
Ashley Down Road
Bristol BS7 9BU
t: 0117 312 5171
e: HEinformation@cityofbristol.ac.uk
// www.cityofbristol.ac.uk

GENERAL INFORMATION

City of Bristol College offers a supportive and professional environment which is popular with both mature students who have family or career commitments and students progressing from school or college. A range of courses are on offer that can lead to a teaching qualification.

UNDERGRADUATE AWARDS

Early Childhood Studies Foundation Degree

This course is designed to make links between early education, child health and the welfare of the child and is aimed at those wanting employment within a wide range of early years settings, including nurseries, schools, children's centres and also in private and voluntary sector work.

Early Years Foundation Degree

The Early Years programme is aimed at those who are currently working as early years practitioners and wish to gain a Level 5 qualification which may lead to management jobs in children's centres, Early Years Professional Status or teaching.

For more detailed information about these courses please visit **www.cityofbristol.ac.uk/coursefinder**, email HEinformation@cityofbristol.co.uk, or call 0117 312 5171.

Applications for these full-time courses should be submitted online to UCAS.

Visit **www.ucas.com** and **www.cityofbristol.ac.uk** for more information.

Teaching qualifications

City of Bristol College also offers a range of part-time courses that can lead to a teaching qualification.

- Additional Diploma in Teaching Literacy, Numeracy and ESOL in the Lifelong Learning Sector Level 5
- Certificate in English Language Teaching to Adults (CELTA)
- Certificate in Teaching in the Lifelong Learning Sector (CTLLS)
- Diploma in Teaching in the Lifelong Learning Sector (DTLLS)
- Professional Graduate Certificate in Education/Certificate in Education (Learning and Skills)
- Professional Graduate Certificate in Education/Certificate in Education (Skills for Life)

For more information visit **www.cityofbristol.ac.uk** or contact the College.

Graduate School of Education
35 Berkeley Square
Bristol BS8 1JA
t: 0117 331 4492
e: ed-pgce@bristol.ac.uk

GENERAL INFORMATION

Whatever your background and experience, if you think that teaching is the profession for you, why not come to the University of Bristol? We offer a one-year Postgraduate Certificate in Education (PGCE) for secondary teaching, in close partnership with schools. This course, which commences in September, is fulltime. You will work in your specialist subject area with pupils aged 11-18 and with other student teachers in university sessions. Evaluations show that the PGCE is hard work, busy and stimulating but that our student teachers have benefited enormously from:

- practical school experience (24 weeks, two contrasting schools)
- personal support from school and university tutors
- reflecting on and evaluating their experiences
- sharing skills with a varied and supportive group of other student teachers on the course.

A life-changing experience!

The Graduate School of Education has good working relationships with education authorities and schools on a local level and with overseas governments and institutions on an international level. The University of Bristol is located in the centre of the city. It has a comprehensive health and welfare service available to all students and excellent sporting and recreational facilities. There is a specialised education library on site. All students have their own personal email account.

Job prospects

Each year the vast majority of Bristol students are successful in obtaining a first teaching appointment of their choice.

ACADEMIC AWARDS

PGCE Secondary - 1 year full-time
Main subjects offered:
- Citizenship
- English
- Geography
- History
- Mathematics
- Modern foreign languages (French, German, Spanish, Italian)
- Music
- Religious education
- Science (biology, chemistry, physics)

The courses are offered at Postgraduate Certificate in Education level and students have the opportunity of gaining 60 credit points at M level as part of successfully completing the course. Should a student experience exceptional difficulties during the course of training, but achieve at least a satisfactory standard in practical teaching and written work below master's level, the student may be awarded a Professional Graduate Certificate in Education.

Funding

In recent years, there have been a number of financial incentives available. Candidates are advised to contact the Teaching Agency.

// www.tda.gov.uk/
t: 0800 389 2500

Applications welcome from all graduates, particularly from under-represented groups. Enquiries: PGCE Office, University of Bristol

Enquiries: PGCE Office, University of Bristol

e: ed-pgce@bristol.ac.uk

Application route : Apply through the GTTR.

Frenchay Campus
Coldharbour Lane
Bristol BS16 1QY
t: **0117 32 83333**
f: **0117 32 82810**
e: **admissions@uwe.ac.uk**
// // **www.uwe.ac.uk**

GENERAL INFORMATION

With high quality ratings of its teacher training provision by Ofsted, the Department of Education at UWE occupies purpose-built accommodation on the main university campus at Frenchay with well-equipped teaching areas and fully resourced workshops.

ENTRY REQUIREMENTS

Please visit our website for specific information about the entry requirements for each programme. In addition to the academic requirements listed, and with the exception of the FdA Educational Support, admission to all programmes is subject to interview to assess suitability for teaching. Applicants will also need to undergo a successful medical assessment and Criminal Records Bureau (CRB) check.

UNDERGRADUATE COURSES

FdA Higher Level Teaching Assistant (FT/2Years)
This foundation degree is designed for teaching assistants and links directly to the work place allowing you to gain credit through work based learning. This means you can still earn while you are learning.

BA (Hons) Primary Education (ITE) (FT/UG/3yr)
This is a three year full-time intensive professional programme including placements in schools. You will study the core areas of mathematics, English, science and information and communication technology (ICT) and also foundation subjects within the National Curriculum, taking a thematic approach. A professional study will be undertaken in one of the following: Art and Design in Education; Language and Literacies in Education; Science and Technology in Education; or People, Places and Change in Education.

BA (Hons) Primary Early Years Education (ITE) (FT/UG/3yr)
This is a three year full-time intensive professional programme including placements in schools and early years settings. You will be trained to teach both 3 to 5 and 5 to 7 year olds, focussing on child development, cognitive processes, children's play and learning and policy developments in Early Years provision.

BA (Hons) Education, Learning and Development (FT/UG/3 year) - to be validated
This programme replaces the BA(Hons) Education Studies and the BA (Hons) Education Studies plus PGCE (3+1). This is an ideal course choice if you enjoy working with people, young and old, and wish to understand how they can learn and develop, but are not certain at this stage about a career in teaching.

The degree programme will also contain within it a supported pathway for those interested in postgraduate study for teaching in primary schools or the FE sector - with specific module options to support such interest. The tailored pathway will allow you to make the very strongest application for a PGCE when the time comes. Provided you achieve a 2:1 degree, can demonstrate suitability for teaching and make an early application, we will give you prior consideration for progression to a relevant PGCE programme at UWE.

POSTGRADUATE COURSES

PGCE Primary
On this one-year full-time intensive course you will learn how to deliver the core National Curriculum subjects and pursue a specialist subject, with time spent on professional placements.

University of the West of England, Bristol

continued

PGCE Primary Early Years

On this one-year full-time intensive course you will focus on nursery/reception within the Primary years and specialise in learning in early childhood, with time spent on professional placements.

Training as a primary teacher is an extremely popular route and competition for places is high, so it is essential you apply early as each year regretfully we disappoint many candidates. The university website gives more detail on the selection process.

PGCE Secondary (11-18 years)

On this one-year full-time intensive course you will learn how to become an effective secondary teacher with subject specialism with time spent on professional placements. The course offers specialisms in the following subjects.

Subjects:
- Art and design
- Design and technology
- English
- Geography
- History
- Mathematics
- Mathematics with business education
- Modern languages
- Science: chemistry
- Science: physics
- Science: physics with maths

All of our teacher training courses are active and practical allowing trainees to develop professional competence through work undertaken in schools and in the university.

PGCE PCET (Post-Compulsory Education and Training)

This one-year full-time intensive course is approved by Lifelong Learning UK (LLUK) and is nationally recognised as an advanced professional qualification for teaching in the post-16 sector. Successful participants will, on completion of the course, meet LLUK professional standards in teaching, reflection on practice and scholarship in education.

APPLICATION ROUTES

Undergraduate - through UCAS.

Postgraduate - through the GTTR.

School of Sport and Education
Uxbridge
Middlesex UB8 3PH
t: 01895 267019
f: 01895 269805
// www.brunel.ac.uk/sse

GENERAL INFORMATION

The School of Sport and Education has a vibrant, dynamic culture, promoting and supporting cutting edge research and a highly professional approach to the education of teachers, sport scientists and related professionals. The school of today proudly builds on the traditions of its founder colleges - Borough Road College (established 1798) and Maria Grey College (established 1878), the first centres of excellence for teacher education in the Commonwealth.

Why choose the School of Sport and Education at Brunel?

PGCert courses for the training of teachers have recently been rated as 'Outstanding' and 'Good with outstanding features' by Ofsted.

The school's programmes are taught by staff who are active researchers in their fields and are recognised experts in a broad spectrum of specialist curriculum areas (see Additional Information below).

Brunel is a leading research centre for work in supportive education, with particular expertise in high-ability children and those with learning difficulties.

The school has a reputation as one of the leading institutions in its field for postgraduate work, with its courses recently praised by external assessors for:

- high quality teaching
- pro-active tutoring system
- ways in which cutting-edge research is used in teaching
- making research integral to students' experience.

The university's location and diverse, well-established primary and secondary school network ensure a vibrant and multi-cultural experience.

The university works in partnership with local schools for initial teacher training through a professional tutor system whereby teachers in school act as mentors during school placements. This ensures the courses meet the needs of the schools and improves the employability of the students.

Brunel's investment in buildings and infrastructure is now approaching £400m, with many new and refurbished social, teaching and sporting facilities, halls of residence and outdoor spaces - see **www.brunel.ac.uk/life** for more information.

ACADEMIC AWARDS

PGCert Primary - 1 year full-time postgraduate level

Students take all the primary National Curriculum subjects through teaching experience at the university and in partnership schools. The course equips students to teach across the primary age range 5-11).

Brunel University

PGCert Secondary - 1 year full-time postgraduate level

Main subjects offered:

- English
- Information and communication technology
- Mathematics
- Physical education
- Physics with mathematics
- Science with biology
- Science with chemistry
- Science with physics.

PGCert Secondary - 24 months part-time - postgraduate level

Main subjects offered:

- English
- Mathematics
- Science with biology
- Science with chemistry
- Science with physics.

Entry requirements:

- Applicants should have, by the start of the course, a good honours degree in a relevant subject from a UK or EU university, together with GCSE passes at grade C or equivalent in English language, mathematics and, for primary, a science subject.
- Applicants for mathematics and physics, whose degrees have insufficient mathematics/physics content, may be asked to complete a recognised full-time enhancement course from January to June, before the start of the PGCert course.

Other qualifications: Some BA/BSc or MA/MSc degrees from institutions outside the EU are acceptable in accordance with Department for Education regulations.

Qualified Teacher Status

Successful completion of the PGCert courses leads to a recommendation for Qualified Teacher Status (QTS).

Financial support

Students classified as 'home' students receive a training salary dependent on the current Teaching Agency (TA) criteria. For further information, please visit **www.education.gov.uk/get-into-teaching**.

Application route: Apply through the GTTR.

Additional information: research areas in education

The school undertakes interdisciplinary research in a diverse range of education related disciplines. It is home to staff with national and international reputations for their research and publications. Research is organised under three research groups:

- Curriculum Adaptation and Educational Interventions (CAEI)
- Education, Identities and Social Inclusion (EISI)
- Pedagogy and Professional Practice (PPP).

For more information about our research areas, please visit **www.brunel.ac.uk/sse/education/research**.

For more information about The School of Sport and Education generally, please visit **www.brunel.ac.uk/sse**.

Bromley Schools' Collegiate

Institution code: B91

Beaverwood School
Beaverwood Road
Chislehurst
Kent BR7 6HE
t: 020 8300 6566
f: 020 8300 6733
e: administrator@gradteach.co.uk
// www.bscteach.co.uk

GENERAL INFORMATION

Bromley Schools' Collegiate is a consortium of 9 local secondary schools based in the London Borough of Bromley. The provider was awarded 'Outstanding' status by ofsted in 2009. Trainees complete two separate placements in partner schools with attendance at a core training session each Wednesday afternoon.

Visit our website for details of the qualification achieved.

ACADEMIC AWARDS - QTS

The course is full-time for one academic year (September to July). A distinctive feature of the training is that the programme is totally school-based, giving trainees the opportunity to become part of everyday school life during each placement. Trainees are assigned to an experienced subject mentor who works closely with each trainee to help him/her develop the competencies required for Qualified Teacher Status. Trainees start by observing lessons and progress through collaborative teaching with their mentor to whole class teaching.

The weekly professional studies sessions develop trainees' theoretical knowledge and its practical application. The subject-specific programme offers the opportunity for trainees to develop subject knowledge for teaching. Assessment of trainees' progress is continuous, based on classroom observation which builds towards an e-portfolio of evidence towards QTS. In addition, trainees must complete written assignments throughout the programme.

Entry requirements:
- A relevant good degree at 2:2 or above
- GCSE English and maths at grade A - C
- Competent ICT skills
- Ability to travel to and between partner schools
- Commitment to teaching and improving the life chances of young people
- Excellent organisation skills
- Enthusiasm and passion for their chosen subject

Subjects offered:
- English
- Geography
- History
- ICT
- Mathematics
- Modern languages (French, Spanish, German)
- RE
- Science (biology, chemistry, physics)

Tuition fees
Visit our website for full details.

Application route: Complete the initial registration form (on our website **www.bscteach.co.uk**) and send with CV to the BSC Administrator and apply through the GTTR.

The Faculty of Education
184 Hills Road
Cambridge CB2 8PQ
t: **Secondary PGCE - 01223 767674**
t: **Primary PGCE - 01223 767679**
e: **pgce-admissions@educ.cam.ac.uk**

GENERAL INFORMATION

The University of Cambridge Faculty of Education offers courses that combine an excellent academic reputation with top-quality professional training for people who wish to become teachers. The faculty and its students benefit from being part of a world-class university where research constantly enhances the quality of taught courses and where students and teachers alike can work at the cutting edge of international knowledge in a wide range of subjects.

Our initial teacher-training courses are designed to be challenging, stimulating and suitable for a broad mix of trainees from different backgrounds and cultures, from different parts of the country and from a variety of universities and colleges. We take pride in the high quality of the PGCE courses which are offered in three different age ranges, and which were graded 'outstanding' by Ofsted in their most recent round of inspections.

Cambridge offers the delights of a very beautiful city and the great variety of intellectual, cultural, sporting and social opportunities afforded by collegiate life.

PGCE programmes
The Postgraduate Certificate in Education is a one-year course. Three different age ranges are offered:

- Secondary (11-18) course
- Primary (5-11) course
- Early years (3-7) course

The Secondary PGCE is a partnership course, offered in conjunction with secondary schools throughout East Anglia. Subjects offered currently are art, classics, design and technology, English (with drama), English, geography, history, mathematics, modern languages, music, religious studies and science (with biology, chemistry or physics as a specialism).

The Primary/Early Years PGCE course recruits students to a partnership scheme which works largely with schools in Cambridgeshire and adjacent counties. Students are prepared to teach across the range of the primary school curriculum, specialising either in the Early Years (3-7 age range) or the Primary (5-9 or 7-11) age ranges.

All courses are offered at postgraduate level. Those who successfully complete the PGCE course may be admitted directly onto the second year of the faculty's MEd course.

Enquiries about entry requirements for PGCE courses should be addressed to Robert Garnett for secondary courses and to Ursula Clarke for primary courses at the above address. For information about the PGCE courses and to download a prospectus, please refer to the faculty website at
www.educ.cam.ac.uk/courses/pgce

Application route: Apply through the GTTR.

Campuses at Canterbury
Medway
Broadstairs
Folkestone and Tunbridge Wells
t: 01227 782900
e: admissions@canterbury.ac.uk
// www.canterbury.ac.uk/courses

GENERAL INFORMATION

Canterbury Christ Church is the largest centre of higher education in Kent for teacher education and is renowned for academic excellence, a warm welcoming atmosphere and community spirit. The university is modern and friendly and offers excellent teaching facilities and residential accommodation within attractive environments.

Halls of residence accommodation on or very close to the campus is guaranteed for all Canterbury-based undergraduate students who live outside the immediate area. Further information can be found on our website.

A great social life centred around a lively students' union coupled with top quality teaching, state-of-the-art library and learning centre, and an excellent student support system ensures that your university experience at Canterbury Christ Church will be both immensely enjoyable and an invaluable start to your chosen career.

ACADEMIC AWARDS

The university offers a wide range of programmes for people who want to work with children and adults. A full list of programmes offered can be found on our website at **www.canterbury.ac.uk/courses**

There are full-time and part-time study routes both for those who want to teach and for those who want to work with children and young people.

Full-time programmes include the three-year degrees in Primary Education, Early Childhood Studies, Education Studies, Mathematics with Secondary Education and Physical Education & Sport Science. Applicants hould consult the UCAS website **www.ucas.com** for further information.

There is also an extensive range of full-time PGCE programmes in the following age ranges: Primary, 7-14, 11-19, 14-19 and Post-Compulsory. Applicants should consult the GTTR website **www.gttr.ac.uk**. Applicants for the PGCE Post-Compulsory apply directly to the university.

There are also part-time and work-based routes into teaching. These include foundation degrees, a two-year part-time top-up route in Primary Education, part-time and modular PGCEs as well as the Certificate of Education, the GTP and RTP schemes.

The Faculty of Education
Recognised nationally as a centre of excellence for teacher education and development, the Faculty of Education is one of the university's leading edge academic units. The faculty has developed as a centre of excellence at the cutting edge of training in education and delivers a range of programmes and courses from access/foundation to doctorate level. Faculty staff are recognised for their skill in responding to school, college and individual needs. Students include traditional and non-traditional learners from local, national and international backgrounds.

Application route: Apply through UCAS for three-year degree courses. Apply through the GTTR for PGCE programmes.

Cardiff School of Social Sciences
Professional Programmes Office
Glamorgan Building
King Edward VII Avenue
Cardiff CF10 3WT
t: 029 2087 4021
PGCE (PCET) Programmes Administrator
e: PGCE@cardiff.ac.uk
// www.cf.ac.uk/socsi/pgce

ACADEMIC AWARDS

The school offers long established (over 30 years) university-based teacher training courses in Post-Compulsory Education & Training. The courses cover and provide for teaching in further, adult and nursing education, as well as vocational training in industry, commerce and other professions, where the demand for qualified teachers continues to be high. The PGCE programmes address a range of teaching placement subjects and vocational areas.

The PGCE teacher training scheme offers

- a one-year full-time Postgraduate Certificate in Education (PCET) at master's level 7
- a two-year part-time In-service Postgraduate Certificate in Education (PCET) at master's level 7. Both of the above courses attract 60 credits at level 7 and 60 credits at level 6
- a two-year part-time In-service Professional Graduate Certificate in Education at honours degree level 6 - this attracts 120 credits at level 6.

The PGCE gives students an opportunity to review educational debates, investigate issues about learning and teaching and develop the higher level analytic and empirical skills. Each course programme provides substantive learning and practical opportunities for professional practice and training for those wishing to become teachers/trainers and for those who are already in service.

The PGCE scheme at Cardiff is endorsed and approved by LLUK and is nationally recognised. All the scheme programmes offer a pathway to QTLS, following the successful award and completion of the PGCE.

Admission

In line with Cardiff University's English Language Policy, all UK applicants are required to hold GCSE English (or equivalent) at grade C or above. Applicants whose first language is not English must obtain a British Council IELTS score of at least 6.5 or equivalent prior to commencement of the course.

For the full-time level 7 programme, you should possess at least a 2:2 degree in the subject you wish to teach.

For the in-service level 7 programme, you should possess at least a 2:2 degree. You must also be actively involved in training or education as a work role or in a voluntary capacity.

For the in-service level 6 programme, you should posses a degree or an appropriate professional qualification or experience.You must also be actively involved in training or education as a work role or in a voluntary capacity.

The Professional Programmes Office will require occupational health clearance for all students. In addition, CRB clearance is required for all students on the full-time programme.

Visit **www.cf.ac.uk/socsi/pgce** for more information about course provision and the application process.

Llandaff Campus
Western Avenue
Cardiff CF5 2YB
t: **029 2041 6044**
f: **029 2041 6286**
e: **admissions@cardiffmet.ac.uk**

GENERAL INFORMATION

The Cardiff School of Education (CSE) at Cardiff Metropolitan University has a long-standing tradition of providing high quality initial teacher education and training (ITET) programmes at both undergraduate and postgraduate levels. These ITET programmes make a significant contribution to shaping the next generation of primary and secondary teachers across Wales and beyond. The CSE's ITET programmes are positioned within the South East Wales Centre for Teacher Education and Training (SEWCTET), which is the product of an on-going collaboration between Cardiff Metropolitan University and the University of Wales Newport.

ACADEMIC AWARDS

CSE's Department of Teacher Education and Training (DTET) offers the following ITET programmes:

- PGCE Primary with pathways in: Foundation Phase (3-8 years) and Key Stage 2 (7-11 years).
- PGCE Secondary with pathways in: art and design, biology with science, chemistry with science, design and technology, drama, English, history, ICT, mathematics, modern foreign languages, music, physical education, physics with science and Welsh. The programme prepares students to teach across the 11-18 age range.
- BA (Hons) Secondary Education with QTS with pathways in Welsh and music. The programme prepares students to teach across the 11-16 age range.

The PGCE Primary and Secondary courses are full-time programmes of 1 year's duration. They incorporate significant periods of work-based learning which are distributed across at least two different schools. Successful students attain 60 credits at Level 7 (ie master's level) and 60 credits at Level 6.

The BA (Hons) Secondary Education with QTS is a 3 year, full-time programme that incorporates a significant period of work-based learning distributed across at least two different schools

ADDITIONAL INFORMATION

- ITET programmes are delivered in conjunction with partner schools where trained mentors work closely with students as they develop their professional skills. Ultimately, students are assessed against statutory standards and successful students are recommended for Qualified Teacher Status.
- School-based and university-based elements of the ITET programmes are carefully integrated and this facilitates the development of students' skills as reflective practitioners.
- All of the university's ITET programmes have very good track records in preparing students for employment and this is evidenced by positive employability statistics and feedback from headteachers and former students.
- Opportunities are available for students to undertake part of their study through the medium of Welsh.

Entry requirements: These include the following:

- For PGCE Primary and Secondary - an initial degree (normally at 2.2 or above).
- For BA (Hons) Secondary Education Music and Welsh -Normally, 280 UCAS points to include grade B/C in the specialist subject.

For further entry requirements please visit:
www3.uwic.ac.uk/english/education/teachedu/pages/home.aspx

Application routes: Undergraduate applications through UCAS, postgraduate applications through the GTTR.

OTHER UNDERGRADUATE PROGRAMMES OFFERED (NON-ITET)

- BA (Hons) Educational Studies & Early Childhood Studies / Sport & Physical Activity / English/ Psychology / Welsh
- BA (Hons) Youth and Community Work.

Central School of Speech and Drama

Institution code: C35

Eton Avenue
London NW3 3HY
t: 020 7722 8183
// www.cssd.ac.uk

GENERAL INFORMATION

Central School of Speech and Drama has the longest established drama ITT in Britain, and a PGCE in Media Studies.

Based in the centre of London, you have the opportunity to experience urban education as well as the rich culture of the city.

Whilst on this course, subject to residential status, you may be entitled to a training salary and a student loan.

There are close links with the English and Media Centre and schools throughout the south east.

ACADEMIC AWARDS

PGCE Drama - 1 year full-time
PGCE Secondary (11-18)
PGCE Media Studies - 1 year full-time
PGCE Secondary (14-19)
Entry requirements: GCSE grade C or above or equivalent in English language and mathematics. Normally a good honours degree in a relevant subject with a degree class of 2:1 or above.

Please note that those without the appropriate English language and/or mathematics qualification will not be interviewed.

Work experience: Evidence of working with children and young people required.

For example, work as a teaching assistant or youth worker would be useful, although not essential.

OTHER INFORMATION

Entry route: PG/FT/1year

Awards: PGCE

Intended intake: 18

Application route: Apply through the GTTR.

Enquiries: Please address all postal enquiries to Admissions and Student Recruitment.

University of Chester

Institution code: C55

Parkgate Road
Chester CH1 4BJ
t: 01244 511000
f: 01244 511300
e: enquiries@chester.ac.uk
// www.chester.ac.uk

GENERAL INFORMATION

The University of Chester has been training teachers since 1839 and offers a range of teacher training courses at both undergraduate and postgraduate level.

The Faculty of Education & Children's Services' staff are committed to the continued development and delivery of high quality education programmes.

Partnership schools are largely located in Cheshire, Wirral, Runcorn, Warrington, Merseyside, Shropshire, Flintshire and Denbighshire with a smaller number beyond these areas.

Local interest/activities

Chester is a vibrant, modern city with a host of pubs, clubs and restaurants to suit all tastes and budgets, and some of the best shopping outside London. Popular attractions include the Roman amphitheatre, River Dee and Chester races.

Warrington is a lively, vibrant centre, with a variety of shops, restaurants, clubs, café bars and more traditional pubs. Popular attractions include the museum and art gallery, Pyramid Centre for the Arts and the Golden Square Shopping Centre, which received a multimillion pound renovation, doubling the size to over 100 shops, cafes and restaurants.

Accommodation

Accommodation at Chester and Warrington includes halls of residence, self-catered houses, private sector renting and private sector lodgings.

Students' union

The university's students' union is the focal point for student representation, information, advice, entertainment and services. It has a site on each campus.

Leisure facilities

The university offers a wide variety of on-campus sports facilities, clubs and societies, including gymnasium and fitness centre, all-weather pitches, sports hall, athletics track, cafés, bistros and student union bar.

ACADEMIC AWARDS

The University of Chester provides teacher training courses leading to the awards of BA with Qualified Teacher Status (BA QTS), GTP and PGCE, covering a range of subjects in both the Primary and Secondary sectors.

Chester Campus - most teaching sessions are held at the Riverside Building

Teacher education
BA Primary Teacher Education (QTS)
BA Early Primary Teacher Education
PGCE Primary (5-11) - teaching focuses on Key Stages 1 and 2
PGCE Secondary (11-16) with sixth form enhancement
- Drama
- Mathematics
- Modern foreign languages (French, German,Spanish)
- Physical education

University of Chester

- Religious education
- Science (biology, chemistry, physics)
- GTP Primary, Early Years and Secondary

In the case of GTP Secondary generally, fully funded places are available in the above subjects though there are opportunities for a school to self-fund in other subject areas.

The PGCE Early, Primary and Secondary courses enable trainees to gain Qualified Teacher Status and are designed at master's level, so successful students will also gain 60 credits towards a master's degree.

Warrington Campus
PGCE Early Years (3-7)
Three assignments will be assessed against master's level criteria giving successful students 60 credits towards a master's degree. Teaching focuses on Early Years Foundation Stage and Key Stage 1

Entry requirements:
- For the BA QTS, we accept a range of qualifications, including GCE A levels, BTEC/OCR National Diploma and CACHE Diploma, and QAA recognised Access to HE Diplomas. For the one year PGCE Primary and Early Years courses, a good honours degree is required (a minimum of 2:1).
- At the time of application, BA QTS candidates must have a GCSE grade C or above (Bs preferred) (or equivalent) in English language, mathematics and science. Primary school experience is also essential.
- For the PGCE Secondary courses, a good honours degree is required (a minimum of 2:2, preferably 2:1), the content of which is appropriate to the secondary school curriculum. All candidates must have a GCSE grade C or above (or equivalent) in English language and mathematics. School experience is also essential. We offer a number of Subject Knowledge Enhancement (SKE) courses

(chemistry, maths and modern languages (ML)) which potential PGCE students can undertake to prepare themselves better for PGCE courses.
- For GTP Early Years, Primary and Secondary see above requirements linked to phases. There is also a requirement that school experience is usually at least a term in length, with applicants sometimes fulfilling the role of a teaching assistant, cover supervisor or unqualified teacher. Career changers will be considered with slightly less direct experience in school.
- All suitable applicants are interviewed prior to an offer of a place being made.
- The health of all successful candidates will be assessed to establish fitness to undertake a teaching course, and an Enhanced Criminal Records Bureau check will also be carried out.

Equivalence tests: The university currently does not provide equivalence tests, though applicants are invited to check the website as there are plans to offer them in the future.

Application routes: BA QTS applicants apply through UCAS. PGCE applicants apply through the GTTR. GTP applicants apply directly to the university.

OTHER INFORMATION

To receive a university prospectus, course leaflet or information about open days, please contact us.

t: **01244 512800**
t: **enquiries@chester.ac.uk**
// **www.chester.ac.uk**

To find out more about our Faculty of Education and children's services, please visit our website at
www.chester.ac.uk/education/index.html

University of Chichester

Institution code: C58

Bognor Regis Campus
Upper Bognor Road
Bognor Regis PO21 1HR
t: Switchboard - 01243 816000
t: Admissions Enquiries - 01243 816002
f: 01243 816161

GENERAL INFORMATION

University of Chichester has about 5,000 students, including part-time and postgraduate. It has one of the largest teacher education departments in the country, and has achieved good Ofsted inspection reports. All initial teacher training courses at Chichester benefit from strong links with regional schools.

ACADEMIC AWARDS

BA (Hons) Primary Education and Teaching leading to QTS - 3 years full-time
Routes offered: Advanced study of early years. Citizenship, English, ICT, mathematics, modern foreign languages, natural science.

Entry requirements:
- BBB including an A level at grade B or above in your subject specialism; or National Diploma at DDD; or merit in an approved Access Diploma.
- Plus: GCSE grade C passes (or equivalent) in English language, mathematics and science. Plus two other GCSE passes (5 in total).
- At least two weeks' recent experience in a UK state sector primary school.
- Pre-entry skills tests.

PGCE Primary - 1 year full-time
Master's level course (60 master's level credits) covering professional studies, curriculum studies and school experience.

Equivalence tests: No.

Entry requirements:
- Honours degree, 2:2 pass or above.
- GCSE/O level grade C passes (or equivalent) including English language, mathematics and science.
- At least two weeks' recent school experience in a state sector primary school.
- Pre-entry skills tests.

Equivalence tests: No.

PGCE Primary - 1 year full-time
Specialist routes: Modern languages (currently French and Spanish). For students who wish to become languages specialist but who will also be able to work as a classroom teacher with the 5-11 age range.

Entry requirements:
- Honours degree, 2:2 pass or above.
- GCSE/O level grade C passes (or equivalent), including English language, mathematics and science.
- Must be proficient to at least A level standard in the specified language.
- At least two weeks' recent school experience in a state sector primary school.
- Pre-entry skills tests.

Equivalence tests: No.

PGCE Secondary - 1 year full-time

Main subjects offered:

- Design technology
- English
- History
- ICT
- Mathematics
- Modern languages
- Physical education
- Religious education
- Science.

Entry requirements:

- Honours degree, 2:2 pass or above, with 50% subject content in your specialist subject or a closely related subject.
- Plus: GCSE/O level grade C passes (or equivalent), in English language and mathematics.
- At least two weeks' recent school experience at a relevant level.
- Pre-entry skills tests.

Equivalence tests: No.

Application route: UG apply through UCAS; PG apply through the GTTR.

Chiltern Training Group
Challney High School for Boys and Community College
Stoneygate Road
Luton LU4 9TJ
t: 01582 493680
e: info@chilterntraininggroup.org
// www.chilterntraininggroup.org

GENERAL INFORMATION

Chiltern Training Group (CTG) is a school-centred initial teacher training (SCITT) provider based at Challney High School for Boys in Luton. It is a consortium of 18 schools in the south Bedfordshire area.

- CTG started in 1993 and is one of the longest running SCITTs in the country.
- Training is entirely school-based in carefully selected schools in the Luton area.
- The Key Stages covered are 3 and 4 but in some cases trainees will have opportunities to work at post-16 level. The business studies course is designated 14-19.
- CTG has strong links with Luton Sixth Form College and also with a wide range of primary schools.
- The consortium has a high rate of employment success for its trainees.

The course relies heavily on:

- structured mentoring and the management of classroom learning
- personal subject mentors who act as role model, professional counsellor and assessor
- individually planned training with carefully supervised teaching.

Teaching experience: We organise the training to ensure that all trainees have the opportunity to teach:

- in two very different high schools
- in a feeder primary school
- with post-16 students.

Entry requirements: Degree class 2:2 or better. GCSE grade C or above in English language and mathematics.

ACADEMIC AWARDS

PGCE Secondary (11-16) - 1 year full-time
We offer both Postgraduate and Professional Graduate Certificate in Education courses for 2013 entry. Please contact us or visit our website for more information.

Subjects offered:
- Art
- Business studies (14-19)
- Design and technology (resistant materials, food and textiles)
- English
- Geography
- Information and communications technology
- Mathematics
- Modern foreign languages (French, German and Spanish)
- Music
- PE (male and female)
- Religious education
- Science (combined).

OTHER INFORMATION

Entry route: PG/FT/1 year
Awards: PGCE QTS
Intended intake: 90
Application route: Apply through the GTTR
Enquiries: Please address all postal enquiries to Jayne Ellery (Administrator).

Sheepen Road
Colchester
Essex CO3 3LL
t: 01206 712000
f: 01206 712800
e: info@colchester.ac.uk
// www.colchester.ac.uk

GENERAL INFORMATION

All our degree level programmes are validated through the University of Essex and are based on the Colchester campus. There is easy access to and from Stansted airport. London is within easy reach by motorway and rail link

The Centre for Education offers

- full-time pre-service and part-time in-service for FE teacher training
- a range of teaching practice placements in a wide variety of vocational areas for the full-time, pre-service course
- skills for life specialist teaching qualifications (literacy/ESOL; Numeracy).

ACADEMIC AWARDS

Undergraduate
Main subjects offered:
- Certificate in Education (Lifelong Learning Sector)
- Professional Graduate Certificate in Education (Lifelong Learning Sector)
- Level 5 Certificate in Continuing Education (Teaching Literacy and ESOL)
- Level 5 Certificate of Continuing Education (Teaching Numeracy)

Entry requirements:
Minimum entry qualifications for ITT: level 2 literacy and numeracy (or equivalent); level 3 specialist subject qualification (Cert Ed) undergraduate degree (Professional Graduate Certificate)

Minimum entry qualifications for level 5 certificates: Teaching qualification and employment in the sector.

Application route: Through UCAS for the Professional Graduate Certificate and Certificate in Education (LLS) full-time, pre-service. Otherwise direct to Colchester Institute.

Colchester Teacher Training Consortium

Institution code: C76

Alderman Blaxill School
Paxman Avenue
Colchester
Essex CO2 9DQ
t: **01206 364728**
e: **enquiries@colchesterttc.org.uk**
// **www.colchesterttc.org.uk**

Colchester Teacher Training Consortium

Colchester Teacher Training consortium (formerly Colchester SCITT and DRB) is a strong partnership of 14 secondary schools and colleges, with a number of distinctive features that contribute to diversity and choice for trainees. The mix of partner schools is varied: the consortium can offer trainees a teaching experience in a mixed comprehensive, an 11-18 school, an 11-16 school, a Roman Catholic school and a grammar school. The range of subject specialisms and awards to be found within the consortium is exceptional. In short, Colchester Teacher Training Consortium has friendly, well-equipped schools that offer a wide range of educational experiences and understand the needs of ITT.

PGCE Secondary

Colchester Teacher Training Consortium offers a Postgraduate Certificate in Education (Secondary 11-16) in:

- English (with drama*)
- Mathematics
- Science
- Physical education
- Information and communication technology (ICT)
- Modern foreign languages (French, German** and Spanish**)
- Design and technology.

*drama 10-20%
**only in combination with French

We offer a total of 36 places for the above subjects. All courses are offered at both professional graduate or postgraduate level.

Entry requirements:

- Degree - degree of which at least 50% should be in the subject you wish to teach***.
- GCSE - English language and mathematics at GCSE grade C or higher (or equivalent qualification).

***Secondary school teachers usually specialise in teaching the subject they have studied for their degree and, therefore, it is usual to train to become a teacher in that subject. We take the view that some degrees in subjects not directly related to the one you wish to teach may provide sufficient coverage in terms of subject knowledge for you to be able to teach that subject. If you are unsure about the suitability of your degree course, please contact us so that we may discuss this matter with you.

- School experience - relevant school experience or other recent experience of working with young people in a secondary school or related setting.

Please contact us if you wish to discuss the entry requirements or other aspects of the application process.

Application route: Apply though the GTTR. You are advised to apply early as places are filled quickly.

Truro College
College Road
Truro
Cornwall TR1 3XX
t: **01872 267092**
f: **01872 267526**
e: **scitt@truro-penwith.ac.uk**
// **www.cornwallscitt.org**

GENERAL INFORMATION

Cornwall SCITT is a consortium of 16 local secondary schools, one special school and one tertiary college committed to offering teacher training of the highest standard. Our aim is to recruit students who have the talent, commitment and enthusiasm to be effective teachers.

The main site of study is Truro College, which is a rapidly expanding tertiary college located on the outskirts of the cathedral city of Truro. The facilities, resources, ICT provision and teaching accommodation are of an extremely high standard.

ACADEMIC AWARDS

This PGCE course is offered at both professional and postgraduate level. Please contact the SCITT directly for more information.

Main subjects offered and intended intake:

- Design and technology - 8
- English - 12
- Mathematics - 10
- Modern foreign languages (French or German subsidiary Spanish) - 8
- Music - 5
- Science (with biology, chemistry or physics) - 12
- ICT - 6
- Media studies - 6

Course structure
The course is designed to include closely linked modules in subject application and assessment, professional studies, curriculum studies and application of ICT.

In the classroom, initial observation and interpretation progress to co-planning, teaching and evaluating parts of lessons. By the end of the course, students will be expected to be involved with 60% of the timetabled week.

OTHER INFORMATION

Enhancement opportunities include visits to local special schools to observe the SEN environment; visits to local primary schools and subject support courses for design and technology, science and mathematics.

Entry requirements:

- A relevant good degree, 2:2 or above, in a National Curriculum core or foundation subject. (Other degrees with appropriate content will be considered alongside relevant experience.)
- Appropriate A level or equivalent qualifications.
- Grade C (or equivalent) in GCSE mathematics and English.
- Confidence in using appropriate ICT skills.
- Evidence of relevant school experience and other recent activities that demonstrate a particular interest in working with children.
- Ability to travel between different training locations within the county.

Application route: Apply through the GTTR.

Cornwall SCITT Partnership
Studio 4
Artist Muse - The Heartlands
Fordh an Bal
Pool
Redruth TR15 3FD
t: **01209 721420**
f: **01209 721401**
e: **SCITT Administrator**
scittpartnership@cornwall.gov.uk

GENERAL INFORMATION

Early Years Course: Foundation Stage/Key Stage 1
(age range 3-7yrs)
or
Primary Course: Key Stage 1 and 2 (age range
5-11yrs) - pending approval and number
of allocated places

The structure of both courses links theory
and practice, with training placements each term
spent in a school and at the course centre. Following
on from training at the course centre, trainees
are given tasks to carry out during their time in school
to support their teaching and learning. Trainees are
assigned a trained school-based tutor within each
school in which they are placed. This person is
responsible for supporting and guiding the trainee's
professional development and ensuring that they have
the opportunities that they need within the school.

A trainee's progress is assessed through
regular formal and informal monitoring of teaching
competences, leading to profile reviews and
assignments, which link education/subject theory
with the teaching and learning in the classroom. Key
personnel linked to the assessment process are the
school-based tutor, liaison tutor, course trainers and
the programme manager.

A considerable amount of reading is required
and there is also a strong emphasis on the use of ICT
throughout the course. Experienced trainers and
practitioners provide training specially designed
to introduce trainees to the needs of children and the
Early Years/Primary curriculum.

The participating schools have been selected on
the basis of their record for providing a quality
teaching and learning environment, their strong
commitment to professional development and
their previous interest and experience of working with
trainees in initial teacher training. The schools have a
much greater role in training than in more traditional
courses that lead to QTS. They are involved in the
selection of trainees as well as their mentoring and
assessing.

Entry requirements:
- A degree (at least a 2:2 or higher) from a
  United Kingdom higher education institution or
  equivalent qualification.
- GCSE at grade C or above in English,
  mathematics and science (or O level at grade C or
  above).

Please note we do NOT accept equivalency tests
eg level 2 numeracy or literacy.

Application route: Applications through the GTTR.
www.gttr.ac.uk

Please visit our website:
 www.cornwall.co.uk/scittpartnership for further
details including entry requirements.

Cumbria Primary Teacher Training (CPTT)

Institution code: C97

High Street
Workington
Cumbria CA14 4ES
t: 01900 325060
f: 01900 325061
e: enquiries@cptt.org.uk
// www.cumbria-scitt.org

GENERAL INFORMATION

CPTT offers a successful school-centred initial teacher training Primary PGCE course, validated by the University of Cumbria. On successful completion of this one-year, full-time course, you will be awarded QTS and a PGCE from the University of Cumbria, qualifying you to teach ages 5-11 years.

Trainees are placed in three different schools, one per term, allowing different experiences of rural and urban, large and small, general primary and single key stage schools, single- and mixed-age classes. All trainees are placed in a minimum of one Key Stage 1 class and one Key Stage 2 class.

Each school has a permanent lead mentor throughout the year to all trainees received into their school. Each trainee also has a support mentor who will provide necessary feedback and advice throughout the placement. All head teachers at the placement schools are members of the CPTT Board, ensuring schools have a very 'hands on' approach to course development.

Fifty per cent of course time is spent in experienced CPTT training schools, all within a 20-mile radius of the training centre, which is in Workington, Cumbria

CPTT ensures a good team atmosphere throughout the year by requesting that all trainees participate in an outdoor residential in the Lake District in the first two days of the PGCE.

Although the college does not have accommodation of its own, there is a wide range of accommodation in the area covered by the schools, details of which will be sent to you if you are successful in gaining a place. With the lakes and fells on your doorstep, the Solway coast and Scotland nearby, the recreational and educational facilities are unsurpassed. Spend a year in Cumbria enjoying weekends in scenery which has inspired many artists and poets. As you will expect from a rural area such as Cumbria, providing your own transport is essential!

Entry requirements: All entrants should have undertaken a minimum of two weeks' work experience in a UK primary school classroom.

Please see our website for a complete list of all of our entry requirements.

Application route: Each year we aim to recruit 30 trainees for the one-year (September to July), full-time course. Apply through the GTTR. Interviews commence in February and continue until the course is full (generally April/May).

Candidates should view our website, **www.cumbria-scitt.org** before applying.

Enquiries: Call us if you have any queries or would just like a general chat about our course. We pride ourselves on our informal and friendly approach and we look forward to speaking to you.

University of Cumbria Carlisle, Lancaster and London

Institution code: C99

Undergraduate - 0845 606 1144
PGCE - 0845 850 0760
www.cumbria.ac.uk

GENERAL INFORMATION

The University of Cumbria brought together the expertise and pedigrees of St Martin's College, Cumbria Institute of the Arts and the Cumbrian campuses of the University of Central Lancashire.

As the largest provider of initial teacher education in England, the University of Cumbria is at the leading edge of teacher education. Our excellent reputation for teacher training is well known in the education sector. We provide encouragement and support at every stage, enabling you to achieve your professional and personal goals. Our aim is to provide innovative, flexible learning that focuses on your needs.

We have excellent school placement relationships and collaborate with schools, colleges and other agencies in the region to offer research, scholarship and knowledge transfer excellence. This ensures that the University of Cumbria is at the heart of social, cultural and economic development in the county.

We offer teacher training courses at our campuses in Carlisle and Lancaster and a specialist teacher-education centre in London and also offer a wide range of continuing professional development provision.

Our student population is a rich mixture of full and part-time, vocational and academic, leading to a vibrant and creative atmosphere on campus. We celebrate our graduates and their success, knowing that they will be creative, enterprising, resourceful and equipped to lead in their fields and in their communities. The following teaching courses are available but please check our website for campus locations:

PRIMARY TEACHING

BA/BSc Honours with QTS: (5-11) - 4 years
BA Honours with QTS - Primary Teaching Education (5-11) - 3 years
BA Honours with QTS - Early Years Education (0-7) - 3 years
Foundation Degrees in Teaching and Learning Support - 3 years part-time
Primary - Postgraduate Certificate in Education, PGCE (5-11) - 1 year
Lower Primary - Postgraduate Certificate in Education, PGCE (3-7) - 1 yearPrimary - Distributed Learning Programme Professional Graduate Certificate in Education, PGCE (5-11) - Routes 1-4

SECONDARY TEACHING

Secondary - Postgraduate Certificate in Education, PGCE (11-18 PGCE, awarding 11-16 QTS) - 1 year (range of subjects)
Subject Knowledge Enhancement courses (ICT, mathematics, chemistry and physics)
Foundation Degree in Teaching and Learning Support - 3 years part-time.
Other courses - QTS direct.

Faculty of Education
Health and Sciences
Kedleston Road
Derby DE22 1GB
t: 01332 591166
e: g.s.maxwell@derby.ac.uk
// www.derby.ac.uk

GENERAL INFORMATION

The initial teacher training provision includes training for teaching in the Primary Sector, the Lifelong Learning Sector (previously Further Education) as well as GTP. Facilities include a newly furnished teacher education centre and a well-equipped learning resource centre. Collaborative partnerships include working with primary and secondary schools as well as further education colleges across several counties. These include innercity, town and rural educational establishments which provides an excellent opportunity to gain a range of cultural and social experiences during training. The university also has strong links with schools and universities in the USA and Europe.

Accommodation

The university has an extensive range of modern residential accommodation well suited for both the university and the city centre. The city has a good supply of private rented accommodation.

ACADEMIC AWARDS

BEd (Hons) with Qualified Teacher Status (QTS), Primary 5-11

The university offers a 3-year and 4-year course leading to Qualified Teacher Status in Primary education with a focus on the 5-11 age phase. The course also offers exciting opportunities and experiences relating to the Early Years Foundation Stage and Special School Education. Both routes enable you to choose a subject enhancement linked to local and national priorities and also one elective module from a range of options, including learning beyond the classroom, SEN, cultural diversity, and other applied areas of Primary education. Rated 'Outstanding' by Ofsted, the BEd at the University of Derby has one of the highest student satisfaction and employability rates in the country. Our partnership schools are at the centre of our BEd and throughout the course we have a strong focus on 'giving back' something to the community. More details can be located at:
www.derby.ac.uk/education-bed-hons

Entry requirements: 300 UCAS points preferred from a maximum of three A levels or equivalent qualification. Only 60 UCAS points can be from general studies. Six GCSEs at a minimum grade C is required, which must include English language, maths, and a science. You must have recent primary school experience. All TDA entry requirements also need to be met; this includes suitability and fitness to teach checks.

Application route: Apply through UCAS. Places are only offered following a successful interview.

PGCE Primary - 1 year full-time or flexible
Students will follow one of the following pathways: Early Years (3-7) or Later Years (7-11) or (5-11). Suitable applicants for the 7-11 pathway may opt for a possible French specialism. Any route may be followed 'flexibly' over two or three years based on a negotiated individual training plan. Students following the Later Years (7-11) with French must complete the specialist French module. Assessment for all pathways is through coursework and practical teaching undertaken

on school placements. The modules carry a total of 60 credits at level 7. More details can be located at **www.derby.ac.uk/pgce-primary**

Entry requirements: UK honours degree (or overseas equivalent) 2:1 classification preferred. GCSEs, at minimum grade C, in English language, maths and a science, which must have been attained at the point of application. Applicants for the French pathway must also hold French at A level, minimum grade C, at the point of application. All applicants are expected to have gained an understanding of teaching in UK primary schools and have some recent experience of teaching in a UK primary school setting.

Application route: Apply through GTTR. Competition for places is very high. Places are only offered to suitable candidates who are successful at interview.

Professional Graduate Diploma: Teaching in the Lifelong Learning Sector - 1 academic year full-time

This programme provides an excellent opportunity to become a teacher, developing knowledge and skills which are applied within a work placement throughout the programme.

On successful completion of the course you will be able to meet the new Government Standards for Teaching in the Lifelong Learning Sector and to gain Qualified Teaching Learning and Skills (QTLS) status.

From the start of the course you will be allocated a tutor at the University of Derby to oversee your personal and professional development. You will also be allocated a mentor in your work placement to develop your subject specialism.

Assessment is assignment-based combined with successful teaching observations and application of reflective practice.

The curriculum subjects offered include vocational and academic subject areas, eg art and design, business and management, science, mathematics, English, public services, engineering.

Entry requirements: UK honours degree (or equivalent) normally with a 2:2 classification or above, in a curriculum subject suitable for the lifelong learning sector. GCSE grade C or above (or equivalent) in English language and mathematics. All applicants need to be aware of the key purpose of the Lifelong Learning Sector and familiar with current teaching within it. More details can be located at:

www.derby.ac.uk/teaching-in-the-lifelong-learningsector-professional-graduate-diploma

Application route: Apply through the GTTR.

Devon Primary SCITT
Tollards Training Centre
West of England College
Topsham Road
Countess Wear
Exeter
Devon EX2 6HA
t: 01392 454359
e: admin@dpscitt.ac.uk
// www.dpscitt.ac.uk

GENERAL INFORMATION

The Devon Primary SCITT course

The Devon Primary SCITT offers a one-year, full-time, school-based route to qualification as a primary teacher, leading to Qualified Teacher Status (QTS) and a Professional Graduate Certificate in Education (PGCE) or Postgraduate Certificate in Education (M level credits) validated by the University of Plymouth.

The SCITT consists of 33 successful primary schools in three clusters in North Devon, South Devon and in, or around Exeter. The course prepares trainee teachers for teaching in the 5-11 age range. It covers the full 195 days of the school academic year, and comprises 45 centre-based training days, 60 school-based training days and 90 days of teaching practice spread throughout the year.

Key features of the course:

- Trainees are based in one partnership school for the autumn and summer terms and a second school for the spring term.
- Experience of teaching in Key Stage 1 and Key Stage 2.
- A structured school-based programme that maximises the power of learning through working alongside successful practitioners.
- A high quality taught course delivered centrally by education consultants, advisers and serving practitioners.
- Assignments that develop trainees' subject knowledge for teaching, linked to practical work in school.

Ofsted (March 2009) awarded the Devon Primary SCITT top grades and concluded that the key strengths included:

- the excellent levels of communication and organisation
- the highly focused support and guidance to meet the individual needs of trainees throughout their course
- the excellent links between the various course modules and the school-based training.

Entry requirements:

- A degree from a United Kingdom university or higher education institution (or equivalent).
- Grade C or above in GCSE (or equivalent) English language, mathematics and science.
- Experience of working with children in schools or in more informal settings.
- A strong recommendation to train as a primary school teacher from an appropriate referee.
- Meet the Secretary of State's requirements for physical and mental fitness to teach.
- Never have been excluded from teaching or working with children.
- Declare any criminal background which might prevent employment as a teacher or working with children or young persons.
- Never having failed a QTS course in the past.

Application route: Apply through the Gttr.

Devon Secondary Teacher Training Group

Institution code: D41

Enquiries: DSTTG
Coombeshead Academy
Coombeshead Road
Newton Abbot
Devon TQ12 1PT
t: **01626 883555**
e: **dsttg@devon.gov.uk**
// **www.devonstt.co.uk**

GENERAL INFORMATION

The Devon Secondary Teacher Training Group is a consortium of secondary schools and Devon County Council, which offers a school-based PGCE. This is a distinctive and practical course of the highest quality, Ofsted category 'outstanding'. Partner schools are located in the south and mid-Devon area. All are known for their exceptional standards and commitment to professional development.

PGCE/QTS

The course leads to Qualified Teacher Status and either a Professional Graduate Certificate in Education or a Postgraduate Certificate in Education as part of a master's qualification awarded by The University of Worcester.

Intended intake: Total intake is 30 trainees. 15 places are available for drama, 5 for music and 10 for modern foreign languages.

- Drama
- French
- German
- Music
- Spanish.

Performing arts

The course in specialist drama teaching offers an opportunity to develop teaching in music to Key Stage 3. Similarly, the course in specialist music teaching offers an opportunity to develop teaching in drama to Key Stage 3. Suitably qualified applicants may also be able to develop teaching in dance and media. The course includes a performing arts week and Key Stage 2 outreach work.

Modern foreign languages

The course in modern foreign language teaching offers an opportunity to develop teaching in a second modern language to Key Stage 3 level (French, German, Spanish), and trainees will benefit from working alongside performing arts trainees to share ideas and develop effective teaching strategies. The course includes an opportunity to do Key Stage 2 outreach work.

Entry requirements
- Honours degree in relevant subject with GCSE English language and mathematics to grade C level.
- Preference will be given to applicants with GCSE English language and mathematics to grade C level. However, equivalence tests are available for those applicants who have received a conditional offer of a place.

Application route: Apply through the GTTR.

OTHER INFORMATION

Employment rates are very good.

From September 2013 entry we are planning to offer the following new subjects: mathematics, chemistry and physics.Please contact us or visit our website for more information.

University Centre Doncaster

Institution code: D52

University Centre Doncaster
High Melton
DN5 7SZ
t: 01302 553610
e: he@don.ac.uk
// www.don.ac.uk

GENERAL INFORMATION

University Centre Doncaster offers a host of education-based courses and has some of the lowest tuition fees in the country.

Its courses are run out of the idyllic countryside campus, six miles west of Doncaster. Set in 126 acres of greenery, the campus is the perfect place to combine study and relaxation - and it even has on-site accommodation. There is a £65m sister campus in the town centre, called The Hub.

As well as enjoying some of the country's lowest tuition fees, local students could get up to £1,200 towards their degree through two unique bursaries. The centre offers foundation degrees, BA (Hons degrees, PGCEs and PGCHEs in education (pre-service and in-service).

Independent reviewers recently praised the establishment for its 'approachable and helpful' staff and its student-staff ratio of approximately 10:1.

As well as accommodation for up to 250 students, the campus is home to a huge learning resource centre, newly-refurbished leisure facilities; including a student bar, a fully equipped gym and even a nine-hole golf course.

Doncaster is a lively town with a plethora of entertainment and leisure choices, and the cities of Sheffield and Leeds are only half-an-hour away. The centre is playing a huge part in the regeneration of Doncaster, which has recently gained a new shopping centre, community stadium, transport interchange and airport. Last year more than a thousand students graduated from University Centre Doncaster. It is hoped that the establishment will receive university college status in the next three to five years - the next step tobecoming an independent University of Doncaster.

Enquiries:
For further details on fees, bursaries and the courses offered at University Centre, Doncaster, call 0800 358 7474 or visit **www.don.ac.uk** to order a prospectus with a free CD.

Dorset Teacher Training Partnership

Institution code: D53

SCITT Director
The Thomas Hardye School
Queen's Avenue
Dorchester, Dorset DT1 2ET
t: **01305 756809**
f: **01305 250510**
e: **josborne@thomas-hardye.net**

GENERAL INFORMATION

The Dorset Teacher Training Partnership comprises approximately 30 local infant, first, primary and middle schools; other partners include The Thomas Hardye School (Managing Agent), Dorset Local Authority and Kingston University. The PGCE (postgraduate level) is validated by Kingston University.

The course is specifically designed for trainees wishing to teach pupils in the 5-11 years age range. Trainees spend approximately 22 weeks in schools, with 19 weeks of centre-based study at The Thomas Hardye School and some distance learning making up the remainder of the course.

School experience in one of our partnership schools is integral to the course. Trainees undertake three placements, with experience in both Key Stage 1 and Key Stage 2. From the third week of the course trainees are welcomed into their base school; this allows them to observe and participate in real situations at a very early stage in their training. They are supported by school-based tutors who play a crucial role in coordinating the trainees' learning and teaching programme within the school.

ACADEMIC AWARD

PGCE Primary (5-11) - 1 year full-time
Entry requirements: GCSE grade C in English language, mathematics and science. Good honours degree, 2:2 or above.

OTHER INFORMATION

Entry route: PG/FT/1 year
Awards: PGCE QTS
Intended intake: 26
Application route: Apply through the GTTR.
Enquiries: Please address all postal enquiries to Judi Osborne or email josborne@thomas-hardye.net

School of Education, Social Work & Community Education

University of Dundee
Nethergate
Dundee DD1 4HN
t: 01382 381400
f: 01382 381511
e: MA Hons - g.french@dundee.ac.uk
e: PGDE - l.buj@dundee.ac.uk
// www.dundee.ac.uk/admissions

GENERAL INFORMATION

The School of Education, Social Work and Community Education is located on our City campus close to the centre of Dundee. Our teaching accommodation offers the very best in up-to-date learning and teaching facilities. We also offer a range of CPD and other postgraduate teaching programmes. See our website for more details.

ACADEMIC AWARDS

MA (Hons) Education - 4 years full-time
Entry requirements:

- SQA Highers at ABBB, including English plus Standard Grade mathematics at credit level 1 or 2, or Intermediate 2 mathematics at grade B or above.
- GCE/VCE A levels at BBC, plus GCSE mathematics at B and English language and literature at grade B.
- Alternative qualifications: A variety of equivalent qualifications such as HNC/HND and Access to Higher Education programmes are considered. Applicants must have Higher English or equivalent plus a credit pass in Standard Grade mathematics, Intermediate 2 mathematics at B or above or GCSE mathematics at grade B or above.

PGDE Primary - 1 year full-time
Entry requirements:

- This one-year (36-week) programme is designed for graduates who wish to qualify as primary teachers.
- The programme starts in mid-August and includes 18 weeks of school experience (placement in schools).
- Applicants must have a degree from a UK higher education institution or a degree of an equivalent standard from an institution outside the UK, and Higher English (grade B) and Standard Grade mathematics at credit level 1 or 2, or GCSE mathematics at A or B or Intermediate 2 mathematics at grade B or above. Relevant and recent experience of working in a primary school context is highly desirable. Competition for places is intense.

PGDE Secondary - 1 year full-time or 2 years part-time
Entry requirements:

- The programme will comprise the required component of school experience (18 weeks), but in a flexible framework that allows some room for negotiation between the student, education department and host school. Delivery will involve a substantial amount of distance learning using ICT-based systems.
- Normal entry requirements for such a course apply, ie a degree validated by a higher education institution in the United Kingdom or a degree of an equivalent standard from an institution outside the United Kingdom. The degree should normally contain passes with a minimum of 80 credit points relevant to the teaching qualification(s) being studied. Applicants must also have Higher grade English at grade B or equivalent.

Application route: PGDE apply through the GTTR. MA (Hons) apply through UCAS.

Old Shire Hall
Durham DH1 3HP
t: 0191 334 2000
// www.dur.ac.uk/education

GENERAL INFORMATION

Our School of Education is one of the best in the UK: we received an outstanding grading in all aspects of our initial teacher training provision in March 2011, and we were included in the 10 best departments for education in the country by The Complete University Guide 2010. Our degree courses are based in the spectacular medieval city of Durham and at the modern, purpose-built Queen's campus in nearby Stockton.

Durham is a collegiate university which means that you will be a member of one of the colleges on campus throughout your course. When you apply through UCAS (undergraduate courses) or through the GTTR, you will need to inform us which college you wish to apply to.

We believe the learning experience of our programmes is enriched where we have students from a variety of different social and cultural backgrounds. We therefore welcome students from all walks of life, including those changing career direction or looking for further professional development.

ACADEMIC AWARDS

Primary teaching courses (undergraduate) BA (Hons)

Based at our Queen's campus, Stockton, this is a three-year course for students who wish to pursue primary teaching as a career and become curriculum leaders in a core subject of the National Curriculum.

Entry requirements: At least ABB at A level or equivalent plus GCSE grade C or above in English, mathematics and science and at least 10 days' experience in a primary school.

PGCE programmes

The PGCE programme is a one-year full-time course, based at Durham, with two distinct routes, at primary and secondary level education. The responsibility for the training of teachers is shared between the University and schools, and a substantial part of students' time is spent in schools.

PGCE Primary

The PGCE Primary course offers professional education for teaching the 5-11 years age range in primary schools. You will undertake a professional studies course which introduces the aims and context of primary education, various approaches to teaching and learning and different patterns of school and classroom organisation alongside subject knowledge of the full primary curriculum and specialised preparation.

Entry requirements: You must have GCSE/GCE O level passes (grades A-C) or equivalent in English language, mathematics and science. You must also have a good honours degree (2:1 level or higher) in a subject that you can demonstrate is relevant to the primary curriculum or related to the education of young children. You must also demonstrate previous experience of working with primary-aged learners

PGCE Secondary

Subject specialist courses are provided as follows:

University of Durham

- Biology
- Chemistry
- English
- Geography
- History
- Mathematics
- Modern languages
- Music
- Physical education
- Physics
- Physics with maths
- Religious education

Within your specialist subject you will examine cross-curricular debates such as classroom management, pastoral care, specialist needs and multicultural and anti-racist education.

Entry requirements: You must have GCSE/GCE O level passes (grades A-C) or equivalent in English language and mathematics at the time of joining the course. Fifty per cent of your degree will be relevant to your main teaching subject. In the majority of subjects we expect you to have a good honours degree (2:1 or higher).

MA in Education

Following successful completion of a Durham University PGCE, students can transfer to the second year of the MA Education. Taken part-time, this course will enable an NQT to acquire an MA (Ed) in the second year of teaching.

Entry requirements: For entry via this route you require the successful completion of a Durham University PGCE. Other students can join the MA in year 1. Please see the website below for details.

Contact details: For further information please contact: Reception, School of Education, University of Durham, Leazes Road, Durham DH1 1TA.

t: **0191 334 8310**
f: **0191 334 8311**
// **www.dur.ac.uk/education**

Application route: Postgraduate apply through the GTTR. Undergraduate apply through UCAS.

Durham Secondary Applied SCITT

Institution code: D87

The Work Place
Aycliffe Business Park
Newton Aycliffe
County Durham DL5 6AH
t: **01325 308 918**
e: **info@durhamscitt.co.uk**
// **www.durhamscitt.co.uk**

GENERAL INFORMATION

Durham Secondary Applied School-Centred Initial Teacher Training (SCITT) course is based in Newton Aycliffe in County Durham, working with a partnership of 37 schools and four colleges across the county.

We are offering this unique opportunity to gain Qualified Teacher Status (QTS) and a Postgraduate Certificate in Education (PGCE) specialising in teaching a range of subjects.

County Durham is a beautiful county, and is well-placed for visiting the Lake District and Northumberland. There are also very good transport links from Durham City and nearby Darlington.

ACADEMIC AWARDS

PGCE and QTS
Main subjects offered:
- Art and design
- Geography
- Health and social care
- History
- Mathematics
- Physics with mathematics
- Science with biology
- Science with chemistry

Centrally based training takes place at The Work Place in Newton Aycliffe - a purpose-built work related learning centre. School-based training will take place in at least two of the partnership schools, selected for their experience and expertise in each specialism. You will also complete two master's level assignments (worth 60 master's credits) for your PGCE award.

Entry requirements:
- A degree which is closely related to the subject that you wish to teach.
- GCSE grade C in English language and mathematics.
- Relevant work experience would be beneficial to anyone wishing to teach health and social care.

OTHER INFORMATION

Durham Secondary Applied SCITT is committed to equality of opportunity and welcomes potential trainees regardless of age, gender, race, ethnic origin, colour, nationality, sexual orientation, marital or parental status, disability, political or religious belief, or socio-economic class.

We welcome applications from career changers and people with a range of experiences, as well as recent graduates.
Application route: Apply through the GTTR.

School of Education and Lifelong Learning
Faculty of Social Sciences
Norwich Research Park
Norwich NR4 7TJ
t: **01603 592855**
f: **01603 591523**
e: **edu.pgce.admiss@uea.ac.uk**
// **www.uea.ac.uk/edu/pgce**

GENERAL INFORMATION

The University of East Anglia is rated as one of the UK's exceptional centres for teacher training. The PGCE is offered at Postgraduate level, leading to Qualified Teacher Status and 60 credits at master's level. The course has been developed in close partnership with schools throughout Norfolk and Suffolk.

ACADEMIC AWARDS

PGCE Primary (3-11) - full-time 38 weeks (September-July)
Teaching Agency Category grade A
The PGCE Primary course (covering the age range 3-9, 5-11) is offered in partnership with nursery, first, primary and middle schools. Students follow programmes in teaching core and noncore subjects, relevant to their age ranges. The 5-11 years option also offers a specialism in the teaching of Primary modern languages: Key Stage 2 (French, German or Spanish).

19 weeks are spent in partnership schools, including substantial teaching practices in the spring and summer terms.

Admission is via application, references and interview. We require you to have a good honours degree (class 2:2 or above) and a GCSE pass at grade C in English language, mathematics and a science subject (or equivalent qualifications accepted by the university).

Students should also gain at least five days' observational experience in school, in the age range they wish to teach, before making their application.

Applicants to Primary modern languages must have also achieved an A level or gained considerable experience working with or using their chosen language.

PGCE Secondary (11-18) - full-time 36 weeks (September-July)
Teaching Agency Category grade A
The PGCE Secondary course places great emphasis on practical skills and on the realities of classroom teaching. Two-thirds (24 weeks) of the course is spent on placement in partnership schools within Norfolk and Suffolk, providing a broad range of practical teaching experience.

Trainees also participate in professional development and pastoral programmes. These focus on aspects of the classroom teacher's role, ie being a form tutor, and contributing to a personal and social education programme.

Main subjects offered:
Biology, Chemistry, English, Geography, History, Mathematics, Modern foreign languages (French, German, Spanish), Physical education, Physics and Religious education.

Admission is via application, references and interview. We require you to have achieved a degree and a GCSE pass at grade C in English language and mathematics (or equivalent qualifications) prior to beginning the course.

Cass School of Education and Communities
Water Lane
London E15 4LZ
Dean of School: Ann Slater
t: **Primary: 020 8223 2832**
e: **primary@uel.ac.uk**
t: **Secondary: 020 8223 2268**
e: **secondary@uel.ac.uk**
// **www.uel.ac.uk/cass**

GENERAL INFORMATION

UEL offers primary, secondary and post-compulsory initial teacher training. In our recent Ofsted Inspection in April 2010 UEL was graded 'good' overall with a number of 'outstanding' elements:

- the outstanding way in which trainees are prepared to teach in a socially and culturally diverse society
- the outstanding way in which resources are used effectively and innovatively to support student outcomes
- the strong links that the university has with its local community and the significant contribution that it makes to its development
- the way the provider anticipates and responds to change.

The PGCE programmes at UEL operate in the context of east London schools where the skills, attributes, knowledge and understanding required to facilitate learning in a multicultural, mulilingual urban enviroment are of paramount importance. Trainees are supported in developing an understanding of outstanding classroom practice, and the ability to reflect critically on practice and sustain professional development.

ACADEMIC AWARDS

PGCE Primary - full-time
- Leads to Postgraduate Certificate in Education (with 60 master's level credits)
- Training focuses on the Foundation Stage and Key Stage 1 (3-7) or Key Stage 1 and 2 (5-11)
- Modern languages (French or Spanish), 5-11 only

Entry requirements: Honours degree 2.2 or above (or equivalent), GCSE grade C or above (or equivalent) in English language, mathematics and science. A minimum of ten days' school experience in a mainstream primary school. A level French or Spanish or a significant amount of French or Spanish content in your degree for the modern languages specialism.

PGCE Secondary - full-time
Leads to Postgraduate Certificate in Education (with 60 master's level credits) in the following subjects

- Biology
- Chemistry
- Design and technology (food, textiles)
- English
- Information and communication technology
- Mathematics
- Modern languages (major European or community languages)
- Physical education
- Physics

Entry requirements: Honours degree (or equivalent). GCSE grade C or above (or equivalent) in English language and mathematics.

Trainees on the Secondary Graduate Teacher Programme (GTP) and Primary and Secondary Overseas Trained Teacher Programme (OTTP) are generally paid by the employing school during their training.

Edge Hill University

Institution code: E42

St Helens Road
Ormskirk
Lancashire L39 4QP
t: **01695 575171**
f: **01695 579997**
// **www.edgehill.ac.uk**

Course information, advice and guidance:
t: **01695 657000**
e: **study@edgehill.ac.uk**
// **www.edgehill.ac.uk**

GENERAL INFORMATION

Main 160-acre campus near Ormskirk in Lancashire, close to Liverpool. Easy access to airports, the M6, national bus routes and a direct rail link with inter-city services.

Faculty of Education
* One of the largest providers of initial teacher training in the UK.
* Purpose-built building with state-of-the-art facilities.
* Grade 1 'Outstanding' across all 33 possible graded areas, covering every phase of initial teacher training (Ofsted).
* Largest provider of postgraduate professional development in the country.

ACADEMIC AWARDS: UNDERGRADUATE

BA (Hons) Early Years Education with QTS
BA (Hons) Primary Education with QTS (full-time and part-time)
BA/BSc (Hons) Secondary Education with QTS
In design and technology, English, information and communication technology, mathematics, modern foreign languages, religious education and science (biology, chemistry, physics).

FdA in Early Years Leadership (part-time)
with possible progression routes to BA (Hons) Teaching, Learning and Mentoring Practice, BA (Hons) Early Years Leadership or EYPS.

FdA in Early Years Practice (offered part-time)
with possible progression routes of the full-time programme to BA (Hons) Early Years Practice and Early Years Professional Status.

FdA in Professional Development (part-time, online learning)
Flexible provision designed for members of the Wider School Workforce with progression route to BA (Hons) in Professional Development.

FdA in Teaching in the Lifelong Learning Sector
This is a progression route from the Cert HE in Post-Compulsory Education and Training only, with further details being offered on successful completion of the CertHE. Provides progression onto the BA (Hons) Lifelong Learning and Skills.

Certificate of Higher Education (part-time)
Post-Compulsory Education and Training (PCET)

Other degree programmes
We also offer degree programmes in Children and Young People's Learning and Development, Teaching, Learning and Mentoring Practice and Early Years Professional Practice and Leadership.

Entry requirements: Minimum entry qualifications apply. Please see our current prospectus or website for specific information: **www.edgehill.ac.uk**

Fastrack provision may be available to support entry into higher education.

Edge Hill University

Application route: Applications must be made via UCAS for full-time programmes. Applications for part-time programmes may be made directly to the university.

All courses are subject to sufficient Teaching Agency (TA) student number allocations.

ACADEMIC AWARDS: POSTGRADUATE

PGCE Early Years
PGCE Primary
PGCE Secondary
Subjects offered:
- Applied Art and design
- Biology
- Business education (14-19 years)
- Chemistry
- Design & technology
- English
- Geography
- History
- Information and communication technology
- Mathematics
- Modern foreign languages (French, German, Mandarin, Spanish and Urdu)
- Music
- Physical education
- Physics
- Physics with mathematics (11-18 years)
- Religious education

Postgraduate Early Years Flexible Programme
Postgraduate Primary Flexible Programme
Postgraduate Secondary Flexible Programmes
Subjects offered:
- Biology
- Business education (14-19 years)
- Chemistry
- Design and technology
- English
- Information and communication technology
- Mathematics
- Modern foreign languages (French, German, Spanish, Urdu, Mandarin)
- Music
- Physics
- Religious education

PGCE in Post-Compulsory Education and Training (part-time)
Entry requirements: Minimum entry requirements apply. Request a copy of our PGCE prospectus or visit our website at **www.edgehill.ac.uk**.

Future Teachers Graduate Teacher Programme
A school-based, salaried programme for trainee physics, chemistry or mathematics teachers.

Subject knowledge enhancement modules are available in a wide range of subjects. Enhancement courses are also available in physics, chemistry and mathematics.

Application route: Full-time undergraduate and foundation degrees apply through UCAS. Part-time programmes apply direct to Edge Hill University. All PGCE (both full-time and part-time) apply through the GTTR.

All courses are subject to sufficient Teaching Agency (TA) student number allocations.

Candidates for undergraduate and PGCE programmes will undergo a compulsory interview.

Candidates offered and accepting a place will be required to complete a medical questionnaire and provide a satisfactory Criminal Records Bureau Enhanced Disclosure.

Edge Hill University

"Outstanding" Teacher Training
- Shortage subjects

Edge Hill University is based at an award-winning campus near Liverpool and is the largest provider of ITT Secondary shortage subjects in the UK.

Our Faculty of Education is renowned for its teaching excellence and in a recent Ofsted inspection it achieved Grade 1 'outstanding' results across all 33 possible graded areas covering every phase of initial teacher training.

We offer a number of programmes in the secondary shortage subject areas of Mathematics and Sciences with training bursaries also available. We also provide subject knowledge training for those who want to teach in an area they do not have a degree in.

Over 92% of Edge Hill University's PGCE trainees secure employment as teachers within six months of graduation. Teachers of Mathematics and Science are in great demand and the Government offers financial incentives to train to teach these subject areas.

Shortage subject opportunities include:

- BSc (Hons) Secondary Mathematics Education with QTS
- BSc (Hons) Secondary Science (Chemistry) Education with QTS
- BSc (Hons) Secondary Science (Physics) Education with QTS
- PGCE Secondary Mathematics
- PGCE Secondary Physics with Mathematics
- PGCE Secondary Chemistry
- PGCE Secondary Physics
- Subject Knowledge Enhancements in Mathematics, Chemistry and Physics
- Future Teachers Graduate Teacher Programme (a school-based, salaried programme covering Mathematics, Chemistry or Physics)

For more information contact our Course Information, Advice and Guidance Team on:

T: *01695 657000*
E: *study@edgehill.ac.uk*

Search for **Edge Hill**

ehu.ac.uk/shortagesubjects

Undergraduate Admissions Office
College of Humanities and Social Science
David Hume Tower
George Square
Edinburgh EH8 9JX
t: 0131 650 3565
f: 0131 650 4678
e: HSSUG@ed.ac.uk
// www.ed.ac.uk

GENERAL INFORMATION

Edinburgh is one of the most beautiful cities in Europe. The University of Edinburgh, founded in 1583, is one of the four ancient universities in Scotland. The School of Education and the University of Edinburgh's main administrative buildings are within easy walking distance of the city centre.

The Moray House School of Education is a lively multidisciplinary school, staffed by eminent specialists in all fields of education, offering a stimulating environment in which to pursue courses of academic and professional development.

ACADEMIC AWARDS

PGDE Primary - 1 year full-time
PGDE Secondary - 1 year full-time
For PGDE Secondary, the main subjects offered are:
- Art and design
- Biology
- Chemistry
- Drama
- English
- Geography
- History
- Mathematics
- Modern languages: Chinese, French and German
- Music
- Physical education
- Physics
- Technical education

Entry requirements
- A degree validated by a higher education institution in the United Kingdom or a degree of an equivalent standard from an institution outside the United Kingdom. For PGDE Secondary, an applicant's first degree must contain at least 80 credits of specific subject study which is relevant to the intended teaching qualification. It must also be of appropriate breadth and depth for teaching the subject in Scottish secondary schools.
- SCE/SQA higher grade award at band C or above in English, GCSE English language and GCSE English literature at grade C or above, or a National Course award in communication at Higher Level and literature 1 at Higher Level (or equivalent).
- For PGDE Primary only, SCE/SQA Standard Grade award in mathematics at grade 1 or 2, GCSE mathematics at grade B, or NQ Intermediate 2 mathematics at grade C.

Closing date
Applicants are advised to apply as soon as possible after mid-September. For PGDE Primary, however, the GTTR closing date is 1 December and only applications received by this date will be guaranteed consideration.

OTHER INFORMATION

Entry route: PG/FT/1year (36 weeks).
Intended intake: Primary 103; Secondary 178.
Application route: Apply through the GTTR.

Essex Primary Schools Training Group

Institution code: E73

Harlow Centre
Partridge Road
Harlow
Essex CM18 6TE
t: 01279 400139
// www.essexteachertraining.co.uk

GENERAL INFORMATION

This course is based on the school-centred model and is provided jointly by a consortium of Essex primary schools and the Essex Local Authority.

ACADEMIC AWARDS

General Primary (5-11) - 1 year full-time
Main subjects offered: Subjects relevant to the National Curriculum. All trainees have the opportunity to gain a Postgraduate Certificate in Education equivalent to 60 M level credits over the duration of the training and NQT year.

Entry requirements: GCSE grade C in English language, mathematics and science. Lower second class degree.

Entry route: PG/FT/1 year

Award: QTS

Intended intake: 28

Application route: Apply through the GTTR.

Exeter College

Institution code: E81

Department of Quality and Higher Education
Hele Road
Exeter EX4 4JS
t: 0845 111 6000
e: teachereducation@exe-coll.ac.uk
// www.exe-coll.ac.uk

GENERAL INFORMATION

Exeter, capital of Devon, is a historic yet modern city with a reputation for an outstanding quality of life.

Exeter College - a great place to study
It's an exciting, friendly and purposeful college in the centre of this vibrant city.

- We make sure we have small tutorial groups, so that we get to know our higher education students as individuals.
- We have a reputation for academic excellence and our partner universities further strengthen our exciting and quality higher education programmes.
- A supportive environment with group teaching, individual support and a comprehensive tutorial system.
- Excellent facilities including award-winning learning centres.

Working with the University of Plymouth
The University of Plymouth is one of the largest in the country, with around 30,000 students, a third of whom are studying at its partner colleges. Teacher education is part of the University of Plymouth Faculty of Education.

In terms of academic study, all UPC Partnership students have the same rights and status as other University of Plymouth students. You will benefit from additional support and resources provided by the university including its library, electronic resources and learning support materials through a web-based student portal. You will be a member of the University of Plymouth Students' Union (UPSU).

Main courses offered:
University of Plymouth partnership:
- University of Plymouth Postgraduate Certificate in Education (PGCE) full-time, incorporating the Diploma in Teaching in the Lifelong Learning Sector
- University of Plymouth Certificate in Education part-time, incorporating the Diploma in Teaching in the Lifelong Learning Sector

We also offer the following City and Guilds qualifications for teachers and assessors:

- Additional Diploma in Teaching English (Literacy) in the Lifelong Learning Sector ADTLLS Literacy: (City and Guilds 7305-15/16)
- Additional Diploma in Teaching Mathematics (Numeracy) in the Lifelong Learning Sector ADTLLS Numeracy: (City and Guilds 7305-17)
- Certificate in Teaching in the Lifelong Learning Sector City and Guilds 7304 (CTLLS)
- Preparing to Teach in the Lifelong Learning Sector City and Guilds 7303 (PTLLS)
- New Assessor and Internal Quality Assurance Qualifications (TAQA).

University of Exeter

Institution code: E84

PGCE Admissions Office
Laver Building
North Park Road
Exeter EX4 4QE
t: 0844 6200012 (UK callers)
t: +44 (0)1392 723009 (EU/international callers)
// www.exeter.ac.uk/education

GENERAL INFORMATION

The Graduate School of Education is based on the St Luke's Campus, walking distance from Exeter city centre and the university's Streatham Campus.

St Luke's has long been the home of teacher education programmes. The school dates back to 1840 under its original name of the Exeter Diocesan Training College. In 1854, the college moved to its current Heavitree Road location and what is now the University of Exeter's St Luke's Campus. Although much has changed over the past 150 years, one thing has remained consistent - a commitment to quality teacher education.

In our most recent Ofsted inspection (February 2010), Exeter received top marks in all inspection categories for both our Secondary and Primary PGCE provision, confirming our position as one of the best providers of teacher education in the country.

Ranked third in The Good Teacher Training Guide 2011 (Higher Education Institution Providers), the school is also recognised by the Teaching Agency and Ofsted as an outstanding provider of Early Years, Primary and Secondary teacher education.

The strength of the PGCE programmes is largely due to the school's ongoing research activities. The 2008 Research Assessment Exercise (RAE) ranked the school fifth in the UK for world-leading and internationally excellent research. It is this expertise which helps set Exeter apart from other leading teacher training providers.

Exeter PGCE trainees are highly sought after - 90% of our graduates who achieve QTS are in a teaching post. Our partnership with over 250 schools and a very active careers and employment service will help to ensure you are given the best possible opportunity to secure your first teaching post.

Facilities

The school has one of the largest education libraries in the UK, modern seminar rooms, restaurant and bar, as well as an indoor swimming pool, two gymnasia and tennis courts.

ACADEMIC AWARDS

PGCE Early Years (3-7)
PGCE Primary (5-11)
Main subjects offered: Art (7-11); English; humanities; mathematics; modern foreign languages (7-11); music; science.

PGCE Secondary (11-18)
Main subjects offered: dance; design and technology; English with drama; English with media; French; geography; German; history; mathematics; physical education; religious education; biology; biology with psychology; chemistry; physics and Spanish.

Intake in 20112/13: 498 (Primary - 212) (Secondary - 286)

Each programme lasts one year and leads to a recognised postgraduate level qualification with recommendation for QTS (Qualified Teacher Status).

Entry requirements:
- graduate or equivalent status
- the relevance of the degree content to the chosen specialist subject(s)
- passes at GCSE in English and mathematics at grade C or above (or equivalent) for those applying for Secondary.
- pass at GCSE in English, mathematics and science at grade C or above (or equivalent), if you are

applying for Primary or Early Years. Please note : although the Teaching Agency minimum requirement is a grade C at GCSE, we will generally only consider applicants with a grade B or above for mathematics and English and a grade C or above for science for the Primary and Early Years programmes

- selection is based on the GTTR application and interview
- a satisfactory medical report
- an enhanced Criminal Records Bureau disclosure which is deemed satisfactory by the institution

Equivalence tests: If you do not possess or expect to obtain suitable formal qualifications in English language, and mathematics, Exeter offers secondary shortage subject applicants (design and technology, mathematics, modern languages and science subjects) the opportunity to undertake the university's equivalence tests.

Application route: Apply through the GTTR. An academic reference is required from any institution of higher education that applicants have attended within the last five years.

Enquiries: For enquiries regarding entry qualifications, contact:

PGCE Admissions Office
Laver Building
North Park Road
Exeter EX4 4QE
t: 0844 6200012 (UK callers)
t: +44 (0)1392 723009 (EU/international callers)
// **www.exeter.ac.uk/education**

'The teaching is excellent. I feel very lucky to have been taught by the tutors on the course - their enthusiasm is infectious!'
Renuka Sivakumaran, Primary Mathematics

Limes Farm Junior School Site
Limes Avenue, Chigwell,
Essex IG7 5LP
Linda Wheatley - Course Administrator
t: 020 8501 2089
e: lindawheatley@fipc.ac.uk
Dr Sonia Burnard - Course Manager
t: 020 8500 2089
e: soniaburnard@fipc.ac.uk
// www.fipc.ac.uk

GENERAL INFORMATION

Forest Independent Primary Collegiate is a primary school-centred initial teacher training provider based at Chigwell, Essex. The college has a positive ethos and a focus on behaviour and learning. The PGCE is validated by Middlesex University.

The partnership consists of local mainstream schools that support the process of training through three teaching practices. All trainees have experience of both KS1 and KS2. The head teachers of the schools have a firm commitment to initial teacher training and create the management committee of the FIPC. We also place trainees for two weeks in affiliated special schools. Trainee representatives sit on the quality assurance and curriculum committees.

Teaching is delivered by qualified tutors who are also practitioners. Educational theory focuses on child development and behaviour management directly but these areas are permeated through all subjects. Trainees become informed and confident in the management of learning and behaviour in the classroom. There is a system of formative and summative assessment in order for trainees to demonstrate that they have met the professional QTS standards and to gain credits towards the MA degree. This is taught at the FIPC in partnership with Middlesex University.

The prospective trainees should be aware that they will be expected to travel to their school placements shown on the website. The school is served by the central line at Grange Hill and Hainault. There are local buses, local shops and a supermarket.

The FIPC also has a Graduate Teacher Programme (GTP): make enquiries at the above email addresses or telephone numbers.

ACADEMIC AWARD

PGCE General Primary (5-11) - 1 year full-time
Entry requirements: GCSE grades A-C in English language, mathematics and science (or equivalents). Good honours degree (2:2 or above).

ACADEMIC AWARD

PGCE General Primary (5-11) - 1 year full-time
Entry requirements: GCSE grades A-C in English language, mathematics and science (or equivalents). Good honours degree (2:2 or above).

Work experience: Work experience that is relevant to the teaching professional is desirable.

Entry route: PG/FT/1 year

Award: PGCE QTS

Intended intake: 26

Application route: Apply through the GTTR.

Enquiries: Please make all enquiries to Linda Wheatley - Course Administrator.

Gateshead 3-7 SCITT

Institution code: G10

Lobley Hill Primary School
Rothbury Gardens
Gateshead NE11 0AT
t: **0191 433 4081**
e: **info@train2teach.net**

GENERAL INFORMATION

The Gateshead 3-7 SCITT provides the opportunity for you to gain Qualified Teacher Status (QTS) and a Professional Graduate Certificate in Education (PGCE), or Postgraduate with 60 credits towards master's level, validated by Northumbria University. This is a school-centred initial teacher training course delivered in primary schools and nursery schools in the north-east region. The Gateshead 3-7 SCITT offers:

- QTS for the 3-7 age range
- the PGCE validated by Northumbria University
- high quality ITT
- the opportunity to train within excellent schools
- a training route matched to your individual requirements
- high quality school-based experiences in the North East region
- all the benefits associated with being a Northumbria University student.

The consortium of schools involved with this course has a high level of expertise and strong commitment to delivering high quality teacher training. The lead school, Lobley Hill Primary, has extensive experience in ITT. In partnership with other north east schools, Northumbria University and Gateshead Council, the SCITT provides excellent facilities and resources. Gateshead is one of the best performing local authorities and Northumbria University has a good reputation for quality teacher education.

Tuition fees
Tuition fees are payable for a full-time postgraduate ITT place. These fees are in line with other ITT regional providers.

Students' union
Students are full members of the Northumbria University's students' union. Although they may never use its facilities, they have a right to do so and will receive all of the student discounts etc, as well as useful access to restricted internet and major libraries.

Entry requirements: The Gateshead 3-7 SCITT is very pleased to welcome applications from graduates (2:2 or above) and prospective graduates and will happily consider applicants whose degrees do not seem to have any major immediate relevance to primary education. All applicants must have GCSE A-C or equivalent in English, mathematics and science on application.

Application route: Apply through the GTTR. The SCITT Manager and SCITT Business Manager are pleased to discuss applications and questions on 0191 4334081 and also to provide the course brochure.

University of Glamorgan
Institution code: G14

Pontypridd
CF37 1DL
t: **08456 434 030**
f: **01443 654 050**
// **www.glam.ac.uk**

GENERAL INFORMATION

The University of Glamorgan is a dynamic institution with an exceptional record for academic excellence, teaching and research. Just 20 minutes from Cardiff, Glamorgan's modern campus continues to grow with state-of-the-art facilities that include a brand new students' union and £20m accommodation development. Glamorgan attracts more than 23,000 students from across the globe. We pride ourselves on courses that are relevant to the real world and 94% of our graduates find employment and/or further study within six months *(Source: HESA 2009/10 Performance Indicators)*.

Undergraduate courses
BSc (Hons) Childhood and Youth
BSc (Hons) Early Years Development and Education
BA (Hons) English with Education
BA (Hons) History with Education
BSc (Hons) Mathematics with Education
BSc (Hons) Psychology with Education
BSc (Hons) Sociology with Education
BA (Hons) Professional Welsh with Education

If you are thinking about teaching or related areas for a future career, these multidisciplinary programmes offer you a valuable theoretical and practical introduction to different aspects of education.

These courses will provide you with a range of academic, personal and professional skills to prepare you for employment, future study or professional training. They are ideal qualifications if you want to work with children and/or young people through teaching, learning support roles, therapeutic play, social work and youth and community work.

For more information please call 08456 434 030 or visit **www.glam.ac.uk**.

ITE Admissions
St Andrews Building
11 Eldon Street
Glasgow G3 6NH
t: **0141 330 2463**
f: **0141 330 3065**
e: **education-admissions@glasgow.ac.uk**
// **www.glasgow.ac.uk/education**

GENERAL INFORMATION

The University of Glasgow is the fourth oldest university in the UK and it has a long-standing international reputation for research, education, and innovation. It is one of only a few UK universities to feature in the top 100 of the *Times World University Rankings*. The University of Glasgow offers access to outstanding academic opportunities as well as superb social, sporting and cultural activities within both the university and the city of Glasgow. The only UK destination to feature in the *Lonely Planet's* top 10 cities list, Glasgow attracts the largest student at population in Scotland.

Entrance to the BEd and BTech Ed is based on academic qualifications and personal statement. Applicants for MA Primary Education, the MA Religious and Philosophical Education and the PGDE will be invited for interview.

ACADEMIC AWARDS

BEd Hons Primary Education*
Entry requirements:
Higher: AAB or ABBB including English. Plus Standard Grade mathematics at grade 2 or above, or Intermediate 2 mathematics at grade C or above.

A level: BBB. Plus both GCSE English language and GCSE English literature at grade C or above, and GCSE mathematics at grade B or above.

Irish Leaving Certificate: Honours AAB/ABBB including English plus Ordinary mathematics at grade B or above.

Access: Approved SWAP Access to Primary Education.

HND: HND Supporting and Managing Learning Needs may be a possible pathway for direct entry into year 2 subject to references. Candidates must also have Higher English at grade B or above and Standard Grade mathematics at grade 2 or above.

MA Primary Education with Teaching Qualification (School of Interdisciplinary Studies)
Entry requirements:
Higher: AAB or ABBB including English. Plus Standard Grade mathematics at grade 2 or above, or Intermediate 2 mathematics at grade C or above.

A level: BBB. Plus both GCSE English language and GCSE English literature at grade C or above, and GCSE mathematics at grade B or above.

Irish Leaving Certificate: Honours AAB/ABBB including English plus Ordinary mathematics at grade B or above.

MA Religious and Philosophical Education with Secondary Teaching Qualification
Entry requirements:
Higher: AAB or ABBB including English.

A level: BBB. Plus both GCSE English language and GCSE English literature at grade C or above.

Irish Leaving Certificate: Honours AAB/ABBB including English.

BTechEd Technological Education
Entry requirements:

Higher: AAB or ABBB including English, and preferably mathematics and a technology or science subject.

A level: BBB including preferably mathematics and a technology or science subject. Plus both GCSE English language and GCSE English literature at grade C or above.

Irish Leaving Certificate: Honours AAB/ABBB to include English, and preferably mathematics and a technology or science subject.

PGDE Primary* and Secondary Education
Description:

This innovative programme will educate together those who intend to teach in primary schools with those who intend to teach in secondary schools so that students gain a greater understanding of the cross-sector working which is becoming more common in Scotland's learning communities. The programme is offered as a qualification worth 90 credits at postgraduate level.

Entry requirements:

- A bachelor degree from a UK university or equivalent. For Secondary Education, the degree should contain 80 SCQF credit points relevant to the subject chosen, 40 of which at year 2 or above.
- Plus Higher English at grade C or above, or both GCSE English language and GCSE English literature at grade C or above, or both communication 4 and literature 1, or Irish Leaving Certificate Honours English at grade C or above.
- For Primary Education, also Standard Grade mathematics at grade 2 or above, or Intermediate 2 mathematics at grade C or above, or GCSE mathematics at grade B or above, or Irish Leaving Certificate Ordinary mathematics at grade B or above.
- Work experience in a school classroom.
- Applicants should consult

www.teachinginscotland.com for general advice.
- and they should consult the Scottish Government's Memorandum on Entry Requirements to courses of initial teacher education in Scotland 2009 which is available at www.scotland.gov.uk/Publications/2010/03/10112435/12

for specific requirements for secondary subjects.

* The Scottish Executive requires that the University of Glasgow continues to provide adequate numbers of teachers to teach in Catholic schools in Scotland. This particular programme provides support for and emphasis on the initial teacher education of those who intend to teach in Catholic schools. The design of the programme necessarily reflects the denominational sector requirements and prospective applicants should consider this before applying. The university welcomes applications from all qualified candidates. In the selection procedures priority is given to those who indicate, in their personal statement, their intention to teach in Catholic schools and to seek the Catholic Teacher's Certificate in Religious Education.

Students on the BTech Ed and the MA Primary Education can take CREDL in the last two years of their degrees.

MATURE APPLICANTS

Mature applicants for undergraduate programmes should contact the university.

Application route: UCAS for undergraduate programmes. GTTR for PGDE.

Gloucestershire SCITT Consortium

Institution code: G48

St Peter's High School
Stroud Road
Tuffley
Gloucester GL4 0DD
t: **01452 509 208**

GENERAL INFORMATION

ACADEMIC AWARD

Gloucestershire SCITT Consortium (GSC) is an accredited school centred initial teacher training (SCITT) provider working with Gloucestershire secondary schools to deliver both QTS and PGCE routes into teaching.

Part of the Gloucestershire Initial Teacher Education Partnership, Gloucestershire SCITT Consortium (GSC) is based in the beautiful county of Gloucestershire where over 48 schools participate in the training of teachers to QTS standard.

GSC offers you the opportunity to train in some of the best schools in the country; you may be training in grammar and comprehensive schools as there are a significant number of selective schools in Gloucestershire. However, many of the comprehensives, despite the presence of grammar schools, perform at a level which puts them amongst the very best schools of this type nationally.

Our aim to 'train the best to retain the best' often results in a large proportion of our trainees gaining employment within Gloucestershire schools.

We offer the following two routes into secondary teaching:

- PGCE (postgraduate certificate in education)
- QTS (postgraduate route to qualified teacher status)

The PGCE is validated by our GITEP partner the University of Gloucestershire and covers the following subjects - business education, design and technology, ICT and music.

The QTS route is provided by schools through Gloucestershire SCITT Consortium and covers the following subjects - chemistry, English, maths, modern foreign languages and physics.

Tuition fees have been set at:
PGCE - £8,250 (eligible SCITT PGCE trainees will receive a SCITT bursary of £250)
QTS - £6,000

Route 1 - PGCE Secondary (11-18) - 1 year full-time
Main subjects offered:
- Business education
- Design and technology
- ICT
- Music

Route 2 - Schools Direct QTS - 1 year full-time
Main subjects offered:
- Chemistry
- English
- Maths
- Modern foreign languages
- Physics

Entry requirements for routes 1 and 2: GCSE grade C in English language and mathematics plus honours degree (2:2 or above).

OTHER INFORMATION

Entry route 1 : PG/FT/1 year
Awards: PGCE QTS
Application route: Apply through the GTTR.

Entry route 2 : School Direct
Awards: QTS
Application route: Apply through
SchoolDirect@st-petershigh.gloucs.sch.uk.

Enquiries: Please send all postal enquiries to Gloucestershire SCITT Consortium at the above address.

Department of Education
Francis Close Hall
Swindon Road
Cheltenham GL50 4AZ
t: 01242 714700
// www.glos.ac.uk

GENERAL INFORMATION

The University of Gloucestershire in its present form was established in 1990 but has a history dating back to 1847 when it was founded as a Teacher Training College. The university now offers a diverse range of courses but maintains its position as an excellent provider of initial teacher education.

ACADEMIC AWARDS

BEd Primary Education Key Stage 1 and Key Stage 2 (5-11) - 3 years full-time
Main subjects offered: National Curriculum subject.

Entry requirements: GCSE grade B in English language, together with grade C in mathematics and science. A levels (or equivalent) 280 points.

Other qualifications: Contact the university.

BEd Foundation Stage and Key Stage 1 (3-7) - 3 years full-time
Main subjects offered: National Curriculum subject.

Entry requirements: GCSE grade B in English language, together with grade C in mathematics and science. A levels (or equivalent) 280 points.

Other qualifications: Contact the university.

Application route: Apply through UCAS.

PGCE /PCE Key Stage 1 and Key Stage 2 (5-11) or Foundation Stage and Key Stage 1 (3-7) - year full-time
Main subjects offered: National Curriculum subjects.

Entry requirements: GCSE grade C in English language, mathematics and science. Honours degree at 2.2 or above (2:1 preferred).

PGCE Secondary (11-18) - 1 year full-time
Main subjects offered: Art and design, Business studies*, Design and technology*, English with drama, Geography, History, Information and communication technology*, Leisure and tourism*, Mathematics, Modern foreign languages, Music*, Physical education, Religious education and Science.

*In partnership with the Gloucestershire Initial Teacher Education SCITT.

Entry requirements: GCSE grade C in English language and mathematics. Honours degree.

Equivalence tests: Contact the university on 01242 714766 or 714767.

PGCE Flexible Modular Secondary (11-18)
Main subjects offered: Geography, Mathematics, Modern foreign languages, Religious education and Science.

Entry requirements: GCSE grade C in English language, mathematics and science. Honours degree.

Equivalence tests: Contact the university on 01242 714766 or 714767.

OTHER INFORMATION

Entry route: UG/FT/3 years, PG/FT/1 year, PG/PT/Modular
Awards: BEd/BEd(Hons) QTS, PGCE/PCE QTS
Intake: UG-125, PG Primary-127, Secondary-110

Enquiries: Please address all postal enquiries to Ms P Liau.

Goldsmiths
University of London
New Cross
London SE14 6NW
t: 0207 078 5300
// www.goldsmiths.ac.uk

GENERAL INFORMATION

Lively, cosmopolitan and innovative, Goldsmiths is a great place to study. We are part of the University of London, and we have been training teachers since the early 1900s. We have developed our programmes in partnership with schools, integrating theory and practice, and supporting your development. Our programmes have a great reputation so our graduates have excellent employment prospects. Applicants must fulfil suitability requirements and will therefore be subject to a CRB enhanced disclosure check and a 'Fitness to train' check.

ACADEMIC AWARDS

BA (Hons) Design, Creativity and Learning with QTS (12-18) - 3 years full-time
Main subjects offered: Design and technology.

Entry requirements: A levels, BBC, or equivalent qualifications. Grade C GCSE or equivalent in English language and in mathematics.

PGCE Primary (3-7, 5-11 or 7-11) - 1 year full-time
Specialisms:
- Early years (3-7 only)
- Citizenship and comparative education
- Creativity and new media
- Linguistic and ethnic diversity
- Special educational needs

PGCE Primary with Modern Languages (5-11 or 7-11) - 1 year full-time
Main languages offered: French, German and Spanish

Entry requirements Primary: First degree, honours usually 2:1 or above. Grade C GCSE or equivalent in mathematics, English language and science.

PGCE Secondary (11-18) - 1 year full-time
Main subjects offered:
- Art and design
- Design and technology
- Drama
- English
- Geography
- Mathematics
- Languages (French, German and Spanish)
- Sciences (chemistry, physics and biology)

Flexible PGCE Secondary (11-18) - 1-2 years
Main subjects offered:
- Languages (including Bengali, Mandarin, Urdu, Panjabi and Arabic)
- Design and technology
- English
- Sciences (chemistry, physics and biology)

Entry is usually in either September or January.

Entry requirements Secondary: First degree, honours ideally 2:1 or above. The degree needs to contain at least 50% of the subject you wish to train in. Grade C GCSE or equivalent in mathematics and English language.

OTHER INFORMATION

PGCE: Please see our website for details of entry requirements. All of our PGCE programmes are offered at both professional graduate and postgraduate levels.

Entry route: UG/FT/3 years, PG/FT/PT/1/2 years

Awards: BA (Hons) with QTS, PGCE QTS

Intended intake: UG Secondary-8, PG Primary-227, Secondary-173

Application route: UG apply through UCAS, PG apply through the GTTR.

The Grand Union Training Partnership

Institution code: G60

Sponne School
Brackley Road
Towcester
Northants NN12 6DJ
t: 01327 350284 - Ext: 253
e: training@gutp.org.uk
// www.gutp.org.uk

GENERAL INFORMATION

The GUTP SCITT Consortium has been training teachersin the south and west of Northamptonshire and in Milton Keynes since 1997. The partnership schools are a mixture of semi-rural schools in Northamptonshire and some newly-built schools in Milton Keynes with Sponne School in Towcester as its training centre. They are all successful 11- 18 co-educational comprehensive schools.

Our trainees are selected from a wide age range and from all sections of society and most come from within a 25-mile radius of the partnership schools.

During the year trainees have experience of working in two of the partnership schools, their host school to which they are attached for most of the year and their placement school in which they do their main teaching practice. In each school their work and progress is closely supervised by one of the schemes mentors. The mentors ensure the trainees are involved in the classroom right from the start of the course, observing experienced teachers teach and then gradually developing their own confidence and ability to take an increasing level of responsibility for the planning and delivery of lessons.

The scheme's training course is very practical in nature and as a result the scheme prepares its trainees to take up their first appointments with confidence and a sound working knowledge of their subjects. Typically, nearly half the trainees progress to full-time employment in partnership schools while a further third start their careers in other local schools.

ACADEMIC AWARD

One-year full-time PGCE Secondary (11-18 years with the exception of business studies which is 14-19).
Main subjects offered are: Business studies, English, French, German, history, mathematics, physics, chemistry and biology.

Entry requirements: GCSE grade C or equivalent in English language and mathematics. Degree class 2:2 or above.

Equivalence tests: Contact institution.

OTHER INFORMATION

Entry route: PG/FT/1 year

Awards: QTS PGCE

Intended intake: 21

Application route: Through the GTTR.

Enquiries: Please address all postal enquiries to Mr P H Laycock. Alternatively, telephone or email using the contact details above.

Avery Hill Campus
Mansion Site
Bexley Road
Eltham, London SE9 2PQ
t: **0800 005006**
e: **courseinfo@greenwich.ac.uk**

GENERAL INFORMATION

The University of Greenwich trains teachers for the primary, secondary and lifelong learning sectors. The School of Education has developed strong partnerships with schools and colleges in the region. Courses are taught by University of Greenwich lecturers, who have strong education experience as well as excellent academic credentials.

ACADEMIC AWARDS

BA (Hons) Primary Education with QTS - 3 years full-time
Entry requirements: GCSE grade C or above in English language, mathematics and science. 240 Tariff points. Ten days' experience in a primary school.

BA (Hons) Secondary Design & Technology with QTS - 3 years full-time
Entry requirements: GCSE grade C in English and mathematics. 200 Tariff points in related area.

PGCE Primary - 1 year full-time
PGCE Primary - 2 years part-time
All PGCE Primary courses are offered at professional graduate and postgraduate level.

Entry requirements: GCSE grade C or above in English language, mathematics and science. Good honours degree class 2:2 or above. Ten days' experience in a primary school.

PGCE Secondary - full-time
Main subjects offered:
- Design and technology (11-16)
- ICT (11-16)
- Mathematics (11-16)
- Physical education (11-16)
- Science with biology (11-16)
- Science with chemistry (11-16)
- Science with physics (11-16)
- Music (11-19)

All the above subjects are offered at professional graduate and postgraduate level.

Entry requirements: GCSE grade C or above in English language and mathematics. Good honours degree class 2:2 or above.

PGCE/PCE Lifelong Learning Sector
Main subjects offered: Our students come from a wide variety of professional/vocational and academic backgrounds, but we particularly seek students from ESOL, literacy, information and communication technology, maths, numeracy, health and social care backgrounds, construction and science.

All the above subjects are offered at professional graduate level.

Entry requirements: Good honours degree class 2:2 or above.

The School of Education also offers BA (Hons) Early Years, BA (Hons) Childhood Studies, BA (Hons) Education Studies, BA (Hons) PE and Sport and BA (Hons) Youth and Community.

Guildford College
Stoke Road
Guildford
Surrey GU1 1EZ
t: 01483 44 85 85
e: info@guildford.ac.uk
// www.guildford.ac.uk

GENERAL INFORMATION

Guildford College is the largest provider of further and higher education in Surrey, offering a wide range of courses from foundation to degree level. Higher education courses are vocationally-focused and can be studied full-time or part-time. The college boasts competitive tuition fees, employer-endorsed qualifications validated by leading universities, tailor-made student support, specialist facilities and a central location.

ACADEMIC AWARDS

Post-Compulsory Education/Lifelong Learning Professional Graduate/Professional Certificate in Education (PGCE) (Franchised from the University of Greenwich)

This course is for those who teach or intend to teach in further education colleges, sixth-form colleges, adult education centres, healthcare or community organisations, commercial or voluntary organisations. It covers the skills needed for teaching and classroom management and the theory underpinning teaching and learning.

Successful completion of the course allows trainees in teaching employment to apply for Qualified Teacher Learning and Skills (QTLS) status. It is anticipated that the Government will allow people with QTLS to work in schools. This is subject to reforms planned for April 2012.

Duration: 2 years part-time.

Entry requirements: Degree or professional/vocational qualification and relevant work experience. You must be employed as a teacher or trainer in the post-compulsory sector and/or be able to complete between 30-75 hours of teaching in the first year and 150 hours of teaching by the end of the course.

Five reasons to study at Guildford College:
- The course fulfils the training requirements of the Institute for Learning, the professional body overseeing teacher training regulations in FE.
- Support from by a college personal tutor and your own subject specific mentor whilst on the course.
- Promotes on-the-job training which allows you to develop professional skills whilst you are teaching.
- Allows you to engage with other professionals who are learning about key aspects of teaching, especially issues that are of great importance to new teachers, eg how to manage students in the classroom, and deal with disruptive behaviour.
- Access to materials at the University of Greenwich, including its web presence with a range of learning resources which students can access at home.

Hastings and Rother SCITT

Institution code: H13

Claverham Community College
Battle
East Sussex TN33 0HT
e: **hastingsandrotherscitt@yahoo.co.uk**
// **www.hastingsandrotherscitt.co.uk**

GENERAL INFORMATION

The Hastings and Rother SCITT offers trainees experience in a range of partner secondary schools, including an independent school and a sixth-form college. Each trainee will spend a block of time in at least two of the schools and will have the opportunity to visit up to six others.

The course
The course has been designed to allow access to those who are not able initially to train full-time. Trainees are offered a five-term course leading to Qualified Teacher Status, which is followed as a part-time evening class model in the first three terms and full-time for the last two terms. The course is ideal for recent graduates, as well as for those graduates who are looking for a career change or are returning to work after a break. This course enables those who are already in employment to commence their training as teachers without initially giving up their current job. All trainees will have a fully qualified mentor to guide their training, as well as a subject tutor and a professional studies tutor to develop their knowledge and skills.

Assessment
Assessment is continuous, beginning with an initial needs analysis and leading to a carefully designed individual programme that profiles standards as they are achieved.

Entry requirements: The entry requirements for our course include:

- a degree or equivalent, ideally in the subject area you wish to study, or with at least 50% of your degree relevant to that subject. A Higher National Diploma is not acceptable.
- GCSE grade C or above in English language, mathematics and (if born after 1979) science.
- experience of working with young people in either paid and/or voluntary work and you must not have been excluded from working with young people by the CRB.
- experience of using your subject knowledge, eg in your job.

Main subjects offered and intended intake:
- Mathematics - 6
- Science - 7
- Modern foreign languages - 6

Comments about ITT in SCITT schools
'This has been an unbelievable placement.'
ITT trainee

'I have been pulled along by the enthusiasm that I have seen around me.'
ITT trainee

'If only all school experience could be like this.'
ITT trainee

Enquiries: For further details, contact the ITT Administrator, Linda Haley, at the Hastings and Rother email address above.

Bursaries available; information on fees available on request.

Application route: Apply through the GTTR.

University of Hertfordshire

Institution code: H36

de Havilland Campus
College Lane
Hatfield
Hertfordshire AL10 9AB
t: 01707 284 800
// www.herts.ac.uk/education

GENERAL INFORMATION

We are a thriving, friendly school that offers first-class professional training for teachers.

ACADEMIC AWARDS

BEd (Hons) Primary - 3 years full-time

We offer two primary pathways: Foundation Stage/Key Stage 1 or Key Stage 1 / Key Stage 2.

Entry requirements:

- 300 UCAS Tariff points - (minimum of two 6-unit awards or one 12-unit award. Specified subjects must include a 6-unit award in a primary school National Curriculum subject, or BTEC ND/NC level - merit/distinction profile in an appropriate National Curriculum subject. If the BTEC ND/NC is not in a National Curriculum subject, an A2 in a primary school National Curriculum subject is also required.
- Access Certificate to include GCSEs or recognised equivalents with an overall merit profile.
- GCSEs at grade C or higher in maths, science and English language or combined English language and literature.
- Two weeks' work experience in a state primary school prior to application.

Application route: Apply through UCAS

PGCE Primary - 1 year full-time postgraduate and professional graduate.

We offer two primary pathways: Foundation Stage/Key Stage 1 or Key Stage 1 / Key Stage 2.

Entry requirements:

- A first degree 2:2 or above. An award recognised as equivalent to a UK degree by the Department for Education is also acceptable.
- GCSE English language, mathematics and science GCSE at grade C or above.
- Two weeks' work experience in a state primary school prior to application.

Application route: Apply through the GTTR.

PGCE Secondary (postgraduate and professional graduate)

This programme is for graduates who want to be secondary teachers in art, biology, chemistry, English, mathematics, modern foreign languages or physics and provides training across the 11-16 age range with enhancement at post-16. For modern foreign languages, mathematics and sciences there is the option of a two-year part-time route.

Entry requirements:

- A first degree at 2:2 or above in a subject closely related to that you wish to teach. An award recognised as equivalent to a UK degree by the Department for Education is also acceptable.
- GCSE English language and mathematics at grade C or above.
- Two weeks' work experience in a state secondary school prior to application.

Application route: Apply through the GTTR.

OTHER INFORMATION

Personal suitability for a career in teaching is essential and will be assessed at interview.

High Force Education SCITT

Darlington and Dales Teacher Training
Green Lane
Barnard Castle
Co Durham DL12 8LG
t: **01833 630487**
f: **01833 690316**
e: **info@highforceeducation.org.uk**
// **www.highforceeducation.org.uk**

GENERAL INFORMATION

High Force Education offers full-time primary-level training over one academic year, leading to Qualified Teacher Status and the award of a Professional Graduate or Postgraduate Certificate in Education with 60 credits towards master's level (validated by the University of Northumbria).

The course is based at Green Lane CE Primary School and is taught in a consortium of 18 very effective primary schools in the Darlington to Teesdale area of south Durham, and into North Yorkshire. There is a wide variety of schools within this consortium: very large to very small, urban and rural, denominational and community schools, separate junior and infant, as well as 3-11 primary schools from diverse socio-economic backgrounds, all of which give students a range of teaching experiences.

High Force Education aims to produce confident, skilled, enthusiastic and innovative practitioners able to teach the 5-11 age range effectively and prepared to continuetheir professional development throughout their career. By the end of the one-year course, students will have good ICT skills and will be trained in the effective teaching of all core and foundation subjects, the widercurriculum and other educational issues.

Application route: Apply through the GTTR.

University of the Highlands and Islands

Institution code: H49

University of the Highlands and Islands
Executive Office
Ness Walk
Inverness
Scotland IV3 5SQ
t: 0845 2723600
f: 01463 279001
e: info@uhi.ac.uk
// www.uhi.ac.uk

ACADEMIC AWARD

PGDE Primary Teaching with Gaelic or English

The Professional Graduate Diploma in Education: Primary Teaching with Gaelic or English course marks a special partnership between the University of Strathclyde and the University of the Highlands and Islands, offering you the best combination of tried and tested methodologies, cutting-edge knowledge and teaching opportunities in Gaelic or English schools to maximise your development.

The PGDE (Primary) is a 36-week taught course that will prepare you for life as a teacher and provide you with the chance to play your part in the regeneration of the Gaelic language.

On successfully completing the course you will be qualified to teach in English or Gaelic-medium streams. The current need for skilled, qualified Gaelic-medium teachers is acutely felt and this valuable course offers graduates the real prospect of filling one of the growing number of available posts appearing across Scotland.

The course comprises the following modules: Environmental studies and health education; expressive arts and physical education; language in the primary school; mathematics in the primary school; religious and moral education; educational studies; planning for effective teaching; and learning - the early years. There is also an optional module.

Student performance is evaluated by continuous assessment based upon performance during school experience placements and course assignments.

The course is available through Inverness College UHI, Lews Castle College UHI, and Moray College UHI as well as selected UHI learning centres.

Entry requirements:

An undergraduate degree validated by a higher education institution in the United Kingdom. Applicants undertaking the Gaelic pathway must be fluent in Gaelic. Experience of working with children in primary school or evidence of an ability to work with children in primary school or related context will be taken into consideration for selection.

University of Huddersfield
School of Education and Professional
Development
Queensgate
Huddersfield HD1 3DH
t: **01484 47 8249**
e: **sepd@hud.ac.uk**
// **www.hud.ac.uk/edu**

GENERAL INFORMATION

We offer one-year full-time courses leading to the award of PGCE (both Postgraduate Certificate and Professional Graduate Certificate in Education) leading to Qualified Teacher Status in the following subjects:

- Business education (with the opportunity for citizenship enhancement)
- Design technology
- Information and communication technology
- Mathematics
- Music
- Sciences: biology, chemistry and physics.

We link with enhancement courses in mathematics, chemistry and physics and offer a subject booster course in design technology.

Our courses have been carefully developed in partnership with schools and colleges over a wide geographical area. The course offers the opportunity to consider the practice of teaching, the development of your own subject specialism and the generic aspects of present day education.

The course is popular with mature students and students from ethnic minority groups and we have a strong support system to help students successfully complete their studies.

The university is close to the centre of town and is easily accessible by road and rail. The school is based in a recently converted mill offering excellent facilities.

Entry requirements

- A degree, a substantial proportion of which (at least half and preferably more) should relate to the subject applied for.
- GSCE/GCE grade C or above, or equivalent qualification, in English language and mathematics.
- Medical and criminal record clearance checks to ascertain suitability for teaching.
- A satisfactory reference and interview.
- For further details on individual subject requirements please see either the university website or course Entry Profiles on the GTTR website.

Application route: Applications for the PGCE are made through the Graduate Teacher Training Registry - www.gttr.ac.uk. We also offer qualifications for teaching in the lifelong learning sector, a three year BA for the early primary sector and various early years courses, many leading to Early Years Professional Status (EYPS). Please see our website for further details of these courses or contact us directly for details.

University of Hull

Institution code: H72

Hull Campus
Cottingham Road
Hull HU6 7RX
t: 01482 466 216
f: 01482 466 137
// www.hull.ac.uk/ces

Scarborough Campus
Filey Road
Scarborough YO11 3AZ
t: 01723 357 313
f: 01723 357 333
// www.hull.ac.uk/sse

GENERAL INFORMATION

The Hull campus accommodates not only all the main teaching buildings, library, computer centre and language institute, but also the main students' union building, theatre, sports and fitness centre and most of the playing fields. The Scarborough campus is 40 miles from Hull and is situated in one of England's most famous coastal towns. Scarborough students benefit from a well stocked library, plenty of IT facilities, performance studios, a sports field and use of the nearby sports centre.

ACADEMIC AWARDS

PGCE Primary (3-7) - Scarborough campus
Intended intake: 64 Early Years

Entry requirements: Degree or equivalent in appropriate subjects (normally at grade 2:2 or above). GCSEs (or equivalent) which must include English language, mathematics and science atgrade c or above plus relevant key stage experience. Access courses or equivalent BTEC, GNVQ (level 3) IB and other qualifications are recognised. Assistance can be offered to help locate English, mathematics and science equivalency test providers.

PGCE Primary (5-11) - Hull campus
Intended intake: 91 General Primary

Entry requirements: as for PGCE Primary (3-7)

PGCE Secondary - Hull campus
Intended intake: 100 Secondary

Main subjects offered: Mathematics, English, Science (biology, chemistry, physics), History, Geography, Modern languages (French, German & Spanish); Mathematics enhancement course or French extension course also available.

Entry requirements: Degree (normally at grade 2:2 or above) or equivalent in the appropriate subjects. Assistance can be offered to help locate English, mathematics and science equivalency test providers.

Undergraduate programmes BA (Hons) Primary Teaching - Scarborough campus - 3 years full-time
Intended intake: 98
Entry requirements: 240 points
GCSEs (or equivalent) which must include English language, mathematics and science at grade c or above. Access courses or equivalent BTEC, GNVQ, IB and other qualifications are recognised.

OTHER INFORMATION

There is an opportunity for those who successfully complete their initial teacher training programmes at the University of Hull to continue their professional development immediately by enrolment on one of a selection of master's options.

Application route: Undergraduates apply through UCAS. Postgraduates apply through GTTR.

Institute of Education, University of London

Institution code: I30

20 Bedford Way
London WC1H 0AL
t: 020 7612 6043
f: 020 7612 6097
e: info@ioe.ac.uk
// www.ioe.ac.uk

GENERAL INFORMATION

The Institute of Education, a college of the University of London, is the largest graduate institution in the UK devoted solely to the study of education and related aspects of the social sciences and professional practice. Founded in 1902, it has earned an international reputation for its world-class teaching and research programmes. The Institute offers an unrivalled range of part-time, full-time and distance postgraduate courses. The Newsam Library at the Institute has the largest collection in Europe of learned books and periodicals on educational studies. Its archive and special collections contain the most comprehensive range of government documents on education in the UK. The Institute of Education is committed to equal opportunities for all and seeks to create an open and supportive environment. Academic and pastoral support is offered to all students through their departments, Registry and Student Support, and the Students' Union.

ACADEMIC AWARD

PGCE courses encompass part-time and full-time routes for people who want to teach in primary schools, full-time routes for prospective secondary school teachers and full- and part-time courses for those who wish to teach in the post-16 sector. In addition, this institute offers individually tailored courses for graduate teachers and overseas-trained teachers.

The institute's PGCE awards are undertaken at master's level, and students may be able to carry up to 60 master's level credits from their PGCE towards a master's qualification at the institute.

The institute runs its PGCE in partnership with over 500 schools and colleges in the Greater London area, working with a diverse range of institutions. It is this great variety of provision, coupled with the high quality of the training offered by institute tutors and staff in partner schools and colleges, that gives students a broad and solid foundation for a successful teaching career. Many PGCE graduates return to the institute to undertake forms of in-service training, or to pursue higher degrees in education including the Master of Teaching course.

In partnership with other universities, the institute also provides the Teach First programme, training graduates to be high quality teachers and leaders. Application for this programme is through Teach First.

Progression routes within the institute include over 50 taught master's degrees in education and related social sciences. The modular structure of our courses allows choice and flexibility in combining required modules with optional elements, enabling you to pursue specific areas of interest. We also offer research-focused master's degrees, which can act as preparation for a doctorate or research career. Our 'special courses' help you achieve your professional development aims, or allow you to follow a particular area of academic interest. Modules at master's level are available as stand-alone 'special courses' and can count towards a master's degree.

Entry requirements: Entry requirements vary, so please check our website or prospectus for the entry requirements for the course you are interested in.

Jewish Teacher Training Partnership

Institution code: J40

Bet Meir
44b Albert Road
Hendon
London NW4 2SG
t: 020 8203 6427

GENERAL INFORMATION

The Jewish Teacher Training Partnership consists of 15 primary schools situated in North London, Middlesex, Hertfordshire, Redbridge and Harrow. The programme is accredited by the Teaching Agency to provide school-centred initial teacher training.

The London School of Jewish Studies is the managing agent. 40% of the training is centre-based and 60% is spent in school. The programme covers all aspects of primary school teaching and prepares trainees to teach in any school in the country. In addition there is a differentiated curriculum focus based on either the teaching of Jewish studies or the integration of Jewish studies with the National Curriculum. School experiences take place in Jewish primary schools. Trainees also spend time in a multicultural school. The programme leads to a Professional Graduate Certificate in Education (PGCE) with some 'M' level credits and Qualified Teacher Status (QTS). The Jewish Teacher Training Partnership SCITT is validated by Roehampton University.

ACADEMIC AWARD

PGCE General Primary (3-11) - 1 year full-time
Current intake: 35

Entry requirements:
- An honours degree, class 2:2 or above.
- Must have achieved a standard equivalent to a grade C in the GCSE examination in English, mathematics and science.
- At least two weeks' recent experience in an English state primary school, to be completed before acceptance on the programme can be confirmed.

OTHER INFORMATION

Application route: Apply through the GTTR

Enquiries: SCITT Administrator
Jewish Teacher Training Partnership
Bet Meir
44b Albert Road
London NW4 2SG

t: 020 8203 6427 Ext:303
e: gill.hornstein@lsjs.ac.uk
// **www.lsjs.ac.uk**

Keele University

School of PPPP - Education
Keele University
Keele
Staffordshire ST5 5BG
t: 01782 733 120
f: 01782 734 428
e: eda00@keele.ac.uk
// www.keele.ac.uk/depts/ed/pgce/

GENERAL INFORMATION

Keele University, established in 1950, stands in a 650 acre estate in north Staffordshire. It is one of the largest and most attractive of Britain's campus universities. There are approximately 60 schools within the Keele Partnership. The majority are within 45 minutes travel of Keele. It is the aim of the Keele Partnership to produce successful and enlightened teachers. Employment prospects of those who are successful are good.

Local interest/activities

The area has excellent leisure-facilities including cinemas, theatres, a Premiership and NPower League football teams and a range of clubs, wine bars and restaurants. For those interested in outdoor activities, the Peak District, North Wales and the Lake District are easily accessible.

Birmingham, Liverpool and Manchester are approximately one hour away by car and there are excellent public transport links.

Accommodation

Accommodation may be available on campus although it may be more convenient for PGCE students to live near to their school/college.

ACADEMIC AWARDS

PGCE Secondary (Teacher Training)

Keele offers a Post/Professional Graduate Certificate in Education (PGCE) - 170 places, which lead to Qualified Teacher Status for graduates wishing to teach in secondary schools.

Keele also offers **Subject Knowledge Enhancement courses**. Successful completion of these courses enables students to move on to a PGCE or other teacher training route.

One year PGCE, subjects offered: biology, chemistry, English, French, geography, geology, German, history, ICT, mathematics, physics, Spanish and Urdu.

Entry requirements: You should be a graduate in your main teaching subject or have followed an undergraduate course of which that subject constituted at least 40%. You must have English language and mathematics at grade C or above, or the equivalent.

All applicants for the MFL Community Language course must be able to offer French as a first or second language; it may be offered in combination with German, Spanish or Urdu.

One-year Subject Knowledge Enhancement courses:

- Chemistry
- ICT
- Mathematics
- Physics.

Entry requirements: Mathematics - any degree plus A level mathematics. Chemistry and physics - a) a science-based degree with one other science at least to A level or equivalent; b) any degree with one or more sciences at A level or equivalent.

OTHER INFORMATION

Equivalence tests: mathematics and English language equivalence tests are available.

Application route: Apply through the GTTR for PGCE; apply direct to Keele University for the Subject Knowledge Enhancement courses.

Kent and Medway Training

Institution code: K30

c/o Leigh Technology Academy
Green St Green Road
Dartford
Kent DA1 1QE
t: 01322 620 518
// www.kmtraining.org.uk

GENERAL INFORMATION

Kent and Medway Training is a consortium of 17 successful schools offering a school-centred initial teacher training course for postgraduates who wish to teach in secondary schools. The course offers a QTS and a PGCE (professional) pathway.

Location
KMT is situated close to the M25/M2 interchange and the Dartford crossing giving access to the rest of Kent, Essex, Surrey and south London. The Bluewater shopping and leisure complex is very close by.

Accommodation
There is a wide variety of rented accommodation available in Dartford and the surrounding area.

Students' union
As trainee teachers, KMT associate teachers are eligible to join the teaching unions.

ACADEMIC AWARDS

This full-time course, lasting one academic year (September to July), is totally school-based. Trainees have the individual support of experienced subject teachers who have been trained as mentors.

Subjects offered: business studies, English, mathematics, modern foreign languages (French, German, Italian, Japanese, Spanish or Chinese) and science (with biology, with chemistry or with physics).

Entry requirements:
- English language and mathematics GCSE (A-C) or equivalent and a good degree which is closely related to the chosen teaching area. Recent experience in a secondary school would also be beneficial. Applicants whose degree subject does not fulfil this requirement should be able to provide evidence of knowledge and experience in that area at an appropriate level.
- Trainees are eligible for the same financial support as HE PGCEs.

Equivalence tests: English and mathematics equivalence tests available.

Application route: Apply through the GTTR

OTHER INFORMATION

Enquiries: Mrs B Smith
Senior Course Administrator
c/o Leigh Technology Academy
Green Street Green Road
Dartford
Kent DA1 1QE
t: 01322 620518
e: bsm@leighacademy.org.uk
// www.kmtraining.org.uk

King's College London
Centre for Arts and Sciences Admissions (CASA)
Room KO.30
Strand Campus
Strand
London WC2R 2LS
t: **0207 848 7207**
e: **pgceadmissions@kcl.ac.uk**
// **www.kcl.ac.uk/pgce**

WELCOME TO KING'S

King's College London is England's fourth-oldest university institution and one of the top 30 universities in the world (QS World Rankings).

Our programmes
King's offers a secondary Postgraduate Certificate in Education (PGCE) programme, which was recently graded 'outstanding' by Ofsted. The programme is one year, full-time and prepares you to become a secondary school teacher. The PGCE is enjoyable, challenging and hugely rewarding. We aim to enable PGCE students to:

- reach the standards required for QTS (Qualified Teacher Status)
- become reflective practitioners who can evaluate their own practice
- become aware of the broader educational contexts.

The department offers a Secondary PGCE in the following subjects:

- Biology
- Chemistry
- Classics
- English
- Information and communication technology with computing
- Mathematics
- Modern foreign languages (French, German, Spanish)
- Physics
- Religious education

Gain credits for a master's through the PGCE
The PGCE offers 60 credits to contribute towards a master's in education once you have qualified. We hope and expect that Newly Qualified Teachers (NQTs) will return to continue master's level study within the department within their first few years of teaching.

Making connections between theory & practice
The King's PGCE programme emphasises learning through critical reflection and makes connections between theory and practice. In the same way that our PGCE students are encouraged to make their pupils think, tutors at King's will encourage you to apply your developing understanding of teaching to your own practice. The PGCE programme links practice in schools to recent and relevant research, including the renowned work undertaken at King's, to update the programme continually in light of findings and national developments.

Employment prospects and professional development
King's NQTs are well placed to find work after completing the programme. Many of our PGCE students gain their first teaching post through contacts they have made during their school placements. The majority who want to go straight into teaching have little difficulty finding posts. Past PGCE students have gone on to become heads of department or take senior management posts in schools, including headships. Some go on to careers in educational administration, museums and the advisory and inspection service, or return to King's for master's or research degrees in education.

Application route: Through the Graduate Teacher Training Registry (GTTR)

Kingston University

Institution code: K84

Admissions
The School of Education
Kingston Hill
Kingston upon Thames
Surrey KT2 7LB
t: **020 8417 5145**
e: **education-admissions@kingston.ac.uk**

GENERAL INFORMATION

Kingston University has offered courses in initial teacher training since 1917. The School of Education is regarded by Ofsted (the government agency that monitors teaching standards in education) as a high quality training provider across its Primary, Secondary and CPD provision. Our Ofsted reports are available on the Ofsted website (**www.ofsted.gov.uk**).

We offer three routes into teaching:

- Primary undergraduate BA (Hons) degree.
- Primary postgraduate PGCE course.
- Secondary postgraduate PGCE course.

Why study at Kingston?
- Relevant, stimulating courses provided in partnership with schools.
- Professional accreditation with subject specialism awarded alongside academic qualifications.
- Commitment to equal opportunities and a supportive learning experience.
- Full modular programmes of study, responsive to new initiatives.
- An established framework for continuing professional development.
- Enthusiastic, well-qualified and experienced staff committed to enabling you to achieve your full potential.
- Excellent resources and location (plus good travel network and on-site parking).
- Consistently rated amongst the top schools of education in the Guardian League table - fifth in 2011

Accommodation

Accommodation is offered to most first year students who live more than 15 miles from Kingston railway station, subject to conditions. You do not have to vacate your room over the Christmas or Easter holidays, which is a benefit if you prefer to work for a longer period than the academic term. Some privately owned accommodation is available for PGCE students within the university's Headed Tenancy Scheme.

Students' union

The students' union has a wide range of activities and clubs, all advertised during Freshers' Week. The union runs bars on three of Kingston's campuses. There is also a second-hand bookshop.

Leisure activities

The university offers competitive and non-competitive sports programmes, together with a full range of student welfare services. Kingston upon Thames is a lively centre within walking distance of the Thames, Hampton Court, Richmond Park and local riding stables and within commuting distance of central London (25 minutes by train).

Intended intake: The planned intake for teacher training in 2012 is 91 undergraduates, with 125 Primary PGCE places, including Primary French, German or Spanish places and 25 Early Years places and 53 Secondary PGCE places.

ACADEMIC AWARDS

Foundation Degree in Early Years
Two year work-based

BA (Hons) in Early Years Training
One year top-up work-based

For more details refer to university website at
www.kingston.ac.uk/education

BA (Hons) in Primary Teaching leading to QTS
Three year full-time teacher training course
leading to QTS

Entry requirements:
- 240 UCAS Tariff points.
- GCSE at grade C or above in English language, mathematics and science or equivalent
- Access course (subject specialism to level 3)

For more details refer to university website at
www.kingston.ac.uk/education

Application route: Apply through UCAS.

Primary PGCE (5-11)
Primary PGCE with French, German or Spanish option (5-11)
Primary PGCE (Early Years) (3-7)

Secondary PGCE

Main subjects offered:
- Mathematics
- Modern languages (French, German or Spanish)
- Science (biology, chemistry or physics)

Entry requirements
- GCSE at grade C or above in English language and mathematics or equivalent.
- For PGCE Primary, science at grade C is also required (or equivalent)
- An honours degree of 2:2.
- For Secondary, an honours degree 2:2 in an appropriate subject specialism
- Proficiency in your chosen language, if applicable

For more details refer to university website at
www.kingston.ac.uk/education

Application route: Apply through the GTTR.

The Learning Institute

Institution code: L19

Launceston Road
Callington
Cornwall PL17 7DR
t: **01579 386 123**
f: **01579 386 125**
e: **info@learninginstitute.co.uk**
// **www.learninginstitute.co.uk**

GENERAL INFORMATION

The Learning Institute's Professional Graduate Certificate in Education (PGCE) is a one-year programme that is entirely school-based, in secondary schools and colleges across Cornwall and Devon. Our partnership schools have driven the national training schools initiative, developed high quality research programmes and led innovative projects.

You will have access to invaluable classroom experience from the beginning of your course, allowing you the chance to put your teaching skills into practice immediately. We believe the best way you can learn is from leading, practising teachers in a friendly and supportive environment.

ACADEMIC AWARDS

Our PGCE leads to Qualified Teacher Status which is awarded by the Teaching Agency (TA). The academic element of the programme is validated by the University of Exeter.

Assessment is continuous and takes the form of a professional portfolio, which you will build up over time, and written assignments.

Qualities we are looking for in our potential teachers

We are seeking creative, energetic, enthusiastic and flexible people with a determination to become an outstanding teacher. Applicants must be good communicators with an aptitude for working with young people. Work experience in a school environment is an advantage but not essential.

Main subjects offered

We offer eight secondary subjects:

- Mathematics
- Science
- Religious education
- Modern foreign languages
- ICT
- Business administration and finance
- Media studies
- Society, health and development

In addition, you will have the opportunity to receive training and experience in specialised diplomas.

Application route: Apply through the GTTR.

School of Education
University of Leeds
Leeds LS2 9JT
t: **0113 343 4524**
f: **0113 343 4541**
e: **pgce@education.leeds.ac.uk**

GENERAL INFORMATION

The University of Leeds is one of the largest and most successful in the country, with a long-established international reputation for the high standard of its teaching and research. Teacher training at Leeds is built on a long and successful history and is run in partnership with many of the region's schools. The University of Leeds PGCE Partnerships provide high quality initial teacher training.

ACADEMIC AWARDS

The School of Education provides Primary and Secondary PGCE courses. The award of the PGCE and passing the national skills tests leads to the recommendation to the DfE for the award of Qualified Teacher Status (QTS).

We offer the following one year full-time PGCE programmes:

- Primary 5-9
- Primary 7-11
- Secondary 11-19 in the following subjects: Biology, Chemistry, Physics, English, Modern foreign languages, Mathematics

Application routes: Apply through the GTTR. All applications are made online. Please note: Interested candidates are strongly advised to make early applications since many courses are frequently oversubscribed.

Information regarding our PGCE courses is available on the website **www.education.leeds.ac.uk**. If you have any further queries or need clarification please email pgce@education.leeds.ac.uk.

The School of Education also runs a masters programme, the MA in Teaching, that is specifically designed to follow-on from the PGCE. This three year part-time programme for newly qualified teachers attracts students who have completed our PGCE programmes and wish to continue their professional and academic development with us. Masters level credits from the PGCE can be used on this programme.

Equal opportunities and teacher training
The University of Leeds is proud to be a multi-cultural community. The School of Education is particularly committed to ensuring that the teaching workforce of the future is representative of the wider community, thereby providing children in schools with the benefits of working with a wide range of people from our multi-cultural society.

We strongly encourage suitably qualified applicants of black or minority ethnic heritage to consider our courses.

School of Education

UNIVERSITY OF LEEDS

The School of Education offers one year PGCE courses in:

**Primary - age ranges 5-9 and 7-11
Secondary - English, Mathematics,
Biology, Chemistry, Physics and
Modern Foreign Languages (French,
German and Spanish)**

For further information visit our website: **www.education.leeds.ac.uk**

Enquiries for PGCE Initial Teacher Education Courses
Admissions Office, School of Education, Hillary Place University of Leeds, LS2 9JT
telephone: 0113 343 4524 email: pgce@education.leeds.ac.uk

Leeds Trinity University College

Institution code: L24

Leeds Trinity University College
Brownberrie Lane
Horsforth
Leeds LS18 5HD
t: **0113 283 7150**
f: **0113 283 7200**
e: **admissions@leedstrinity.ac.uk**
// **www.leedstrinity.ac.uk**

GENERAL INFORMATION

Leeds Trinity University College is a great university community in a great city. For further details about student life, accommodation, leisure, sports, students' union and campus facilities, visit our website:
www.leedstrinity.ac.uk

ACADEMIC AWARDS

BA (Hons) Primary Education in the Early Years (3-7)

You will develop a sound understanding of the subject areas taught in the National Curriculum and Early Years Foundation Stage frameworks, and will also receive training in the standards needed to attain Qualified Teacher Status.

Entry requirements: UCAS typical offer B, B, C at A level. English, mathematics and science GCSEs at grade C or above. Apply through UCAS.

BA (Hons) Primary Education in the Junior Years (7-11)

This course will help you to gain the practical skills and theoretical knowledge you'll need to educate and inspire children, and also provides training in the standards needed to attain Qualified Teacher Status.

Entry requirements: UCAS typical offer B, B, C at A level. English, mathematics and science GCSEs at grade C or above. Apply through UCAS.

PGCE Secondary Education

Leeds Trinity University College is the premier provider of Secondary teacher training in the region, offering comprehensive and highly-respected programmes of training for aspiring teachers. Professional Graduate Certificate of Education (PGCE) (FHEQ Level 6) initial teacher training in:

- Business studies
- English
- History
- Mathematics
- Modern foreign languages (French, German, Spanish)
- Religious education

A Postgraduate Certificate in Education qualification (PGCert) (FHEQ Level 7) is also available.

Entry requirements: Relevant honours degree and GCSE English and mathematics at grade C or above or equivalent qualification. Apply through the GTTR.

Leeds Trinity University College
Brownberrie Lane
Horsforth
Leeds LS18 5HD
t: 0113 283 7150
f: 0113 283 7200
e: admissions@leedstrinity.ac.uk
// www.leedstrinity.ac.uk

GENERAL INFORMATION

The Leeds SCITT is a partnership between Leeds Trinity University College and schools in the north of Leeds. The university college is a great university community in a great city. For further details about student life, accommodation, leisure, sports, students' union and campus facilities, visit our website: **www.leedstrinity.ac.uk.**

ACADEMIC AWARDS

We provide school-centred initial teacher training at secondary level, that leads to a Professional Graduate Certificate of Education (PGCE) and Qualified Teacher Status (QTS).

Courses start early in September, last for ten months and are open to graduates wishing to teach:

- Design and technology (resistant materials or food)
- ICT
- Music
- Science

The schools offer a 'hands on' experience where you will be able to watch and develop your teaching skills. With training placements in at least two different schools during your training year you will be able to lead yourself into teaching and begin your teaching career as a confident and effective practitioner. You will have a dedicated specialist subject lead tutor and a school-based specialist subject tutor to support you.

To be accepted onto the course you will need:

- an honours degree with a significant element of the subject that you wish to teach
- advanced level qualifications (or equivalent experience) in the subject you wish to teach
- GCSE grade C or above in English and mathematics (or equivalent)
- the ability to read effectively and communicate clearly and accurately in spoken and written standard English
- confirmation that you have not been excluded from teaching nor from working with children, nor have been registered with the Criminal Records Bureau as unfit for working with children or young persons
- the suitable personal and intellectual qualities required for teaching in secondary schools.

Apply through the GTTR: **www.gttr.ac.uk**

Carnegie Faculty
Carnegie Hall
Headingley Campus
Leeds
LS6 3QQ
t: **0113 812 3113**
e: **course-enquiries@leedsmet.ac.uk**

GENERAL INFORMATION

Leeds is an enterprising, exciting, and expanding city. Not surprisingly it is very popular with students.

Accommodation
The city of Leeds has for many years housed a large student community and is geared to meeting student needs. The university offers a wide selection of accommodation, and there is a plentiful supply of student houses available in the private sector.

University accommodation has been specifically designed to meet the needs of disabled students.

Please contact the Accommodation Office on 0113 812 5972 for further information.

Students' union and leisure
The SU feeds, entertains, informs, and most importantly represents the student body at the university. The union runs shops, cafes, cashpoints, bars, and the student advice bureaus.

The university also offers quality playing fields, courts and athletic tracks, and full gym facilities at numerous sites.

Teaching and learning facilities
The Headingley Campus houses all the facilities for teacher education. Teaching takes place in a well planned modern environment with appropriate specialist equipment.

The university maintains a strong partnership with a large number of local schools, offering our students a wide variety of practical teaching experience in order to boost their skills and employment potential upon completion of the course.

Courses
The university offers a number of teacher training courses, at both undergraduate and postgraduate level. These courses all lead to Qualified Teacher Status (QTS)

Undergraduate:
BA (Hons) Early Childhood Education
BA (Hons) Early Childhood Education (2 year route)
BA (Hons) Primary Education

Postgraduate:
PGCE Early Child Education
PGCE Primary Education
PGCE Secondary Physical Education

Entry requirements: Entry requirements differ on each course for more detailed information visit **www.leedsmet.ac.uk** or contact Course Enquiries.

University of Leicester

School of Education
21 University Road
Leicester LE1 7RF
t: **0116 252 3677 (Primary PGCE)**
t: **0116 252 3689 (Secondary PGCE)**
f: **0116 252 3653**
e: **secondary.pgce@le.ac.uk**
e: **primary.pgce@le.ac.uk**
// **www.le.ac.uk/departments/education/pgce**

GENERAL INFORMATION

"The university has a well-deserved reputation for training high quality teachers." OfSTED 2008

Since its formation in 1962 the University of Leicester School of Education has enjoyed an enviable reputation for being in the forefront of educational research andthe professional education of teachers. The School of Education works in partnership with over 250 local schools. They represent an unusually diverse and interesting range of institutions, from small rural primary schools to large multi-ethnic comprehensives.

ACADEMIC AWARD

PGCE Primary and Secondary programmes
Successful completion of the courses gives students either the university's Postgraduate Certificate in Education (60 credits at master's Level) or Professional Graduate Certificate in Education (see website for further information) and a recommendation for Qualified Teacher Status. The courses are full-time for one year.

Main courses offered and intending intake:
Primary PGCE: The total target intake for the Lower Primary (3-7), Upper Primary (5-11) and Primary with French is 150. All students are required to undertake a specialist study. The specialist options are likely to include: citizenship, early years, English, ICT, mathematics, PSHE, science and special educational needs.

Secondary PGCE: The total target for the secondary course is 130, divided between citizenship, English, geography, mathematics, mathematics with physics, modern languages, physics with mathematics, social science (sociology and psychology) and science (biology, chemistry, physics and co-ordinated sciences).

Entry requirements
Minimum entry requirements apply. Primary applicants from all degree subject backgrounds will be considered with a 2:1 degree or above. GCSEs in English, mathematics and science at grade C or above are needed in order to apply.

Secondary applicants would normally be expected to have studied the subject they wish to teach, or a closely-related one, to first degree level, with a 2:2 or above. Secondary applicants can apply without GCSEs in mathematics and English but they must have them by the start of the course.

All applicants must also have experience of working with children in schools.

Equivalence tests: Equivalence tests in lieu of GCSE English and mathematics are only available for secondary candidates lacking the requisite qualifications.

Application route: apply through the GTTR

OTHER INFORMATION

The PGCE brochure can be obtained on request from the Primary or Secondary PGCE offices at the School of Education either by telephone or email. Further details about the courses and the extensive resources, accommodation and additional opportunities provided by the university can be found on the website.

Dovelands Primary School
Hinckley Road
Leicester LE3 0TJ
t: 0116 254 3187
e: scitt@dovelands.leicester.sch.uk
// www.leics-scitt.co.uk

GENERAL INFORMATION

The Leicester & Leicestershire SCITT is a school-based postgraduate programme that is managed by the headteachers of ten successful primary schools. Senior management in these core partner schools contribute to all aspects of the design and running of the programme. Training takes place within the schools and is largely provided by local authority consultants and practising teachers who are experts in their fields and at the cutting-edge of innovation and best practice in primary education.

ACADEMIC AWARDS

The SCITT training leads to Qualified Teacher Status, and a Postgraduate Certificate in Education (PGCE), with 60 master's level credits, accredited by the University of Wolverhampton.

We believe that the SCITT is able to offer a unique opportunity for trainees. Our partnership of schools and extremely effective teaching staff offer trainees high quality centre-based and school-based training. Strengths within the programme include:

- three substantial periods of teaching experience across the range of Key Stages 1 and 2 in at least two contrasting schools
- the attraction of a wide field from ethnic minority groups, men, classroom assistants and NNEBs. Leicester has a uniquely diverse community - well over 50% of families come from an ethnic background
- immersion of trainees in teaching and learning through linking innovative, current theory with effective, tried and tested classroom practice
- assignments that offer research that will extend knowledge and test understanding of the nature of high quality teaching and learning, at master's level
- relevant and up-to-date school-based experience, working alongside existing effective practitioners in schools that are at the cutting edge of innovation and self-evaluation
- all trainees are treated as fellow professionals within effective schools in a high-quality, well structured training programme.

OTHER INFORMATION

Enquiries: Please contact the SCITT directly for further information and visit the SCITT website.
www.leics-scitt.co.uk

Application route: Apply through the GTTR.

Student Administration Office
Liverpool Hope University
Hope Park
Liverpool L16 9JD
t: 0151 291 3331
// www.hope.ac.uk

GENERAL INFORMATION

Liverpool Hope has been involved in ITT for over 160 years and, in February 2005, it was awarded a Grade 1 from Ofsted for the Quality Assurance and Management of all its primary and secondary teacher training courses. The BA (QTS) and full-time PGCE courses are delivered at Hope Park, Childwall, and the Creative Campus, which is near the city centre.

ACADEMIC AWARDS

Main subjects offered:
- Biblical studies
- Biology
- Christian theology
- Early childhood studies
- English language
- English literature
- Fine art
- Geography
- History
- Human biology
- Information technology
- Mathematics
- Music
- Special educational needs
- Sport studies
- Teaching modern foreign languages in the primary school
- World religions

Entry requirements: GCSE grade C in English, mathematics and science (or equivalent). 300 points of which applicants must achieve 240 points at A2 (or equivalent) with passes in 2 x grade C or above at A2 (or equivalent). Equivalent level from non A level qualifications required. Plus any specific entry requirements for the area of special interest. Recent experience in a primary classroom is essential.

PGCE Primary, Choices FS/KS1 or KS1/KS2 or KS1/KS2 with MFL (French or Spanish) - 1 year full-time
The courses focus on generic issues and training across the primary curriculum. Students also develop an area of special interest, eg Early Years Education, MFL, National Curriculum subject (eg mathematics in the primary years), Special Educational Needs etc. Areas of special interest must be supported by academic qualifications (see website for details).

Entry requirements: Applicants must already possess GCSEs (grade C or above) in English, mathematics and science at the time of application. Degree content: must offer support for an area of special interest. Degree class 2:1 or above is preferred (minimum degree 2:2 may be considered for Primary with MFL).

Work experience: Recent experience in a primary classroom is essential (minimum ten days over the previous 18 months).

PGCE Secondary (QTS 11-18) - 1 year full-time
Main subjects offered
- Biology
- Chemistry
- English
- Geography
- History
- Information and communication technology
- Mathematics
- Modern languages (French, French with German, French with Spanish, German, German with French, Spanish, Spanish with French)
- Music
- Performing arts
- Physics

- Physics with mathematics
- Religious studies
- Religious studies and philosophy

Entry requirements: GCSE Grade C in English and Mathematics. Good Honours Degree 2:1 or above (minimum Degree 2:2 may be considered for specific PGCE subjects where candidates have additional skills/attributes/experiences to offer). Specific subject entry criteria apply.

Work experience: Observation/experience in a comprehensive secondary school (minimum 10 days over the previous 18 months).

OTHER INFORMATION

Entry route: UG/FT/4 years, PG/FT/1 year, PG/ Professional Graduate Certificate.
Awards: BA (QTS) Honours, PGCE
Intended intake: UG-220; PG Primary-251 FT, Secondary-254

Application route: UG apply through UCAS, PG FT apply through the GTTR, Professional Graduate Certificate apply through the GTTR.

Enquiries:
t: 0151 291 3111
e: enquiry@hope.ac.uk

Student Recruitment Team
IM Marsh Campus
Aigburth
Liverpool L17 6BD
t: **0151 231 5340**
f: **0151 231 5379**
e: **traintoteach@ljmu.ac.uk**
// **www.ljmu.ac.uk/teaching**

ACADEMIC AWARDS

BA (Hons) QTS
● Primary Education (3 years full-time)*

PGCE Primary - 1 year full-time
● Early years (3-7)*

PGCE Secondary (11-18) - 1 year full-time
● Art and design
● Design and technology: resistant materials, design and technology: food and textiles
● Information technology (computing)
● Mathematics
● Modern languages (French, Spanish, German)
● Physical education*
● Physics with mathematics
● Science (biology, chemistry, physics)

PGCE Vocational (14-19) - 1 year full-time
● Engineering

* These courses will require GCSEs in place **prior** to application.

All PGCE's are offered at postgraduate level and carry up to 60 master's level credits.

Entry requirements: All entry requirements can be found at **www.ljmu.ac.uk/courses** or by contacting the Student Recruitment Team direct.

GCSE equivalence tests: For further information on English language, mathematics and science GCSE equivalence tests (AEFIT, ASFIT, AMFIT), contact the Student Recruitment Team.
t: 0151 231 5340
// **www.ljmu.ac.uk/teaching/gcse**

All suitable applicants are interviewed prior to an offer of a place being made.

OTHER INFORMATION

Application route: BA: apply through UCAS. PGCE apply through the GTTR.

Coleg Llandrillo Cymru

Institution code: L53

Coleg Llandrillo Cymru
Llandudno Road
Rhos-on-Sea
Colwyn Bay
LL28 4HZ
t: 01492 546 666
// www.llandrillo.ac.uk

GENERAL INFORMATION

Academic Awards: Undergraduate
- BA(Hons) Post-compulsory Education and Training
- Professional Graduate Certificate in Education / Certificate in Education
- Preparing to Teach

ACADEMIC AWARDS

BA (PCET) Honours - 2 years part-time
Flexible part-time course to give those working in post compulsory education and training the opportunity to achieve a full honours degree in education and training through part-time study.

Entry requirements: Minimum entry qualifications apply. Please see our current prospectus or website for specific information: www.llandrillo.ac.uk

Application route: Applications for BA (Hons) Postcompulsory Education and Training courses will undergo a compulsory interview and will have to produce evidence of having completed a relevant teacher training programme and of having substantial professional development.

Professional Graduate/Certificate in Education
This is a nationally recognised qualification for those working in the lifelong learning sector. The part-time programme is suitable for college lecturers, adult/community education providers, military and public service trainers, training officers and others who have a teaching or training role. Successful completion of the course provides the mandatory qualification for those wishing to teach within Further Education. Those who successfully complete the course may progress to complete a BA(Hons) Post-compulsory Education and Training

Those who successfully complete the course may progress to complete a BA(Hons) Post-compulsory Education and Training

Entry requirements: Minimum entry qualifications apply. Please see our current prospectus or website for specific information: www.llandrillo.ac.uk

Application route: Applications for part time teacher training courses will undergo a compulsory interview and will have to meet the entry criteria.

All applicants offered and accepting a place on the Professional Graduate Certificate in Education / Certificate in Education programme will have to have an enhanced criminal record bureau clearance before they can commence teaching practice.

Preparing to Teach
This is the threshold qualification for those starting work in the lifelong learning sector. The short part-time course is suitable for those who wish to become teachers, trainers or lecturers in the lifelong learning sector. Successful completion of the course provides the threshold qualification for those wishing to teach within Further Education.

Entry requirements: Minimum entry qualifications apply. Please see our current prospectus or website for specific information: **www.llandrillo.ac.uk**

Application route: Applications for part time teacher training courses will undergo a compulsory interview and will have to meet the entry criteria.

All applicants offered and accepting a place on the programmes will have to have an enhanced criminal record bureau clearance before they can commence teaching practice.

LDBS
St Mary Magdalene Academy
Liverpool Rd
London N7 8PG
t: **020 7502 4780**
f: **020 7700 4218**
e: **Kamar.Fadiga@smmAcademy.org**

GENERAL INFORMATION

The LDBS SCITT is a one-year full-time postgraduate course.

The LDBS SCITT was developed in 1998/9 by a consortium of Church of England primary schools. These schools wished to contribute to teacher training and were keen to support the training and recruitment of teachers for London schools. We took our first cohort of trainees in September 1999. Although the consortium schools have changed over the years, we currently operate in more than forty London primary schools.

We aim to recruit high quality graduates and to train them to become successful, confident, effective teachers, well equipped to teach in a range of urban primary schools. We are especially keen to recruit candidates from black and ethnic minority backgrounds, and male candidates.

On a SCITT programme, a substantial part of the training takes place in school and the course presents an opportunity to acquire much fuller experience, not only of teaching and learning, but of all other aspects of school life than is possible on a conventional PGCE route. All the training on the course revolves round work in school where you are regarded as (trainee) members of staff.

The taught part of the programme is based at St Mary Magdalene Academy in Islington. The course is accredited by the Teaching Agency (TA) and validated by the University of Roehampton. It leads to the award of Qualified Teacher Status (QTS) and of the Professional Certificate of Education (PGCE).

Entry requirements:
These are the qualifications that you must have:

- a United Kingdom first degree or a recognised equivalent qualification
- GCSE English language, mathematics and science at grade C or above.

In addition to the requirements for English, maths and science, the DfE Circular 02/02 also contains high expectations for the subject knowledge of trainees in ICT. So, we recommend that potential trainees familiarise themselves with ICT techniques in preparation for their work in school.

These are some of the qualities and experiences that are also required:

- good written and oral communication skills
- commitment to Primary Education
- experience relevant to working with young children
- willingness to work hard
- reliability and punctuality
- resilience, flexibility and a sense of humour.

How do I apply?
Application for a place on the LDBS SCITT is made through the Graduate Teacher Training Registry (GTTR).

For further information, please contact the Administration Manager, Mrs Kamar Fadigaat:
LDBS
St Mary Magdalene Academy
Liverpool Rd
London N7 8PG
t: 020 7502 4780
f: 020 7700 4218
e: Kamar.Fadiga@smmAcademy.org

London Metropolitan University

Institution code: L68

166-220 Holloway Road
London N7 8DB
t: **020 7133 4200**
f: 020 7133 2677
// **www.londonmet.ac.uk/teach**

GENERAL INFORMATION

The Department of Education has been training teachers to meet the needs of inner-city schools for over 30 years. Our courses prepare you for a career in teaching in urban, multilingual schools, and we aim to recruit students who reflect the cultural and linguistic diversity of London schools.

The majority of our graduates teach in London schools. Many keep in touch with us and report that the training they received here equipped them very well for the opportunities and challenges of the profession.

Reflective practice is central to our courses and enables you to apply the theoretical elements of the course to the practicalities of the classroom, and integrate educational and professional issues within your teaching.

ACADEMIC AWARDS

Primary education - undergraduate
- BEd (hons) Early Years Teaching

Primary education - postgraduate
- PGCE Primary Education: Early Years (3-7)
- PGCE Primary Education: Primary (5-11)

Secondary education - postgraduate
- PGCE Citizenship
- PGCE English with Media/Drama
- PGCE Mathematics
- PGCE Modern Languages
- PGCE Physical Education
- PGCE Science - routes available in science with biology, science with chemistry and science with physics. Subject Knowledge Enhancement (SKE) courses are also available in chemistry, maths, modern languages and physics.

Our PGCE courses have awards at professional and postgraduate levels. These are determined by the quality of work submitted during the course.

Entry requirements:
- As part of the selection process, you will be invited to attend an interview. Prior to this you are expected to have visited a school to observe the teaching of the appropriate subject/level and to inform yourself about the teacher's role.
- Undergraduate courses: The BEd Early Years requires 260 UCAS points.
- Postgraduate courses: All PGCE courses require a degree. For Secondary courses, it should be relevant to the subject you will be teaching.
- All courses require GCSEs (grade A to C) or equivalent qualifications in English language and mathematics. Applicants also need GCSE grade C or above in science for the Early Years and Primary courses. For Secondary applicants we offer an internal equivalency test in English language and mathematics for those who do not have the GCSE grade C or equivalent qualification, but who currently hold a grade D or equivalent.

Application routes: Undergraduate (BEd) apply through UCAS. Postgraduate (PGCE) apply through the GTTR.

OTHER INFORMATION

Enquiries: For further information, please contact Admissions.
t: 020 7133 4200 e: admissions@londonmet.ac.uk

London South Bank University

Institution code: L75

Department of Education
London South Bank University
London SE1 0AA
t: 020 7815 8071
// www.lsbu.ac.uk

GENERAL INFORMATION

London South Bank University is situated in central London, just south of the River Thames. The university has strong links with partner schools and nurseries and is committed to train teachers to work creatively in inner city, multilingual settings.

ACADEMIC AWARDS

PGCE Primary (5-11) either full-time or part-time
Award: PGCE/QTS
School experience: KS1/2

Entry requirements: GCSE grade C or above (or equivalent) in English language, mathematics and science. A degree in any subject. Experience of and commitment to working with young or adult learners in a formal/informal setting and an appreciation of diversity and how equality is promoted through education. (Applicants are strongly advised to gain recent experience in a state school setting prior to application).

PGCE Early Years (7-11) - 1 year full-time only
Award: PGCE/QTS
School experience: KS2 only

Entry requirements: GCSE grade C or above (or equivalent) in English language, mathematics and science. A degree in any subject. Experience of and commitment to working with young or adult learners in a formal/informal setting and an appreciation of diversity and how equality is promoted through education. (Applicants are strongly advised to gain recent experience in a state school setting prior to application).

PGCE Early Years (3-7)- 1 year full-time only
Award: PGCE/QTS
School experience: Foundation Stage/KS1

Entry requirements: GCSE grade C or above (or equivalent) in English language, mathematics and science. A degree in any subject. Experience of and commitment to working with young or adult learners in a formal/informal setting and an appreciation of diversity and how equality is promoted through education. (Applicants are strongly advised to gain recent experience in a state school setting prior to application).

PGCE Secondary Mathematics (11-16)
- 1 year full-time only
School experience: KS3/4

Entry requirements: GCSE grade C or above (or equivalent) in English language. A mathematics degree or a degree with significant mathematics content, such as physics or engineering. We also consider other degree subjects where mathematics is applied such as psychology, business, accountancy or finance providing applicants have a good mathematics A level.

Experience of and commitment to working with young or adult learners in a formal/informal setting and an appreciation of diversity and how equality is promoted through education. (Applicants are strongly advised to gain recent experience in a state school setting prior to application.)

We particularly welcome applications for all courses from mature students, people from the local community and from minority ethnic communities.

Application route: Apply through the GTTR.

Teacher Education at Loughborough
Loughborough University
Leicestershire LE11 3TU
t: 01509 222762
f: 01509 223912

GENERAL INFORMATION

Loughborough University has been involved in teacher education since 1930 and has extensive experience of specialist courses for teachers. Our programmes attract successful students who have enjoyed excellent career prospects, and many of our graduates have progressed to senior posts throughout the education service.

Local interests/activities
Loughborough University has a student population of over 17,000. It is situated on a single-site campus, surrounded by beautiful countryside, in the heart of England. Only 90 minutes by train from London, Loughborough has relatively inexpensive living costs and is less than 20 miles from Nottingham and Leicester. The campus is a thriving community on the edge of a friendly student-orientated town with good local amenities.

Accommodation
It is recommended that PGCE trainees contact the Student Accommodation Centre about private rented properties in and around Loughborough. They offer value for money and are regularly inspected to maintain quality.

Students' union
Loughborough students' union is the on-campus focus of social life with its numerous societies and sports clubs and regular entertainment events. The campus has the most extensive sports facilities of any university in the UK and the facilities and recreation classes are open to students at all levels.

Leisure facilities
The union is one of the largest music and dance venues in Leicestershire and the biggest provider of entertainment in Loughborough. There are over 50 different clubs within the Athletics Union providing both competitive and recreational sport. With access to some of the best sporting facilities in the country, the Athletics Union ensures access to sport for all Loughborough students.

ACADEMIC AWARDS

The PGCE course lasts for 36 weeks, of which 24 weeks are spent undertaking teaching and related activities in partnership schools. At the heart of the course is the development of classroom teaching competence. Experienced school teachers work alongside university tutors to provide mentoring and support through a programme which is designed to develop specialist subject teaching skills, and the wider professional role of a teacher.

Main courses offered:
- Design and technology
- Physical education
- Science (biology, chemistry, physics, physics with maths).

On this course, trainees will learn to teach and relate to young people in a variety of learning situations, and will gain the skills to plan, teach and manage pupils effectively. Trainees will gain the confidence and competence to undertake a full role as members of a secondary school's staff, and they will develop sufficient knowledge and understanding of educational issues to be able to contribute effectively to the highest standards of teaching.

The PGCE course contributes towards half of a master's degree (90 credits). Individuals wanting to complete the master's degree can do so on a part-time basis during their early teaching career. Entry requirements: Applicants require a degree in their chosen teaching subject or a degree with over

50% of its content closely related to that subject. Entrants also require English language and mathematics at GCSE grade C or equivalent.

Application routes: Apply through the GTTR.

The University of Manchester

Institution code: M20

School of Education
University of Manchester
Oxford Road
Manchester M13 9PL
e: pgce@manchester.ac.uk

GENERAL INFORMATION

The University of Manchester has a long tradition as a centre of excellence in teacher training. Building upon your existing strengths and ambitions, we aim to empower you to develop your knowledge, understanding and skills so that as a teacher, you make a lasting positive impression upon young people in an exciting and fast-changing profession.

Greater Manchester is a culturally, socially and ethnically diverse area, and as such is an excellent location in which to prepare for a career in teaching. The PGCE programmes work closely with a wide range of partner schools and colleges in Greater Manchester and surrounding areas, including Cheshire, Derbyshire, Lancashire, Merseyside and West Yorkshire.

Postgraduate open days for the programme are held in the autumn and spring terms, please see the university open day pages for further information at: **www.manchester.ac.uk/postgraduate/opendays**

For further information about Primary and Secondary PGCE courses, please visit the School of Education website at: **www.education.manchester.ac.uk/postgraduate**

ACADEMIC AWARDS

PGCE General Primary (5-11) - 1 year full-time, postgraduate level
Main subjects offered: General Primary.
Entry requirements: GCSE grade C or above, or an equivalent qualification, in English language, mathematics and science. A good honours degree, preferably a National Curriculum subject. Strong background at A level, preferably including two A levels at grade C or above in National Curriculum subjects.

Work experience: A minimum five days' experience (from within the last three years) in a UK state primary school (this experience must have been completed prior to application).

PGCE General Primary (5-11) with a Language Specialism - 1 year full-time, postgraduate level
Main subjects offered: General Primary with an option to specialise in either French, German or Spanish.
Entry requirements: Same as for the General Primary course, Language specialists must also hold a good A level in a relevant modern language or an equivalent qualification.
Work experience: Same as for the General Primary course.

PGCE Secondary (11-18) - 1 year full-time, postgraduate level
Main subjects offered: Business education, design and technology (resistant materials and systems control), English, mathematics, modern languages (French, German and Spanish), science (biology, chemistry and physics).
Entry requirements: GCSE grade C or above, or an equivalent qualification, in English language and mathematics. A good background at A level or an equivalent qualification. A first or second class honours degree. Degree content minimum 50% relevant to specialism.
Work experience: A minimum two days' recent experience in a UK state secondary school is recommended.

OTHER INFORMATION

Entry route: PG/FT/1 year
Awards: PGCE QTS
Intended intake: Primary-136, Secondary-257
Application route: Apply through GTTR.
Enquiries: Please see the FAQs section of our website:
www.education.manchester.ac.uk/postgraduate
or email pgce@manchester.ac.uk.

Course Enquiries
All Saints Building (GMS)
All Saints Campus
Manchester M15 6BH
t: 0161 247 6969
e: courses@mmu.ac.uk
// www.mmu.ac.uk

GENERAL INFORMATION

The Institute of Education is one of the largest providers of initial teacher education in the country. It is based on two campuses: Didsbury in south Manchester (campus code D for UCAS, campus code M for GTTR) and Crewe in south Cheshire (campus code A for UCAS, campus code C for GTTR) and provides a full range of courses with high quality ratings.

Manchester is a vibrant city with unparalleled opportunities for cultural, sporting and leisure activities. Crewe is a lively town with a thriving social and cultural scene.

ACADEMIC AWARDS

BA (Hons) Primary Education (3-11) - 3 year full-time
Intended intake: 273
Campus: A or D

Trainees study all areas of the primary curriculum.

PGCE Primary Education (3-7/5-11) - 1 year full-time
Intended intake: 255
Campus: C&M

Trainees specialise in teaching either 3-7 or 5-11.

PGCE Secondary Education (11-16) - 1 year full-time
With preparation for ages 16-19.
Intended intake: 436
Main subjects offered:

- Art and design (M)
- Biology (M)
- Business and information and communication technology (C)
- Chemistry (M)
- Design and technology: food and textiles (M)
- Design and technology: resistant materials (M)
- Drama (M)
- English (C, M)
- English with special educational needs (M)
- French (M)
- Geography (C, M)
- German (M)
- History (M)
- Mathematics (M)
- Music (M)
- Music with specialist instrumental teaching (M)
- Physical education (M)
- Physics (M)
- Physics with mathematics (M)
- Psychology (M)
- Religious education (M)
- Social science with citizenship (M)
- Spanish (M).

Entry requirements:
- BA (Hons) Primary Education: GCSE English language, mathematics and science must be achieved before submitting an application, with one grade B and two grade Cs. Two additional GCSEs at grade C are also required, a modern language is desirable. Also, 300 Tariff points at A2 or equivalent A levels at grades BBB are required, excluding general studies. BTEC National Diploma grades DDM. CACHE Diploma grade B.
- PGCE Primary: GCSE maths, English language and science at grade C or above achieved before application. Also, 2:1 honours degree. Minimum

Manchester Metropolitan University

continued

two weeks' experience within a mainstream primary school undertaken before application within the last two years.

- PGCE Secondary: GCSE English language and maths at grade C or above must be achieved before application. Also, 2:1/2:2 honours degree (depending upon subject) in a relevant subject or a degree containing substantial related content (minimum 50%).

International students: Equivalent qualifications are accepted. Those interested in applying should contact NARIC to establish equivalencies **(www.naric.org)**. Also, IELTS 6.0 or equivalent for BA (Hons). IELTS 7 or equivalent for PGCE.

Equivalence tests: Available in maths and English for secondary candidates offered a place for PGCE biology, chemistry, French, German, mathematics, physics or Spanish only.

Application route: Undergraduate apply through UCAS. PGCE apply through the GTTR

Mid Cheshire College

Institution code: M77

Hartford Campus
Chester Road
Northwich
Cheshire
CW8 1LJ
t: 01606 74444
e: info@midchesh.ac.uk
// www.midchesh.ac.uk

GENERAL INFORMATION

Graded 'Outstanding' by Ofsted in December 2008 and awarded Beacon status in 2009, the college's inspection profile is one of the very best in the country. In fact Mid Cheshire College is in the top 10% of colleges in England.

Mid Cheshire College has a tradition of providing quality education to all sections of the community. Our higher education courses are no exception and support our reputation for excellence in a friendly and supportive environment. We are one of the largest providers of higher education in further education in Cheshire and Warrington.

Foundation Degree (FdA) Supporting Teaching & Learning - 2 years part-time, one evening per week
Students will have the opportunity to apply to progress on to the second or final year of an honours degree in a related area at any university. Students can apply to progress to the part-time route of the BA (Hons) Education at Manchester Metropolitan University (**www.mmu.ac.uk**) as a top-up to honours degree from this foundation degree. Applications will be considered based on performance on the foundation degree.

The Burroughs
London NW4 4BT
t: 020 8411 5555
e: enquiries@mdx.ac.uk

GENERAL INFORMATION

Middlesex University provides a range of high quality initial teacher training programmes for those wishing to train as primary or secondary teachers. All programmes are based at our flagship Hendon campus, which has been the focus of the largest development in the university's history, with over £95 million invested. Our purpose-built venue for students includes places to study, eat, socialise and relax, and has excellent public transport links with nearby tube, rail and bus.

Teacher training at Middlesex is based upon a strong partnership between the university and schools in the area. Schools in north London and Hertfordshire provide trainees with a range of experiences in urban, suburban and rural schools. All programmes lead to Qualified Teacher Status. The training we provide is rigorous and challenging and designed to give you the support and assistance which you will need to reach the required professional standards.

Accommodation
There are four halls of residence, either next to the campus or within a short walking distance.

Students' union/leisure facilities
Middlesex University students union (MUSU) runs a wide range of entertainments, sports and societies. We offer a modern gym and outdoor courts.

Primary programmes
BA (Hons) Primary Education
PGCE Primary Education
PGCE Early Years - Foundation and Key Stage 1
Graduate Teacher Programme

Secondary programmes
PGCE Business Studies
PGCE Citizenship
PGCE Drama
PGCE English
PGCE Geography
PGCE Information and Communication Technology
PGCE Mathematics
PGCE Modern Foreign Languages
PGCE Physics with Mathematics
PGCE Music
PGCE Science with Biology, Physics or Chemistry
Graduate Teacher Programme

Entry requirements:
For all PGCE Secondary programmes:

- A 2:2 degree or equivalent in an appropriate subject area (2:1 or above for drama)
- A GCSE (A to C) or equivalent in English language and mathematics.

For the PGCE Primary and Early Years programmes
- An honours degree, 50% of which should be in a National Curriculum subject
- GCSE grade C or above in English, mathematics and science
- Two weeks' work experience in a primary setting.

For BA (Hons) Primary Education:
- GCSE (A to C) or equivalent in English language, mathematics and science
- 260 Tariff points
- Access to Primary Teaching course.
- Two weeks' work experience in a primary setting.

Application route: Undergraduate apply through UCAS, **www.ucas.ac.uk**. Postgraduate apply through the GTTR, **www.gttr.ac.uk**.

Mid Essex SCITT Consortium

Institution code: M82

c/o Shenfield High School
Alexander Lane
Brentwood
Essex CM15 8RY
t: 01277 249288
e: s.sale@shenfield.essex.sch.uk
// www.midessexitt.com

GENERAL INFORMATION

The Mid Essex Consortium for school-centred initial teacher training (SCITT) is made up of 12 partnership schools offering a Professional Graduate Certificate in Education in one of seven subjects.

All of our PGCE courses have been planned and developed in consultation with the partnership schools and our accrediting HEI (Greenwich University)

As a school-based ITT programme, emphasis is on the placements and partnership schools and the high quality mentoring provided throughout the course.

General professional studies sessions and subject specific training is held weekly, usually at the lead school (Shenfield High School). Subject specialist sessions are hosted by one of the consortium schools.

The different components of the course come together neatly in order to create a programme that is balanced in providing the necessary theory and practice involved in training to become a teacher.

Mid Essex ITT is also working in partnership with Edge Hill University in order to allow those who gain QTS to also gain master's level credits.

The local area

The Mid Essex Consortium stretches from Brentwood on the M25 to Dunmow, approximately 15 miles north of Chelmsford. Most of the schools are in areas within easy reach of outer London and enjoy excellent transport links with the capital and surrounding areas.

Other local features include Lakeside and Bluewater shopping areas, the county town of Chelmsford and miles of beautiful countryside.

ACADEMIC AWARDS

PGCE Secondary (11-18) - 1 year full-time
- Art and design
- English
- Geography
- Information communication technology
- Mathematics
- Modern foreign languages
- Science

Entry requirements
- An honours degree (2:2 or above) from a recognised university, at least half of which should be in the subject you wish to teach. (For ICT, the degree may be in any relevant discipline, where ICT has been an integral part of the study.)
- GCSE English language and mathematics at grade C or higher. We can offer advice on where to obtain information about equivalence tests.
- Applicants are strongly advised to spend time observing lessons in a local secondary school prior to application.

Application route: Apply through the GTTR

School of Education
University of Nottingham
Jubilee Campus
Nottingham NG8 1BB
t: 0115 951 4396/4464
f: 0115 951 4499

GENERAL INFORMATION

This is your chance to gain Qualified Teacher Status and a Postgraduate Certificate in Education (PGCE) by school-centred training in some of the best primary schools, working with one of the best universities in the country.

A consortium of primary schools, located in most regions of England and previously recognised by Ofsted as nationally outstanding, together with the University of Nottingham, offer a one-year programme of teacher training to individuals who have:

- a commitment to teaching as a career
- a desire to work with primary age children
- the personal and intellectual qualities needed to be an excellent primary teacher
- the confidence to be part of an innovative and prestigious programme.

Introduction

The course is 39 weeks long with two additional weeks for a summer and an Easter study school. There are three periods of dedicated teaching practice, totalling 11 weeks. There are four study weeks where you will be required to read and reflect on your school experience. For the remaining weeks you will spend four days a week in your home school on directed activities. Each week you will have a study day to work on the study materials and associated tasks. It is possible to accrue master's level credits which may be used towards an MA in Education at the University of Nottingham.

Age-range and specialisms

Schools involved in the SCITT cover the 3-11 Primary age range. Directed study time is aimed at ensuring that trainees acquire understanding, knowledge and skills for teaching and learning across this age range. In some schools, you will be able to follow an Early Years/Key Stage 1 course. All of our schools offer a Key Stage 1/Key Stage 2 course. You will be invited to express an age-range specialism at the interview stage. Throughout the course you will be expected to develop an understanding of appropriate practice for the age range in which you intend to apply for your first post. Professional studies are generic to the Primary age range in all areas.

You can choose to specialise in maths, English, science or modern languages or to take a purely generalist course. In either case you will cover the full curriculum and a wealth of whole-school issues.

Mentor arrangements

Mentors have a key role in supporting trainees within their school and have regular tutorials with their trainees. One day per week is designated to undertake reading and writing assignments linked to the study materials. It is expected that some time to prepare for teaching activities will be provided as 'non-contact' time while you are in school, in line with that ordinarily offered to teachers in school. You will also have a designated tutor who is based at the university.

If you choose to train with the National Primary SCITT and are successful in your application, you will have already made a successful start to your teaching career. PGCE training in schools will demand hard work and commitment, spirit and imagination. In return, all who are involved in the National Primary SCITT partnership will ensure you have a rewarding and worthwhile training year which equips you to take your place in the profession as a qualified teacher, ready to benefit the children placed in your care.

PGCE Office
Newcastle University
School of Education
Communication and Language Sciences
Newcastle upon Tyne NE1 7RU
t: 0191 222 6581
e: pgce-education@ncl.ac.uk
// www.ncl.ac.uk/ecls

GENERAL INFORMATION

Our School of Education, Communication and Language Sciences is one of the largest centres of postgraduate teacher training in the country, with over 100 years of successful experience. Despite its size (approximately 250 students complete the PGCE each year), the well-established tutorial arrangements and the active social life combine to make it a friendly, stimulating and secure environment from which to embark upon a career in teaching.

ACADEMIC AWARDS

PGCE Primary (5-11) - 1 year full-time
This is a Postgraduate Certificate in Education with a weighting of 60 credits at master's level.

Main subjects offered: Primary National Curriculum subjects with a limited number of places (16) for those wishing to teach Primary French.

Entry requirements: A 2:2 honours degree. GCSE grade C or above in English language, mathematics and a science subject before applying.

Candidates should have at least two weeks' recent experience in a UK primary school prior to application. Applicants for primary French normally require an A level in French although a good GCSE pass may be considered. Candidates who demonstrate that they meet the university's French speaking competence requirements may also be considered.

PGCE Secondary (11-18) - 1 year full-time
This is a Postgraduate Certificate in Education with a weighting of 60 credits at master's level.

Main subjects offered subject to government allocation: Biology, chemistry, English (with drama), geography, history, mathematics, modern foreign languages (French, German, Spanish), physics and religious education.

Entry requirements: GCSE grade C or above in English language and mathematics before commencement of the course. A 2:2 honours degree in a relevant subject (normally at least 50% of the degree content should be in the subject you wish to teach; closely related subjects may be accepted; please contact the university for specific queries). Candidates should have recent experience in a UK secondary school prior to application. An additional requirement for applicants to the modern foreign languages PGCE is that they must have spent a year abroad.

OTHER INFORMATION

Entry route: PG/FT/1 year

Awards: PGCE QTS. The PGCE carries 60 master's level credits, equivalent to one third of the 180 credits for the Master's in Education course. Successful completion of the PGCE gives the option, whilst teaching, of direct entry to year two of the university's part-time MEd Practitioner Enquiry programme.

As a result of their teaching placements, trainees must demonstrate compliance with all Qualified Teacher Status standards.

Newcastle College

Institution code: N23

Rye Hill Campus
Scotswood Road
Newcastle upon Tyne
NE4 5BR
t: **0191 200 4000**
f: **0191 200 4349**
e: **enquiries@ncl-coll.ac.uk**
// **www.newcastlecollege.co.uk**

FACT FILE

- Lead organisation in Success North, a centre for excellence in teacher training.
- Career focussed courses - right balance of classroom learning with hands-on experience.
- Clear progression route - with honours degree programme and masters' level study.
- Support for new and experienced teachers - helping you succeed.
- Tailor made courses - so you get the best learning experience.
- A range of delivery modes, including a blended learning option - flexibility for you.

AREAS OF STUDY

We offer a full range of programmes ideally suited to both experienced teachers and those who want to teach in any area of the post-16 sector. The teaching development team allows us to offer training in any subject and provide fully integrated courses for ESOL/literacy and numeracy teachers.

Our courses lead to a full teaching qualification and we can offer progress onto our honours degree programme, masters' level courses and a range of CPD opportunities which will help you to maintain QTLS (qualified status).

Professional placements/live projects/careers

We offer placements in a range of teaching contexts, alongside careers guidance. There will be observations of experienced teachers and taster days - which give you a snap shot of what teaching is like.

OUR COURSES INCLUDE:

Certificate of Education in Teaching in the Lifelong Learning Sector part-time (DTLLS)*
Certificate of Education in Teaching in the Lifelong Learning Sector full-time (DTLLS)*
Postgraduate Certificate in Teaching in the Lifelong Learning Sector* (subject to validation)
Certificate of Education in Teaching in the Lifelong Learning Sector (DTLLS Literacy)*
Certificate of Education in Teaching in the Lifelong Learning Sector (DTLLS Numeracy)
Diploma of Higher Education Lifelong Learning (Teacher Education)*
Diploma in English Language Teaching to Adults DELTA (Cambridge)
Diploma in Teaching English (ESOL) in the Lifelong Learning Sector (Cambridge)
Additional Diploma in Teaching English ESOL in the Lifelong Learning Sector (Cambridge)
Foundation Degree in Teaching in the Lifelong Learning Sector (subject to validation)
BA (Hons) Lifelong Learning and Professional Development (Year One)*
BA (Hons) Lifelong Learning and Professional Development (Year Two)*
MA Lifelong Learning and Professional Development (two year part-time)*
*validated by Leeds Metropolitan University

All candidates apply direct to Newcastle College and will undergo a compulsory interview.

For entry requirements, course codes, duration, and timetable, please visit
www.newcastlecollege.co.uk.

Newman University College

Genners Lane
Bartley Green
Birmingham B32 3NT
t: 0121 476 1181
// www.newman.ac.uk

GENERAL INFORMATION

Newman University College, Birmingham has an established reputation for producing high quality teachers, who understand the needs of the children they teach, and develop creative and effective practice. Newman offers a range of teacher training courses at Early Years, Primary and Secondary level through our undergraduate, postgraduate and employment-based programmes.

In recent years very positive inspection reports have been received from the QAA and Ofsted, including an 'outstanding' grade, the highest possible, for its latest inspection for Employment Based Initial Teacher Training (Graduate Teacher Programme).

Undergraduate teaching BA (Hons) with QTS
- Primary Education: Early Years
- Key Stage 2/3 (7-14) in: ICT and Science

Secondary: Through a partnership with Aston University there is the opportunity to study for a combined honours degree in mathematics or chemistry at Aston and gain QTS in maths or science through Newman.

PGCE - Postgraduate and Professional Graduate Certificate
- Primary (3-7) and (5-11)
- Primary (5-11) with EAL
- Primary (5-11) with French, German or Spanish

Secondary
- Citizenship
- English
- Information and communications technology
- Mathematics

- Modern foreign languages
- Physical education
- Religious education
- Science

Employment-based training
- Graduate Teacher Programme (GTP)
- Overseas Trained Teacher Programme

Other education-related courses
- Early Childhood Education and Care BA (Hons) full and part-time routes, Foundation Degree and MA
- MA Education
- Education Studies BA (Hons) and MA
- MA Physical Education and Sports Studies
- Teaching and Learning Support Assistants (Foundation Degree)
- Theology for Education BA (Hons) and Contemporary Christian Theology MA
- MA Colonial and Post-colonial Literature

Entry requirements:
Undergraduate: A minimum of 280 to 300 UCAS points including at least two grades C or above at A2, or equivalent. Plus GCSEs in English, mathematics and science at grade C or above (or equivalent) are also required before applying. Shortlisted candidates must attend an interview and pass literacy and numeracy tests. CRB clearance and school experience in a relevant Key Stage are required prior to interview.

PGCEs: In addition to the above, a good first degree in a relevant area, experience in school and an understanding of current educational issues.

Postgraduate - master's degrees: A good relevant first degree and equivalent previous experience.

Caerleon Campus
Lodge Road
Newport NP18 3QT
t: **01633 432 432**
e: **uic@newport.ac.uk**
// **www.newport.ac.uk**

GENERAL INFORMATION

Teacher training at Newport is provided for by the South East Wales Centre for Teacher Education and Training, a collaboration between the University of Wales, Newport and Cardiff Metropolitan University. Teacher training at Newport has a long established reputation for the quality of its training that includes Primary and an innovative undergraduate route into Secondary teaching. Furthermore, the university has responded to the major changes which have occured nationally, where there is a greater focus on education in a wider social context, by developing a thriving range of education and humanities degree courses. These open up a variety of employment opportunities beyond that of the traditional classroom teacher.

ACADEMIC AWARDS

BA (Hons) Primary Studies with QTS
BA (Anrh) Astudiaethau Cynradd gyda SAC
BA (Hons) Education, Early Years, Education Studies or Inclusive Education
BA (Hons) Creative and Therapeutic Arts
BA (Hons) Applied Drama
BSc (Hons) Secondary Teaching Design and Technology with QTS
BSc Secondary Teaching (2-year shortened degree with QTS)

Four course choices:

- 2 year BSc (Hons) Mathematics with Science
- 2 year BSc (Hons) Science with Mathematics
- 2 year BSc (Hons) Mathematics with ICT
- 2 year BSc (Hons) Science with ICT

with the additional award 3 year BSc (Hons) Design and Technology.

Entry requirements - for 2 year BSc degrees only
These include the successful completion of one year of higher education or equivalent.

For the 3 year BSC (Hons) Secondary Teaching Design and Technology with QTS course, applicants need to check the university prospectus for the current UCAS points needed.

Introduction to Secondary Teaching - Certificate of Higher Education
Entry requirements
Formal academic qualifications are not essential. Successful completion of this course will meet the academic entry requirements to progress to one of the four BSc Secondary Teaching 2-year degrees.

Entry requirements
*Minimum 2.2 honours degree. Maths and English GCSE grade C. (equivalency tests offered.) The varied nature of design and technology means our PGCE design and technology student teachers have degrees in a variety of related subjects. These include, graphics, product design, engineering, building, food science, textiles and fashion to name just a few.

PGCE Adult Basic Skills (ESOL, Literacy or Numeracy)
PGCE Post Compulsory Education
PGCE Secondary Design & Technology*

Boughton Green Road
Northampton NN2 7AL
t: 01604 892 203
f: 01604 713 029
e: admissions@northampton.ac.uk
// www.northampton.ac.uk

ACADEMIC AWARD

PGCE
Early Years
The course prepares trainees to become teachers of EYFS and the National Curriculum at Key Stage 1.

Primary
The course prepares students to teach the National Curriculum (Key Stages 1 & 2) with an emphasis on the core subjects.

Both courses contain two interlinked strands - professional and modules at MA level. Teaching approaches are highly interactive and a substantial part of the course will be spent in partner schools. This will include at least four different placements in three different Key Stages by the end of the course.

Entry requirements:
- Minimum 2:2 honours degree (2:1 preferred)
- GCSE English language, mathematics and science at grade C or above or equivalent with higher grades preferred. These must be secured prior to application
- A minimum of ten days school/setting experience in a UK state primary school or Early Years setting that follows the National Curriculum /Early Years Foundation Stage approach to practice. This must have been gained within the last two years.

Intended intake:
Early Years - 26
Primary - 104

Application route: Apply through the GTTR

Contact: justine.edwards@northampton.ac.uk

BA (Hons) Early Years (QTS)
This is an intensive full-time programme over three years which has been designed for those wishing to teach three to seven year old children.

BA (Hons) Primary (QTS)
This is an intensive full-time programme over three years which has been designed for those wishing to teach in the primary sector (5-11).

Both courses include significant school experience and are assessed by examinations, observation of practical teaching and dissertation. QTS is awarded at the end of the course.

Entry requirements:
- a minimum of ten days recent experience in a UK state primary school/early years setting that follows the National Curriculum/Early Years Foundation Stage approach to practice
- GCSE English language, mathematics and science at grade C minimum (or equivalent) with higher grades preferred. These must be secured prior to application (applicants studying towards Access Diplomas are exempt from this specific constraint).
- a broad and secure profile of academic attainment alongside a general capability in literacy, numeracy and ICT.

Intended intake:
Primary - 115
Early Years - 26

Application route: Apply through UCAS.

Contact: katrina.turvey@northampton.ac.uk

Northampton Teacher Training Partnership

Institution code: N42

c/o Northampton School for Boys
Billing Road
Northampton NN1 5RT
t: **01604 258 662**
f: **01604 258 659**
e: **nttp@nsb.northants.sch.uk**
// **www.nttp.org.uk**

GENERAL INFORMATION

The NTTP is a school-centred initial teacher training provider based in Northampton. Partner schools include secondary schools (11-18) and rural 11-18 and 11-16 comprehensive schools.

All schools involved in the partnership have gone through rigorous selection procedures.

The Northampton Teacher Training Partnership has an enthusiasm for the delivery of high standards of teaching and learning, and the responsibility for delivering them. The partnership, an exciting consortium comprising secondary schools, is committed to making a full contribution to the recruitment and training of high quality teachers to the profession to ensure effective teaching and learning in the future. The partnership has an outstanding record of trainee employment.

Delivery

You will spend 36 weeks with the partnership, 26 of which are based in schools learning the craft of teaching and classroom management. You will spend up to two weeks at a primary school looking at your subject at Key Stage 2.

In addition, you will have subject and general professional studies sessions looking more specifically at the academic rigour of the profession.

There will be occasions throughout the course when you can evaluate your experiences both in the classroom and in the more formally taught studies.

Tuition fees

Fees from September 2012 will be set at £8,100 pa for eligible 'home' trainees. Fees for non-eligible trainees are set at a higher rate (see our website **www.nttp.org.uk** for further details).

ACADEMIC AWARD

PGCE (validated by the University of Bedfordshire) and QTS. Trainees with the partnership will obtain the dual awards of PGCE/QTS at the end of a successful year. The PGCE is professional (P level). Applicants may ask about this choice at interview.

Main subjects offered and intended intakes:

- Biology - 2 trainees
- Chemistry - 2 trainees
- Design technology - 4 trainees
- English - 5 trainees
- Mathematics - 5 trainees
- Physics - 2 trainees

The lead school also has:

- Modern foreign languages - 3 places
- Music - 2 places
- Physical education - 3 places

under the Schools Direct scheme. Contact Northampton School for Boys on 01604 230240.

Entry requirements:

- GCSE/equivalent C or above in English language and mathematics.
- A relevant degree of which at least 50% is in your chosen subject.
- A degree plus relevant recent experience in the subject you wish to teach.

Application route: Please apply through the GTTR.

OTHER INFORMATION

All trainees who successfully achieved the award of PGCE/QTS, for the last seven years, gained employment in good mainly local schools.

North Essex Teacher Training (NETT)

Institution code: N46

Clacton Coastal Academy
Jaywick Lane
Clacton on Sea
Essex CO16 8BE
t: 01255 431949
f: 01255 421377
e: teach@coastalscitt.co.uk
// www.coastalscitt.co.uk

GENERAL INFORMATION

The confederation offers a school-centred training route into teaching which suits mature entrants and young graduates alike. Our 10-month training programme leads to an 11-18 Secondary PGCE award as well as Qualified Teacher Status, and is amongst the longest running and most successful schemes in the country.

Last year 100% of trainees gained teaching posts.

ACADEMIC AWARDS

PGCE Secondary (11-18) - 1 year full-time
Courses are offered at Professional Graduate level in conjunction with University Campus, Suffolk and validated by the University of East Anglia and University of Essex.

Main courses offered:
- English
- History
- Information technology
- Mathematics
- Science

Entry requirements
- GCSE grade C in English language and mathematics
- Award of 2:2 honours degree or equivalent

OTHER INFORMATION

Entry route: PG/FT/1year
Awards: PGCE QTS
Intended intake: 24
Application route: Apply through the GTTR
Enquiries: Please use the above contact details for any queries.

North East Partnership PGCE Physical Education SCITT

Institution code: N55

Northumbria University
School of Health
Community and Education Studies
Coach Lane Campus
Coach Lane
Newcastle upon Tyne NE7 7XA
t: **0191 243 7900**
f: **0191 227 4561**
e: **hs.admissions@northumbria.ac.uk**

GENERAL INFORMATION

The North East Partnership is a consortium of local secondary schools in the north east of England, providing school-centred initial teacher training in secondary physical education. Northumbria University is the managing agent for the partnership.

This specialist physical education programme, leading to the award of Professional Graduate Certificate in Education, is designed for those wishing to achieve Qualified Teacher Status at Secondary level. The course is structured to develop the skills required to teach across the spectrum of activities in the National Curriculum for physical education, with trainees acquiring the knowledge, skills, understanding and professional standards necessary to teach pupils within Key Stage 3, Key Stage 4 and beyond.

Teaching is a diverse, creative and dynamic activity, and this is reflected in the design of the course. A strong foundation of experiential learning in the school environment is complemented by a comprehensive support system of mentoring and guidance. Trainees are encouraged to experiment with a range of teaching styles and strategies and reflect upon their practice in order to achieve high professional standards.

Students are assessed against the standards for the award of Qualified Teacher Status. Professional practice is undertaken and assessed in two different schools within the north east region and in addition, coursework assignments, a curriculum project and a professional portfolio provide further evidence of suitability to enter the teaching profession.

Entry requirements: Applicants should usually have:
- GCSE grade C in English language and mathematics
- a 2:1 honours degree or equivalent with a substantial sport or physical education content
- a broad and balanced physical education, sport or dance background, particularly in activities associated with the National Curriculum for physical education
- the ability to swim a minimum of 400 metres continuously using two different strokes (evidence of swimming ability required)
- work experience in a secondary school physical education department
- competence in information and communication technology.

Intended intake: 20

Application route: Apply through the GTTR.

The Langdale Centre
Langdale Gardens
Howdon
Wallsend
Tyne and Wear
NE28 0HG
t: 0191 643 8855
f: 0191 643 8596

GENERAL INFORMATION

This course is constructed around a strong partnership between North Tyneside Local Authority (LA) as the managing agent, and a consortium of local schools. The partnership brings together a strong school practice base and the expertise of the LA School Improvement Service, in a high quality postgraduate programme for initial teacher education (ITE) which is validated by Northumbria University.

The course is taught at the Langdale Centre in North Tyneside, a high quality training and development centre. Students have access to a range of practice loan resources and books as well as the facilities of Northumbria University library.

The programme is structured around elements that will enable all the standards for the award of Qualified Teacher Status (QTS). These elements include:

- subject knowledge and its application in the Early Years Foundation Stage and Key Stage 1;
- professional issues in teaching;
- early childhood pedagogy - how children learn;
- placement - students will undertake assessed placements in two different North Tyneside schools and in addition will experience a range of other school-based training.

A variety of assessment methods are used, including written assignments, presentations and practical work in school. The final school placement represents a vital component of this assessment. The standards for QTS require trainees to be successful in all areas, and from the outset each trainee is involved in auditing their own learning and setting targets for their own professional development.

Entry requirements: Entrants must hold a good honours degree from a UK university or a recognised equivalent qualification. Applicants previous education must provide the necessary foundation for work as a primary school teacher. Applicants must also have GCSE (or a recognised equivalent) grade C or above in mathematics, English and a science subject. Applicants will be expected to have had at least two weeks' recent and relevant experience of work with young children in a school (3-7 years) before attending interview.

Candidates invited for interview are provided with an opportunity to experience a consortium school at first hand. School and SCITT staff are members of the interviewing panels. Trainees must be prepared to demonstrate their own suitability for an offer of a place. Interview results are communicated as soon as possible after the interview takes place, but any offer or acceptance of a place is conditional upon receipt of a satisfactory medical report and police clearance.

Intended intake: 35

Application route: Apply through the GTTR.

Northumbria University
School of Health
Community and Education Studies
Coach Lane Campus
Benton
Newcastle upon Tyne NE7 7XA
t: **0191 243 7900**
f: **0191 227 4561**
e: **hs.admissions@northumbria.ac.uk**

GENERAL INFORMATION

This 36-week school centred initial teacher training (SCITT) programme is delivered by a consortium of local secondary schools with Northumbria University acting as managing agent. The programme simultaneously meets the requirement for the award of Qualified Teacher Status (QTS), and successful trainees gain a Professional Graduate Certificate in Education (PGCE) validated by the university, and a recommendation for QTS. The SCITT partnership delivers:

- training and teaching in two secondary schools across the whole ability range and in the requisite Key Stages
- subject group workshops to enhance, acquire and apply subject knowledge and skills
- teaching experience in PHSE/citizenship and the role of form tutor
- training in general professional studies and National Curriculum: design and technology
- training in assessment and standardisation, class management, and legal and contractual responsibilities
- easy and regular access to pupils, teachers, tutors and parents
- a group design and technology workshop in a primary school (awareness of transition between Key Stages 2 and 3)
- training and experience in special educational needs, including the gifted and talented.
- training in CAD/CAM.

The course recruits to and develops trainees' specialist skills in two of the five areas of design and technology, or one vocational subject. Candidates study one strand from the five offered:

- Food and textiles 11-16
- Product design and textiles 11-16
- Food and health and social care 11-16
- Health and social care and food 14-19
- Material component technology and product design 11-16.

Candidates enter the programme with one area of specialism, which they will train to teach to the higher Key Stage in the strand. The programme enables the development of knowledge and skill in the second subject to teach Key Stage 3 but for strand 3, Key Stage 4. Trainees' individual needs are identified and met through audit, individualised training programmes and review.

Entry requirements: Applicants should have a 2:1 honours degree from a UK university or an equivalent qualification in a subject that strongly relates to at least one of the two subjects in the chosen strand, plus GCSEs in mathematics and English language at grade C or above.

Entrants will be expected to test their career choice by visiting secondary schools, preferably prior to the interview. A longer period of time in school with secondary age pupils is highly desirable.

Intended intake: 25

Application route: Apply through the GTTR.

Northumbria University
School of Health
Community and Education Studies
Coach Lane Campus
Benton
Newcastle upon Tyne NE7 7XA
t: 0191 243 7900
f: 0191 227 4561
e: hs.admissions@northumbria.ac.uk

GENERAL INFORMATION

Northumbria University has gained an enviable reputation for the high quality of its initial teacher training courses. Teaching is a diverse, creative and dynamic activity and the design of all of the courses offered within the School of Health, Community and Education Studies reflects this. Trainees are encouraged to experiment with a range of teaching styles and strategies and to reflect upon best practice in order to achieve high professional standard.

ACADEMIC AWARDS

BA (Hons) Early Primary Education
PGCE Primary Education (Full Time)
PGCE Early Years and Primary Education (Flexible)
PGCE Secondary Art
Graduate Teacher Programme (GTP)

PGCE programmes lead to the award of a Postgraduate Certificate in Education with QTS.

All primary education programmes have been graded as category A by Ofsted.

Northumbria University also validates and is the managing agent for the SCITT provision in design and technology and physical education (see entries for N55 and N76).

As well as courses leading to Qualified Teacher Status, the university offers a range of other education programmes at undergraduate, postgraduate and professional graduate level, including some which lead to Early Years Professional Status. Further information can be found on our website at
www.northumbria.ac.uk.

Entry requirements
All courses require the achievement in English language and mathematics at GCSE grade C or above. In addition, applicants to Primary education must also have GCSE grade C or above in science.

BA (Hons) Early Primary Education
280 UCAS Tariff points. Candidates should have studied subjects to an advanced level which reflect the content of the Primary National Curriculum. In addition, candidates must have recent and relevant experience in mainstream UK primary schools (including work in an Early Years setting). It is also advantageous to have experience of working with children in an informal setting, for example Sunday school, guides or cubs.

PGCE
Applicants must hold a good honours degree (normally 2.1 or above) from a UK university or a recognised equivalent qualification. For PGCE Primary (and flexible), within the previous year and prior to application, applicants must normally have at least 15 days of experience in mainstream UK schools in Key Stage 1 and/or Key Stage 2 and this should be itemised on the application form.

Application routes
Undergraduate applications through UCAS
Postgraduate applications through the GTTR

School of Education
The Dearing Building
Jubilee Campus
Nottingham NG8 1BB
t: 0115 951 4543
f: 0115 846 6600
// www.nottingham.ac.uk/education

GENERAL INFORMATION

The School of Education is situated on the state-of-the art Jubilee Campus in central Nottingham. As well as training a large cohort of new teachers each year in partnership with schools across the region, we offer higher degrees and courses to large numbers of serving teachers.

Local interest/activities
Nottingham is renowned for its excellent social and cultural facilities and is one of the most popular cities for students in the country. The sporting facilities include the National Ice Stadium and the tennis centre.

Accommodation
Most PGCE students live in privately-rented accommodation near to the university. There is some university accommodation available.

Leisure facilities
The University of Nottingham has superb sports facilities based in the sports centre on the University Park campus. These facilities include a swimming pool, gym, a nationally-renowned tennis centre and a football pitch.

ACADEMIC AWARDS

Students on PGCE courses will normally complete two 30-credit master's level modules in addition to QTS.

Please note: intended intakes are subject to change depending on Teaching Agency allocations for 2012-13.

PGCE (11-19)
Intended intake based on 2011-12 allocations:
226

Main subjects offered:
- English
- Geography
- History
- Mathematics
- Modern languages
- Physics with mathematics
- Science (biology, chemistry, physics)

Graduate Teacher Programme (GTP)
(full-time, 11-16) with PGCE - one year and
school-based training with a salary
Intended intake based on 2011-12 allocations: 39

Main subjects offered:
- English
- Mathematics
- Languages
- Science (biology, chemistry, physics)

The self-funded GTP is also offered. Please contact us for details.

Application route: GTP applications through the TDA. PGCE applications through the GTTR. Early application is advisable for both programmes.

Enquiries: Please make all enquiries to the address above.

School of Education
Ada Byron King Building
Clifton Campus
Clifton Lane
Nottingham NG11 8NS
t: 0115 848 4200
f: 0115 848 8967
e: ask.ntu@ntu.ac.uk
// www.ntu.ac.uk/edu

GENERAL INFORMATION

Visit our website **www.ntu.ac.uk.**

ACADEMIC AWARDS

BA (Hons) Primary Education
This four year degree is designed for students who wish to become a primary school teacher and leads to both a recommendation for Qualified Teacher Status (QTS) and an honours degree.

Entry requirements: Grades BBC achieved from three A levels (one of which should be in a Primary National Curriculum subject or one related to child development) or equivalent, general studies is not accepted. A minimum of five GCSE passes including English, and mathematics at minimum grade B and science at grade C or above. School observation experience is essential.

Application route: Apply through UCAS using code X101.

BSc(Hons) Secondary Design and Technology Education
This three year degree prepares you to teach design and technology within a secondary school in two specialist areas and leads to both a recommendation for Qualified Teacher Status (QTS) and an honours degree.

Entry requirements: 240 UCAS Tariff points typically achieved from a maximum of three A levels or a combination of two A levels and two AS levels or equivalent (one of which must be in a design and technology related subject); GCSE mathematics and English at minimum grade C or equivalent. These must have been gained prior to application. School observation experience is essential.

Application route: Apply through UCAS using code XWC2.

BSc (Hons) Secondary Physical Science Education
This three year course focuses on the core curriculum subjects of physics and chemistry at secondary school level, and leads to a recommendadtion for Qualified Teacher Status (QTS) and an honours degree.

Entry requirements: 220 UCAS Tariff points typically achieved from three A levels or a combination of two A levels and two AS levels, one A level must be physics or chemistry. General studies is accepted as an A level. GCSE English and maths at minimum grade C.

Application route: Apply through UCAS using code XF19.

PGCE Primary
This one year course is offered at both professional and postgraduate award level. It is designed for graduates who wish to become a primary school teacher and leads to a recommendation for Qualified Teacher Status (QTS).

Entry requirements: A good UK honours degree or equivalent, preferably at a minimum 2:2 which can be related to the Primary National Curriculum. GCSE English, mathematics and science at minimum grade C or equivalent. These must have been gained prior to application. School observation experience is essential.

Nottingham Trent University
continued

Application route: Apply through the GTTR.

PGCE Secondary
This one year course is offered at both professional and postgraduate award level. It is designed for graduates who wish to become a secondary school teacher, specialising in a subject area. The course leads to a recommendation for Qualified Teacher Status (QTS). Secondary specialisms include: biology, business education, chemistry, design and technology, engineering, English, ICT, applied ICT, mathematics, music and physics.

Entry requirements: A good UK honours degree or equivalent, preferably at a minimum 2:2 in a related subject. GCSE English and mathematics at grade C or equivalent. These must have been gained prior to application. School observation experience is essential.

Application route: Apply through the GTTR.

Graduate Teacher Programme (Primary and Secondary)
This one year employment-based route into teaching requires applicants to have had some experience in school. GTP trainees follow the Postgraduate Certificate in Education (PGCE) with Qualified Teacher Status (QTS) route. Secondary specialisms include: business education, biology, chemistry, design and technology, English, ICT, mathematics, music, PE and physics among others.

Entry requirements: A good UK honours degree or equivalent at a minimum grade 2:1 (primary) or 2:2 (secondary). Secondary teacher trainees usually need a degree in a subject related to the one they want to teach. GCSE English or mathematics grade C minimum or equivalent. Primary teacher trainees need GCSE physics, chemistry or biology grade C minimum or equivalent. These must have been gained prior to application. School observation experience is essential.

Subject Knowledge Enhancement course in Chemistry, Physics or Mathematics
These courses are for graduates who need to develop their subject knowledge prior to beginning a PGCE or GTP course.

Entry requirements for enhancement courses: You will only be considered if you have applied for a GTP or a PGCE course through GTTR.

Application route for enhancement courses: For further information contact the university direct. **www.ntu.ac.uk/edu**

Nottingham City Primary SCITT

Institution code: N/A (Do not recruit through UCAS or GTTR)

c/o The Nottingham Wildcats Arena
Greenwood Road, Bakersfield
Nottingham NG3 7EB
t: 0115 9155633
f: 0115 9155628
e: info@teachnottingham.co.uk
// www.teachnottingham.co.uk

GENERAL INFORMATION

Qualify to teach with Nottingham City Primary SCITT:

- An innovative partnership with inner city primary schools.

Our course is distinctive because:

- our training is in the inner city
- our course is taught by experienced and exceptional inner city teachers
- the majority of our training is 'hands on' school-based training
- we offer specific training on meeting the needs of inner city children in order to give them the life chances which are their entitlement
- we are proactive in supporting successful trainees in gaining teaching appointments in inner city schools.

Course organisation:

- school experience with mentor support
- subject specific lecture input
- block teaching practices in at least two SCITT schools in Key Stage 1 and Key Stage 2.

ACADEMIC AWARD

Successful completion of the course will lead to the award of Qualified Teacher Status, General Primary.

Entry requirements: Academic and non-academic, can be found in the application pack, but broadly include:

- * a degree minimum level 2.1
- * GCSE grade B or equivalent in English language, mathematics and science.
- * We reserve the right to interview candidates with a level 2.2 degree or GCSE grade C.
- 10 days' relevant and recent primary school experience (preferably in an inner city school)
- good written and verbal communication skills
- positive attitudes to inner-city teaching.

Overseas trained students must seek evidence of qualification equivalence from NARIC.

*Please refer to our application pack on our website for a full comprehensive list of entry requirements and general information regarding our course.

Application and enquiries route: Apply direct to Nottingham City Primary SCITT. Applications are particularly welcome from minority ethnic and male candidates who are currently under-represented within our city schools. Please phone or email with your name and address for an application pack.

The Open University

Institution code: N/A (Do not recruit through UCAS or GTTR)

The Open University
PO Box 197
Milton Keynes
MK7 6BJ
t: +44 (0)845 300 60 90
e: general-enquiries@open.ac.uk
// www.open-university.co.uk

GENERAL INFORMATION

The Open University (OU) offers the Professional Graduate Certificate in Education (PGCE) in England, Wales and Northern Ireland. We also offer a similar qualification, a Professional Graduate Diploma of Education (PGDE), in mathematics in Scotland.

With our partners in schools we¿re offering a different route into profession, one that opens up a host of opportunities to graduates who want to teach but who, for one reason or another, require a more flexible and individualised approach to Initial Teacher Education (ITE).

THE COURSE

Studying for a PGCE with The Open University can provide the foundations of a successful and rewarding career as a secondary school teacher. Our flexible Professional Graduate Certificate in Education (PGCE) incorporates Qualified Teacher Status (QTS) and offers courses in six secondary subjects: design and technology, geography, mathematics, modern foreign languages (French, German, Spanish), science (biology, chemistry, physics) and music. You could also be eligible for a bursary of up to £20,000 (conditions apply).

The course is divided into three levels: Familiarisation (Level 1), Consolidation (Level 2) and Autonomy (Level 3). The levels are designed to help you to progress from a highly supportive context at Level 1, through to collaborative experiences at Level 2, towards

extended sequences of solo teaching at Level 3. At each level you will complete module study using online materials on the course website.

At each level, you will also complete a school-based placement . The Level 1 placement lasts for five weeks. Level 2 for eight weeks and Level 3 for ten weeks. At each level you will submit an assessment portfolio which includes evidence that you meet the Professional Standards and PGCE/PGDE outcomes at each level. Throughout the course, you will be supported by a personal tutor.

If you have already successfully completed a Professional Graduate Certificate in Education (PGCE) either with the OU or another institution, you can convert your professional level qualification into a Postgraduate Certificate in Education by completing our 60-credit master's module, Reflecting on professional learning in education.

The course requires you to reflect on your experience and learning from the Professional Graduate Certificate in Education. You will also have to complete an extended, analytical piece of writing that relates your theoretical understanding to your thought processes and practice as a teacher.

Credit from successful completion of this course can also be counted towards our Master's degree in Education.

Applications are accepted at any time of the year. Admission is selective and involves assessing your qualifications and the information you provide on your application form. As part of the selection process, candidates will be interviewed and will complete a subject-related task.

If you are interested in this route into the teaching profession, see our Professional Graduate Certificate in Education qualification description for full details or for further information, visit
www.open-university.co.uk.

Oxford University

Institution code: O33

Department of Education
15 Norham Gardens
Oxford OX2 6PY
t: 01865 274 020/179
f: 01865 274 027
e: pgce.office@education.ox.ac.uk
// www.education.ox.ac.uk/

GENERAL INFORMATION

The Oxford Internship Scheme (through which the PGCE is offered) involves a close partnership between the university department and local comprehensive schools. This enables all aspects of the course to be planned, carried out and evaluated jointly by university and school staff. This partnership results in a course which integrates work in the university and in school throughout the year.

In the most recent Ofsted inspection it was awarded the highest grades in all categories.

The scheme prepares graduates to teach in the following subjects: English, geography, history, mathematics, modern foreign languages (French, German, Italian and Spanish), physics with mathematics, religious education and science (biology, chemistry, physics).

ACADEMIC AWARD

The course at Oxford is a Postgraduate Certificate in Education and includes three assignments assessed at master's level, for which students can gain 60 credits towards a full master's degree of 180 credits. The course is full-time for one year, focussing on the 11-18 age range.
Planned intake: 190

Entry requirements:
- Minimum requirements: Candidates wishing to teach a particular subject in school would normally be expected to have studied that subject, or a closely related one, to degree level. Each applicant is considered on merit.
- All applicants must have obtained GCSE or O level passes (grades A-C) in English language and mathematics (or their equivalents) before starting the course. We do not offer equivalence tests.

Application route: GTTR only.

OTHER INFORMATION

Applications are received throughout the academic year or until each subject is full, which in some cases may be as early as December. It is recommended that you apply as early as possible as competition for places on the programme is strong.

All successful applicants will be interviewed in person before acceptance and will have to comply with all government requirements (ie medical fitness, declaration of criminal convictions and appropriate background checks).

The university admissions policy and criteria for interview can be viewed on the department website.

The Oxford University Department of Education positively encourages applications from all sections of the community. It is vital that the teaching profession fully reflects our diverse and pluralistic society.

The School of Education
Oxford OX2 9AT
t: 01865 488600
f: 01865 488356
e: query@brookes.ac.uk
// www.brookes.ac.uk/schools/education

GENERAL INFORMATION

The School of Education is located at Harcourt Hill, to the west of the city of Oxford. Situated on an attractive 110-acre campus overlooking the city, the institute offers the benefits of a complete community on one site. We appeal to those who don't want to be a nameless face in the crowd, and who are looking for a friendly, supportive environment in which they can develop to their full potential. As such, we attract a wide range of students of all ages, religious backgrounds (or none), and from different areas of both this country and abroad.

ACADEMIC AWARDS

BA Hons in Primary Teacher Education - 3 years full-time
Intended intake: 90
Pathways can be chosen during year two and developed in year three to focus on communication and languages, well being or inclusion.

Entry requirements: GCSE English language, mathematics and science at C or above, and three A levels or the equivalent. Experience of primary school classrooms.

Entry route: BBC at A level; BB at A level plus CC at AS level; one 12-unit vocational A level at B plus one A level, IB Diploma 30 points. BTEC DMM, Cache Diploma B or Access to HE Pass.
Application route: Apply through UCAS.

BA Hons in Primary Teacher Education - 4 years work-based part-time
Intended intake: 30
Please contact The School of Education for details.

Postgraduate Certificate in Education (Primary)
Professional Graduate Certificate in Education (Primary) - 1 year full-time
PGCE Primary with two age phase routes: 3-7 (Foundation Stage/Key Stage 1) and 5-11 (Key Stage 1/Key Stage 2).

Students will be enrolled and initially assessed at M level in two modules. This award will give the student 40 M level CATS.

Intended intake: 250
Entry requirements: Normally a recognised degree at 2:2 or above or degree equivalent and GCSE English, mathematics and science at grade C or above. Recent primary classroom experience required.
Application route: Apply through the GTTR.

Postgraduate Certificate in Education (Secondary)
Professional Certificate in Education (Secondary) - 1 year full-time
Intended intake: 85

Main subjects offered:

- English
- Mathematics
- Modern languages (French, French with German, French with Spanish, German with French)
- Physics and mathematics
- Science with chemistry
- Science with physics

Entry requirements: Recognised degree in an area of study related to the subject specialism at 2:2 or above and GCSE English and mathematics at grade C or above. All applicants are encouraged to enquire direct concerning their particular qualification mix.
Application route: Apply through the GTTR.

Two-year Subject Knowledge Enhancement (SKE) courses in mathematics and science are also offered.

The Priory Centre
63 Newnham Avenue
Bedford MK41 9QJ
t: 01234 408590
f: 01234 408591
// www.pilgrim-partnership.org.uk
Principal: Martin Thompson

GENERAL INFORMATION

The Pilgrim Partnership is a consortium of Bedfordshire nursery, lower and middle schools. The course has well-established links with the continuing professional development undertaken by practising teachers and the wider school workforce in the Foundation Stage, Key Stage 1 and Key Stage 2.

ACADEMIC AWARDS

The one-year full-time course, covering three school terms, leads to Qualified Teacher Status for primary teaching. We offer three routes into teaching. Early Years with PG Cert (60 master's credits), General Primary and Primary with Mathematics or MFL. Further details are available on our website.

Entry requirements:

- A UK first degree or equivalent qualification, 2:2 or above
- GCSE grade C or equivalent in English language, mathematics and science.
- Clear communication skills.
- The ability to work as part of a team.
- Self-motivation, self-evaluation and self-organisation.
- An understanding of, and positive attitude to, equal opportunities.
- Significant professional potential.
- A willingness and ability to travel between different training locations within Bedfordshire.

OTHER INFORMATION

A distinctive feature of the school-centred initial teacher training is that the course is focused on carefully staged and appropriately supervised practical classroom experience within at least two schools, which is further supported by academic study in the form of lectures and workshops held at the study centre in Bedford. There are excellent resources both in terms of access to study materials (including ICT facilities) and the experience of staff in delivering teacher training to meet current QTS requirements. The partnership was rated as good with outstanding features by Ofsted in 2010.

Details of bursaries offered and fees to be charged are available on our website.

Intended intake: 75
Application route: Apply through the GTTR.
Enquiries: Mrs Jackie Atkin (Director of Operations)
The Priory Centre
63 Newnham Avenue
Bedford MK41 9QJ
t: 01234 408590
e: jackie.atkin@pilgrim-partnership.org.uk

Plymouth University

Institution code: P60

Faculty of Health, Education and Society
Drake Circus
Plymouth
Devon PL4 8AA
t: 01752 586863

GENERAL INFORMATION

The Faculty of Health, Education and Society at Plymouth University has long enjoyed a distinguished reputation for the training of teachers. Furthermore, the school of education was rated as Outstanding in the 2011 Ofsted inspection and is recognised by the Teaching Agency as a Grade A provider. It is also proud of its excellent graduate employment rates.

Located between the counties of Devon and Cornwall, Plymouth is a vibrant and cosmopolitan city graced with a setting amongst the finest in Europe. Its arts scene is lively; its entertainment eclectic; and its history is rich.

The South West offers unsurpassed beauty and unparalleled opportunity for enjoyment. From secluded sandy coves to wild and rugged moors, there is more scope for sport and leisure than almost anywhere else in Britain.

Accommodation
The University of Plymouth offers a variety of rooms in halls of residence. All halls are self-catered, of mixed gender and are situated in the city centre within ten minutes' walk of the campus, main shopping areas and nightlife.

We also offer a large and varied selection of university-approved accommodation. Our accommodation database contains over 5,000 rooms and each property is inspected and graded by trained staff to ensure safety and quality standards are maintained.

Students' union and leisure facilities
As well as a lively social scene, there are plenty of opportunities for students to pursue hobbies and interests. All of our students have access to sports facilities and fitness suites either on campus or locally. On the Plymouth campus, there is a fully-equipped fitness complex with squash courts and cardiovascular and weight resistance equipment.

With 600 miles of coastline, the South West is one of the country's best locations for watersports. Naturally, the university helps you make the most of this by offering you a fantastic range of activities. We have a selection of watersports crafts including two new J80 class keel boats. You can train for a wide range of Royal Yachting Association qualifications including powerboating, BCU canoeing, BWSF waterskiing and wakeboarding or you can just take part in recreational watersports.

ACADEMIC AWARDS

BEd (Primary) with Honours
Main subjects offered:
- Art and design
- Digital literacy
- Early childhood studies (3-7)
- English
- Humanities
- ICT
- Mathematics
- Music
- Physical education
- Science
- Special educational needs (SEN)

PGCE (incorporating the Diploma for Teaching in
the Lifelong Learning Sector)
PGCE Primary and Early Years
PGCE Secondary

Main subjects offered:

- Art and design
- Drama
- English
- Geography
- Mathematics
- Music
- Science (biology, chemistry, physics)

Graduate Teacher Programme (GTP)

This programme is run by the South West Consortium
which covers Somerset, Devon and Cornwall, Torbay
and Plymouth LAs, Plymouth University, Exeter
University and the University College Plymouth St Mark
and St John.

Non-QTS Awards

- BA (Hons) Education Studies
- BA (Hons) Early Childhood Studies
- FdA Children's Workforce

Entry requirements:

- BEd: A level/AS level/Vocational A level: minimum
  240 points (to include two 6-unit or one 12-unit
  award at grade C, one of which must be directly
  relevant to the subject specialism) plus English
  language, mathematics and science GCSE at grade
  C or above. Non-A level qualifications considered.
- BA: A level/AS level/Vocational A level: minimum
  240-280 points (to include two 6-unit or one
  12-unit award at grade C). Non-A level
  qualifications considered.

- PGCE Primary and Early Years: An honours degree
  (2:1 or above) or equivalent from an approved
  institution, plus a GCSE pass at grade C or above in
  English, mathematics and science.
- PGCE Secondary: An honours degree or equivalent
  in a relevant subject from an approved institution,
  plus a GCSE pass at grade C or above in English
  language and mathematics.

All applicants for initial teacher training courses are
required to undertake some observation in schools,
please contact the admissions team for further
information.

OTHER INFORMATION

Application route: BA/BEd/FdA: UCAS; PGCE: GTTR;
GTP: Apply through the GTP.

Address:
South West Consortium
County Hall
Exeter
Devon EX2 4QD.
t: 01392 383578

University College Plymouth St Mark & St John
(UCP Marjon) Institution code: P63

Derriford Road, Plymouth
Devon PL6 8BH
t: 01752 636890
e: admissions@ucpmarjon.ac.uk
// www.ucpmarjon.ac.uk

GENERAL INFORMATION

UCP Marjon's commitment to quality teacher training is reflected in its excellent Ofsted grades. We are one of only 22 institutions rated "outstanding" by Ofsted.

UNDERGRADUATE PROGRAMMES

BEd (Hons) Early Years with QTS
We offer a three-year training course in Early Years to prepare you for teaching children aged from 3 to 8 years in Nursery and Key Stage 1 settings. This course is school-based with student teachers spending two to three days a week in school.

BEd (Hons) Primary with QTS
We also offer a 3-year general training course to prepare you for teaching in primary schools with children aged 5-11. The course will train you to teach all primary curriculum subjects. Teaching practices take place in both Key Stage 1 and Key Stage 2.

BEd (Hons) Secondary Education and Physical Education
Secondary education and physical education with QTS (11-16 with enhancement)

Entry requirements:
Visit **www.ucpmarjon.ac.uk** for full details. Please apply through UCAS.

Pre-PGCE - Subject Knowledge Enhancement Courses
- Chemistry
- French
- Mathematics
- Physics
- Spanish

Postgraduate programmes
- PGCE Early Years
- PGCE Primary
- PGE Primary with Modern Foreign Languages

PGCE Primary and PGCE Primary with modern foreign languages. All graduates embarking on these courses will undertake teaching practices in both key stages.

PGCE Secondary
Main subjects offered:
- English
- Geography
- Mathematics
- Modern foreign languages
- Physical education
- Physics with maths
- Religious education
- Science

Qualified Teacher Status (QTS)
Students undertake examinations set by the Teaching Agency (TA) at the end of their programme. Successful completion of these examinations will lead to the award of QTS.

Entry requirements:
Visit **www.ucpmarjon.ac.uk** for full details. Please apply through the GTTR.

Poole SCITT

Poole SCITT
Ad Astra First School
Sherborn Crescent
Canford Heath
Poole
Dorset BH17 8AP
t: 01202 660822
e: h.best@poole.gov.uk
// www.poolescitt.co.uk

GENERAL INFORMATION

Poole SCITT offers a full-time 5-11 years, primary course leading to a PGCE with Qualified Teacher Status.

The scheme is a partnership between the primary schools of the Borough of Poole and some Bournemouth and Dorset schools, Poole Local Authority and Kingston University to offer initial teacher training at primary school level for up to 30 suitably qualified graduates.

The SCITT is accredited by the Teaching Agency as a provider of initial teacher training, and the course is validated for PGCE status and M level credits, by Kingston University, Surrey. We have consistently excellent graduate employment rates.

Trainees will have experience in three local primary schools during training and will be supervised in each school by a trained school-based tutor. A professional co-ordinator, with expert knowledge and experience of teacher education will oversee and co-ordinate the training during the course under the direction of the SCITT Management Board.

Trainees are automatically registered as students of Kingston University and have access to KU facilities.

Poole SCITT is committed to the inclusion of all eligible participants and welcomes applications from ethnic minority and under-represented groups.

ACADEMIC AWARD

One year full-time PGCE Primary (5-11) with M level credits
Entry requirements:
- GCSE grade C or above in English, mathematics and a science subject.
- An honours degree of class 2:2 or above
- Evidence of recent work experience in primary schools.

Variable tuition fees:
£9,000 for year 2012-2013

OTHER INFORMATION

Entry route: PG/FT/1 year
Award: PGCE, with M level credits
Intake: 30
Applications: via GTTR only
Enquiries: Visit the website for more details about the course and how to apply.

The University of Portsmouth

Institution code: P80

School of Education and Continuing Studies
St George's Building
141 High Street
Portsmouth
Hampshire PO1 2HY
t: 023 9284 5204
e: secs.enquiries@port.ac.uk
// www.port.ac.uk

GENERAL INFORMATION

The historic city of Portsmouth, with its neighbouring seaside town of Southsea, is an ideal place in which to live and study. The university's excellent academic reputation, up-to-date facilities and lively social scene, together with the city's colourful past and its optimism for the future, offer students a stimulating atmosphere in which to learn.

Transport links include rapid rail connections with London (85 minutes) and excellent ferry services to France, Spain and the Isle of Wight, with many discounts for students. Southampton International Airport is 30 minutes away by rail or road; Heathrow International Airport is 1 hour 30 minutes by rail or road; and Gatwick International Airport is 1 hour 30 minutes by rail or road.

Portsmouth PGCE courses are suitable for both recent and mature graduates who wish to become secondary school teachers. The course is designed to enable students to become capable, confident and imaginative teachers at secondary level. Abilities to teach the National Curriculum and encourage learning are developed alongside the skills and understanding required of effective teachers.

The School of Education and Continuing Studies works with over 80 schools throughout Hampshire, the Isle of Wight, Dorset, West Sussex and South Hampshire. Job prospects are excellent: about 80% obtain posts in our local partnership schools.

We offer both the Professional Graduate Certificate in Education and the Postgraduate Certificate in Education, the latter of which will enable trainees to accumulate 60 master's level (M level) credits towards a master's degree.

ACADEMIC AWARD

PGCE Secondary (11-16, except Business Studies 14-19) - 1 year full-time
Main subjects offered:
- Business studies (14-19)
- English
- Geography
- Mathematics
- Modern foreign languages (French, German and/or Spanish, with options in Italian, Japanese, Mandarin and Russian)
- Science (with biology, chemistry or physics)

Additional opportunities
- German and French enhancement courses.
- Subject Knowledge Enhancement courses in physics, chemistry and mathematics.

OTHER INFORMATION

Entry route: PG/FT/1 year
Entry requirements: GCSE grade C or above in English language and mathematics. Relevant degree. All applicants are subject to Criminal Records Bureau clearance and occupational health clearance.
Awards: PGCE QTS - both Professional Graduate Certificate and Postgraduate Certificate (with 60 M level credits)
Intended intake: 100
Application route: Apply through the GTTR.
Enquiries: Please address all postal enquiries to the PGCE Course Administrator.

Portsmouth Primary SCITT

Institution code: P82

Mr M Honour, Training Manager
Ms L McNulty, Course Co-ordinator
Paulsgrove Primary School
Cheltenham Road
Portsmouth PO6 3PL
t: 023 9237 3432
// www.portsmouthscitt.co.uk

GENERAL INFORMATION

Portsmouth Primary SCITT runs a one-year course that qualifies 29 successful students to teach children aged 5-11 years in primary, junior and infant schools. We also provide excellent training for seven early years students per year who work alongside our primary phase trainees, which qualifies them to teach children aged 3-7 years in primary, infant and nursery schools.

All the schools in the partnership are among the best that Portsmouth has to offer. They have been selected for the quality of education they were already providing for Portsmouth children. Each school serves a different catchment area. In practice, this means that Portsmouth SCITT is able to offer a range of training experiences to prospective candidates.

ACADEMIC AWARD

The partnership is able to offer the Postgraduate Certificate of Education (60 level 3 credits and 60 master's level (M level) credits) or the Professional Graduate Certificate in Education (120 level 3 credits) and QTS validated in partnership with Portsmouth University.

The planned intake each year is for 36 trainees.

The course
Trainees will have half a term of lectures in Primary or Early Years subjects, based mainly at Paulsgrove Primary School followed by half a term of teacher training in school. A total of three teaching practices is required and will cover the Primary age range of 5-11, or Early Years age range of 3-7. Two practices will

take place in one school and one practice in another, which should have a contrasting key stage and catchment area to the first school.

In school, each trainee will be placed with a mentor. The mentors are very experienced teachers who have been selected for their competence as well as their ability as primary practitioners. Trainees spend a total of 22 weeks each in the classroom working alongside not only their designated mentors, but also other teachers in the school who are subject experts in their field.

Assignments
Trainees are required to write these assignments based on action research embedded in Primary or Early Years practice.

Entry requirements:
- A minimum of a 2.2 degree.
- GCSE at grade C or above in English, mathematics and science.
- A minimum of two weeks' experience working in a school.
- To be competent in the use of information technology.

Start date and terms: All courses start at the beginning of September and finish with graduation in July. We follow the school year in Portsmouth.

Application route: Apply through the GTTR. Visit our website **www.portsmouthscitt.co.uk** for further details about the course.

Primary Catholic Partnership

Institution code: P85

c/o Holy Family Catholic Primary School
Mansel Road West
Southampton SO16 9LP
t: 023 8077 9753
e: admin@pcp-scitt.org.uk

GENERAL INFORMATION

The Primary Catholic Partnership SCITT is a highly successful teacher training provider based in Southampton. It was awarded outstanding by Ofsted in 2011 for its capacity to consistently secure high quality outcomes for trainees. Its strengths include the thoroughness with which trainee teachers are prepared and the quality of the schools they are placed in. Trainees' record of employment on completion is very high. The partnership is made up of 32 primary schools in the Portsmouth Diocese.

Training takes place over a year, with slightly longer being spent in schools than the training base. The schools where placements are arranged range from Portsmouth in the east and Bournemouth in the west to Basingstoke, Andover and Farnborough in the north. They also include five on the Isle of Wight and two in Wiltshire. Most are within 45 miles of Southampton.

Start date and terms
The course starts in early September and finishes in July. We work alongside school term-dates and half-terms are generally in line with Southampton schools.

Accommodation
Trainees are expected to find their own accommodation. As Southampton is a university city, accommodation is usually available quite readily.

ACADEMIC AWARD
The Primary Catholic Partnership offers one programme for around 30 trainees. It leads to the award of QTS and a PGCE with master's level credits for the primary sector. Qualifications are awarded by St Mary's University College, Twickenham.

The course
Trainees train to teach all subjects for the primary range of 5-11. Trainees are expected to achieve a pass in two school experiences (one in Key Stage 1 and one in Key Stage 2) and a number of assignments, which assess subject knowledge for teaching. In order to qualify with QTS, it is also necessary to pass the QTS Skills Tests in literacy and numeracy. The Catholic Certificate of Religious Studies (CCRS) is introduced as part of the course and trainees are expected to pass two modules by the end of the year.

Entry requirements: An honours degree classification of 2:2 or above. English language, mathematics and science GCSE at grade C or above or equivalent. At least two weeks' experience in a mainstream English primary school.

Those with significant experience in schools will be looked on favourably, as will those who contribute to the mission of the partnership: "To provide teachers for Catholic education."

OTHER INFORMATION

The partnership works hard to keep tuition fees below the maximum allowed to ensure high quality trainees from a variety of backgrounds are able to apply. There is a range of financial help for qualifying trainees, including, maintenance grants, students loans and bursaries. For further information and details of our tuition fees, please visit our website:
www.pcp-scitt.org.uk.
Application route: Apply through the GTTR.

Institute of Education
London Road Campus
4 Redlands Road
Reading RG1 5EX
t: 0118 378 2600
// www.rdg.ac.uk/education

GENERAL INFORMATION

The University of Reading Institute of Education offers a range of high quality teacher education and professional development programmes within a context of a strong profile in educational research, a thriving continuing professional development programme and many collaborative projects. The institute has over 40 full-time academic staff representing a wide range of expertise in education. The institute particularly welcomes entrants from all sections of the community and encourages applications to teacher training which reflect the social and cultural diversity of modern Britain.

ACADEMIC AWARDS

BA (Ed) Hons QTS Primary (5-11) - 3 years full-time
Main subjects offered: Art, English, and music.
Entry requirements and enquiries: Please contact Undergraduate Admissions.
t: 0118 378 8187
e: ugadmissions@reading.ac.uk

PGCE Early Years (3-7) and Primary (5-11) - 1 year full-time and Primary with French Specialism (5-11)
Main subjects offered: For all students, the National Curriculum for Primary Schools and Early Years Foundation Stage.

PGCE Secondary (11-19) - 1 year full-time
Main subjects offered: Art, drama, English, history, ICT, mathematics, modern foreign languages, music, physical education and science.

Entry requirements and enquiries: Please contact Yvonne Woodward
t: 0118 378 5254
e: y.m.woodward@reading.ac.uk

Subject Knowledge Enhancement (SKE) courses
Main subjects offered: Maths, chemistry, physics and French.

These courses are available for students who already have a place on a PGCE course

Entry requirements and enquiries: Please contact the SKE Office
t: 0118 378 2622
e: ske@reading.ac.uk

Foundation Degree in Children's Development and Learning
This is a two-year modular programme of employment-based learning and day release.

Enquiries: Please contact Undergraduate Admissions.
t: 0118 378 8066
e: ugadmissions@reading.ac.uk

BA (Children's Development & Learning)
The BA provides progression from a FD to honours within a model of vocational higher education.

Early Years Professional Status (EYPS)
This training is funded by CWDC and enables graduates to gain Early Years Professional Status whilst working in 0-5 settings.

Entry requirements and enquiries for both of the above courses: Please contact Mrs Angela Mason.
t: 0118 378 2608
e: a.m.mason@reading.ac.uk

OTHER INFORMATION

Entry route: UG/FT/3 years, PG/FT/SC/ 2 years, PG/FT/1 year, UG/FT/2 years.
Awards: BA (Ed) Hons with QTS, PGCE QTS, FD (Ed), BA Hons.
Application route: UG apply through UCAS, PG apply through the GTTR.

The Robert Owen Group

Robert Owen House
18 Burgess Street
Leominster
Herefordshire HR6 8DE
t: 01568 615510
f: 01568 620386
e: admin@robertowen.org
// www.robertowen.org

SECONDARY SCITT ROUTE

Formerly The Marches Consortium, a large consortium of schools and colleges in the counties of Herefordshire, Worcestershire, Shropshire, West Midlands and Wales. Fully accredited by the Teaching Agency for the award of Qualified Teacher Status. As an integral part of the programme, PGCE accreditation is offered at both level 6 and level 7, professional graduate and postgraduate levels.

Academic award
PGCE - 1 year full-time 11-16/14-19

Main subjects offered:
- Citizenship
- Design & technology
- Geography
- History
- ICT
- Maths
- MFL
- Music
- PE
- RE
- Science

Entry requirements:
GCSE grade C or above or equivalent in English language and mathematics. Award of first degree or equivalent.

Equivalence tests: English language and mathematics offered.

Other information
Entry route: PG/FT/1year
Awards: PGCE and QTS
Intended intake: 76
Application route: Apply through the GTTR
Enquiries: Please address all initial enquiries to the Academic Services Office.

PRIMARY SCITT ROUTE

Formerly The West Mercia Consortium, a large consortium of schools and Early Years providers in thecounties of Herefordshire, Worcestershire, Shropshire, West Midlands and the Welsh Borders. Fully accredited by the Teaching Agency for the award of Qualified Teacher status. As an integral part of the programme, PGCE accreditation is offered at both level 6 and level 7, professional graduate and postgraduate levels.

Academic award
PGCE - 1 year full-time
Early Years (3 - 7) and
Primary (7 - 11)

Entry requirements:
GCSE grade C or above or equivalent in English language, science and mathematics. Award of first degree or equivalent.Equivalence tests: English language, science and mathematics offered. An interest in working with young children

Other information
Entry route: PG/FT/1year
Awards: PGCE and QTS
Intended intake: 40
Application route: Apply through the GTTR
Enquiries: Please address all initial enquiries to the Academic Services Office.

University of Roehampton

Institution code: R48

Erasmus House
Roehampton Lane
London SW15 5PU
t: 020 8392 3232
f: 020 8392 3470
e: enquiries@roehampton.ac.uk

GENERAL INFORMATION

Situated in south-west London, the University of Roehampton is London's longest established teacher education provider. Its superb location provides a parkland campus only 20 minutes away from one of the world's most cosmopolitan cities. Roehampton has more than 9,000 students studying education, humanities and social and life sciences. Roehampton also provides good teaching quality assurance scores and an extensive research profile.

Roehampton is one of the largest providers of initial teacher education in the UK and recent Ofsted inspections of all our secondary subjects have been extremely positive.

Roehampton's four colleges: Dibgy Stuart, Froebel, Southlands and Whitelands, have their own accommodation and student facilities, and a strong support structure for all academic and social requirements.

Accommodation

Getting a place in halls is a great way to meet people. Our accommodation office can provide lists of available accommodation, put you in touch with other students who want to share, and advise you on your legal rights and responsibilities.

Students' union

The students' union offers access to some of the best local clubs and bars, as well as the well-oiled on-campus line-up including club nights, boat parties and comedy nights. The unmissable summer ball has hosted a variety top performers and DJs.

Leisure facilities

As well as on-campus gym RoeActive, there are facilities for boxercise and martial arts. There is also a wide range of societies and clubs to join.

ACADEMIC AWARD

Initial teacher training students are awarded a BA QTS, a BSc QTS, or Postgraduate Certificate in Education. Subject areas cover the arts, education, humanities, and social and life sciences.

Entry requirements:
Applicants are generally expected to meet Roehampton's minimum entry requirements which can be found at:
www.roehampton.ac.uk/admissions/apply/entryre quirements_ug.html
However, the University of Roehampton also welcomes application to most programmes from individuals who can demonstrate the same academic potential as applicants with conventional qualifications. Please note that there are a number of courses where the entry criteria are not flexible - typically where these are governed by outside bodies.

In order to gain admission, the university requires evidence in a field related to the programme to which admission is sought. This experience could have been gained through relevant paid employment, voluntary work or other substantial life experience.

Application route: Apply through UCAS. PGCE apply through the GTTR.

Enquiries: For more information on entry requirements for initial teacher training, call the enquiries hotline on 020 8392 3232 or email: enquiries@roehampton.ac.uk

Royal Academy of Dance

Institution code: R55

36 Battersea Square
London SW11 3RA
Programme Officer
t: **020 7326 8095**
Admissions Officer
t: **020 7326 8086**
f: **020 7924 8040**
e: **faculty@rad.org.uk**

The Royal Academy of Dance

- Accredited by the Teaching Agency to offer the award of Qualified Teacher Status for the training of specialist dance teachers for the 14-19 age range.
- Highly respected international organisation with over 18,000 members in 84 countries around the world, and 900 students enrolled across seven teacher education and training programmes.
- Offers a portfolio of highly acclaimed dance teacher education programmes to increase recognition of the importance of dance in the education of young people.
- Programmes are subject to the full range of quality assurance measures for higher education;
- Thriving dance community comprising students, trainees, experienced teachers and professional artists passionate in their commitment to the art.
- Ideally located in south west London with easy access to theatres and arts venues in and around London.

PGCE Dance Teaching

The Postgraduate Certificate in Education: Dance Teaching (PGCE: DT) awarded by the University of Surrey is designed to provide trainee dance teachers with depth of subject knowledge, and the expertise to deliver the multiplicity of dance curricula and qualifications for the 14-19 age range. The full-time programme comprises 36 weeks: 12 weeks based at academy headquarters in London and 24 weeks gaining teaching experience in selected schools and colleges across London and the South East.

The programme, delivered jointly by the RAD and schools and colleges, comprises three modules covering three interrelated areas derived from the QTS standards. Teaching experience will be offered across the 11-19 range.

Trainee teachers will be assessed throughout the year through assignments such as presentations, seminars and teaching assessments. Successful students are awarded a PGCE from the University of Surrey.

Entry requirements

- An appropriate UK undergraduate degree or equivalent qualification in dance or a related subject with substantial dance components.
- A minimum of grade C in GCSE English language and mathematics.
- Candidates will be invited to attend an audition and interview day.

Application route: Apply through the GTTR.

Royal Conservatoire of Scotland

Institution code: R58

100 Renfrew Street
Glasgow G2 3DB
t: 0141 332 4101
f: 0141 332 8901
e: musicadmissions@rcs.ac.uk
// www.rcs.ac.uk

Enquiries: Contact the conservatoire about entry requirements, auditions and open days.

GENERAL INFORMATION

In 1994, the Privy Council granted degree-awarding powers to the Royal Conservatoire of Scotland for taught programmes. We are the only conservatoire in the UK offering music, drama and dance.

ACADEMIC AWARD

Bachelor of Education in Music (Hons)

The BEd Music is offered by the Royal Conservatoire of Scotland in collaboration with the University of Glasgow's School of Education and is accredited by the General Teaching Council for Scotland. The straight-through honours programme is designed primarily for students wishing to become classroom teachers of music. All students pursue a principal performance study and also focus on keyboard and vocal skills, alongside education studies and school experience.

All incoming students will maintain (for the school experience sector of the course) a Personal Development Plan, which will have a strong vocational focus.

Application route: Apply online through the Conservatoires UK Admissions Service (CUKAS). Visit their website at **www.cukas.ac.uk**.

SCITTELS Lead School: Colegrave Primary
Henniker Road
Stratford
London E15 1JY
t: 020 8534 0243
f: 020 8519 9485
e: scittels@colegrave.newham.sch.uk
// www.scittels.co.uk

GENERAL INFORMATION

This is a course that is designed by teachers, delivered by teachers and evaluated by teachers in the interest of pupils and teachers now and in the future.

We offer: 15 - 20 Foundation Stage and Key Stage 1

(3-7) places and 20 - 25 Key Stage 1 and Key Stage 2 (6-11) places.

Training takes place in and around the regenerated area of Stratford in London, a gateway to Europe, and home to the lead school and the University of East London.

SCITTELS is a friendly consortium that provides quality school-based training in the London Borough of Newham. 38 trainee teachers are recruited each year to work within a professional partnership of primary and nursery schools, and the PGCE will be awarded by the University of Roehampton. The schools involved are all committed to contributing to high quality initial teacher training.

ACADEMIC AWARD

The course is modular and offers general and specialised Primary and Foundation stage study within the context of educational inclusion. All modules are linked and there are also explicit links between coursework and school-based tasks. Over the year, the balance of time shifts from being largely centre-based to being wholly school-based. Aspects covered in the modules include bilingualism, special educational needs and learning within the social context. The course is delivered by highly qualified, serving teachers andvisiting specialists, and aims to supply East London schools with teachers of equally high calibre.

Throughout the course, students complete several school-based tasks, three teaching practices in different schools and across a minimum of two age ranges, as well as six written assignments.

Entry requirements

- A degree (2:2 and above)
- GCSE level C or equivalent English language, mathematics and science.
- Candidates in the process of acquiring any of these qualifications will still be considered. Please enquire.
- School experience is a requirement or evidence of relevant experience transferable to a school environment.

The consortium is committed to equality of opportunity for all and will not intentionally discriminate on grounds of race, sex, age, disability, religion or socio-economic circumstances.

Application route: Apply through the GTTR.

University of Sheffield
Institution code: S18

School of Education
388 Glossop Road
Sheffield S10 2JA
t: 0114 222 8177
f: 0114 222 8105
e: edu-enquiries@sheffield.ac.uk
// www.shef.ac.uk/education/courses

GENERAL INFORMATION

The School of Education is on the main university site, less than one mile from Sheffield city centre. The school has a wide-ranging teaching and research programme with a commitment to research-led teaching in all its courses. The Postgraduate Certificate in Education course has a very good reputation both locally and nationally. It has been developed in partnership with over 30 schools in the Sheffield region and there are very strong links between university tutors, teachers in schools and students. The 2011 Ofsted report stated 'the innovative features of the training contribute strongly to developing trainees who are reflective, self-critical and capable of working independently'.

From September 2011, the school also offers a BA in Education, Culture and Childhood. The degree is truly interdisciplinary, drawing on psychology, sociology, politics, cultural studies, history and philosophy in order to provide a full and varied exploration of education and childhood. The degree, which includes a work placement module, will enable graduates to work across traditional disciplinary and professional boundaries.

ACADEMIC AWARD

Postgraduate Certificate in Education Secondary (11-19)
Intended intake: 107

Main subjects offered:
- English
- Geography
- Languages (French, German, Japanese, Mandarin, Russian, Spanish, Urdu)*
- Mathematics
- Physics with maths
- Science with biology
- Science with chemistry
- Science with physics

* only available in limited combinations; please see our website for details.

Entry requirements: Applicants should have a degree (2:2 or above) in the subject they wish to teach, or have studied the subject for a substantial part of their degree. They should also have GCSE grade C or above, or equivalent, in English language and mathematics.

Equivalence tests: There are equivalence tests in English language and mathematics for those without the necessary qualifications at GCSE.

Application route: PGCE apply through the GTTR.

BA Education, Culture and Childhood
Intended intake: 28

Entry requirements: A levels BBB. At least two of these should be in acceptable subjects. Guidance on our A level subject requirements can be found at: **www.sheffield.ac.uk/undergraduate/policies**. For alternative requirements, see: **www.shef.ac.uk/education/courses/cultchildhood/entryrequ.html**

Application route: All candidates for the full-time degree programme need to apply through UCAS.

Sheffield Hallam University

Institution code: S21

Faculty of Development & Society
Sheffield Hallam University
City Campus
Sheffield S1 1WB
t: **0114 225 5555**
f: **0114 225 2167**
e: **admissions@shu.ac.uk**
// **www.shu.ac.uk**

GENERAL INFORMATION

Sheffield Hallam University is one of the largest providers of teaching education in the UK.

Initial teacher training courses have a strong practical flavour with long periods of supervised teaching experience in schools. All initial teacher education courses are run in partnership with around 600 local and regional schools and colleges that play a key role in teaching and assessment.

For further information regarding Sheffield Hallam University and our courses, including full course entry requirements, please visit our web page.

TEACHER TRAINING COURSES

- BA Primary Education
- PGCE Primary Education
- BA Early Years Education
- PGCE Early Years Education
- BSc Secondary Design and Technology with Education 2 and 3 years full-time
- BSc Secondary Mathematics with Education 2 and 3 years full-time
- BSc Secondary Science with Education 2 and 3 years full-time
- PGCE Secondary Business Education
- PGCE Secondary Citizenship - flexible
- PGCE Secondary Design and Technology
- PGCE Secondary Design and Technology (Engineering)
- PGCE Secondary Design and Technology (Food Technology)
- PGCE Secondary Design and Technology (Textiles)
- PGCE Secondary English
- PGCE Secondary Information and Communication Technology
- PGCE Secondary Mathematics - 1 and 2 years fulltime, 2 year flexible
- PGCE Secondary Modern Foreign Languages
- PGCE Secondary Physical Education
- PGCE Secondary Religious Education
- PGCE Secondary Science - 1 and 2 years full-time
- PGCE Learning and Skills

The two-year undergraduate route is for applicants with at least one-year full-time higher education study or equivalent. The two-year PGCE route is for applicants whose first degree is not closely enough aligned to a National Curriculum subject to qualify for the one-year route. Students spend one year on a Subject Knowledge Enhancement course before progressing onto the one-year PGCE.

OTHER INFORMATION

- BA Childhood Studies
- BA Children and Playwork
- BA Early Childhood Studies
- BA Education and Disability Studies
- BA Education Studies and Sociology
- BA English and Education Studies
- BA Education Studies with Psychology and Counselling
- BA TESOL and Education Studies

The Shire Foundation

Institution code: S25

c/o Hillborough Junior School
Hillborough Road
Luton LU1 5EZ
t: 01582 522121
f: 01582 613332

What is the Shire Foundation?

The Shire Foundation offers you school-centred training in a consortium of local schools, predominantly located in the Luton area. These schools reflect the whole Primary phase 3-11. Over the course of the year, trainees will be based in one school, but will complete teaching practices in at least one other school. As the course is school-centred trainees are able to address current education issues working alongside experienced practitioners.

The course is accredited. It meets the requirements of the Teaching Agency, and on successful completion of all components parts trainees will be awarded Qualified Teacher Status. This is the only qualification that ensures a registration number and access to professional contracts and rates of pay.

The course is also validated for PGCE (Professional Graduate Certificate in Education) through the University of Bedfordshire.

What are the elements of the course?

The course consists of:

Centre-based training

Professional studies providing an introduction to current educational issues, broad curriculum studies covering both theory and practice and with a close study of the National Curriculum subjects at Key Stages 1 and 2 and the Foundation Stage. These training sessions take place in Shire's outstanding lead school.

School-based training

A large percentage of trainee time is spent in school putting theory into practice. Experience in Key Stages 1 and 2 and the Foundation Stage will assist trainees to make an informed choice of focus. Trainees are supported throughout by a qualified teacher.

Entry requirements

- Good honours degree (2:2 or above) in a core or foundation subject, or a degree with appropriate and relevant modules (or equivalents).
- All trainees must have GCSE grade C or above in English language, mathematics and science (or equivalents).
- Trainees must demonstrate an ability to communicate clearly and grammatically in spoken and written English.
- In addition to your academic qualifications you will need to show experience of working with primary age children, preferably in a school setting and a range of interests, skills and hobbies, both practical and intellectual.

Application route: Apply through the GTTR.
Enquiries: Jane Morrissey,
Administration Officer (01582 522121)
or Lesley Cuandu,
Senior Administration Assistant (01582 522121).

Solihull College

Institution code: S26

Higher Education
Blossomfield Road
Solihull B91 1SB
t: 0121 6787007
//: www.solihull.ac.uk

GENERAL INFORMATION

Local interests/activities

Solihull is a vibrant town on the outskirts of
Birmingham offering the best of both worlds - you can
enjoy the local history and relaxed surroundings or
throw yourself into the lively atmosphere of the town.
You'll be spoilt for choice with a top shopping centre
and a great mix of pubs, bars and restaurants.

Accommodation

Located at Blossomfield Campus, the halls of
residence offer self-catering rooms set in leafy
surroundings. All rooms include en-suite facilities and
internet connection. The halls have an appealingly
safe and spacious environment with 24-hour security
and management support.

ACADEMIC AWARDS

HND/HNC Advanced Practice in Work with Children and Families (Education)

This course is ideal for people who want to embark on
a career as an Early Years practitioner, teaching
assistant or primary school teacher. With the
emphasis on work-based learning, in addition to time
in the classroom, this qualification will develop your
ability to work with children and families through the
effective use of a range of skills, theory and
techniques.

Foundation Degree Early Years

This is a sector endorsed foundation degree which
leads to senior practitioner status. Students need to be
working with children (0 to 8 years) in an appropriate
Early Years setting for a minimum of two days
each week.

Foundation Degree Support for Learning

Foundation degrees provide professional development
opportunities for those who wish to follow a
programme where workplace learning is accredited.
This programme offers career development for
support staff in primary and secondary schools and
colleges.

Certificate in English Language Teaching to Adults

The Certificate in English Language Teaching to Adults
(CELTA) is ideal. CELTA is an initial qualification for
people with little or no previous teaching experience
and helps to open up a whole host of exciting
teaching opportunities around the globe.

Certificate in Teaching in the Lifelong Learning sector

The Certificate in Teaching in the Lifelong Learning
Sector (CTLLS) is ideal for new
teachers/assistants/assessors who have some
experience but whose teaching role does not
include curriculum design.

Diploma in Teaching in the Lifelong Learning Sector

This course is aimed at those who are employed in a
full teaching role in the post-16 sector and leads to
full qualification at Level 5.

Initial Teacher Education Office
School of Education
Southampton SO17 1BJ
t: 023 80 592413 - Secondary
t: 023 80 596231 - Primary
// www.southampton.ac.uk/education

GENERAL INFORMATION

Teacher training builds on a 100-year tradition of research-led teacher education and has strong partnerships with local schools and colleges.

All PGCE courses at the University of Southampton can be exited at either postgraduate level (with 60 master's credits) or professional graduate level.

ACADEMIC AWARDS

PGCE Primary (5-11) - 1 year full-time
Main subjects:
- French
- General primary

Entry requirements: GCSE grade C or above in English language, mathematics and science. Degree with 2:1 classification preferred.

PGCE Secondary (11-18) (11-16 with QTS) - 1 year full-time
Main subjects:
- English
- Geography
- History
- Information technology
- Mathematics
- Modern languages (French, German, Spanish)
- Physical education
- RE
- Sciences (biology, chemistry, physics).

Entry requirements: GCSE grade C or above in English language and mathematics. Degree in relevant subject. For German and Spanish, A level French or equivalent experience.

Subject Knowledge Enhancement (SKE) courses in Mathematics (6 months FT) or Physics (6 months FT)
Entry requirements: GCSE grade C or above in English language and mathematics for mathematics, A level mathematics (or equivalent) for physics A level in science and a degree. SKE courses are designed to prepare applicants who are otherwise suitable but have insufficient mathematics or science in their degree for direct entry onto the one-year PGCE.

Apply as for 1 year courses.
SKE course eligibility advised on application.
SKE courses are not currently available to international applicants.

OTHER INFORMATION

Entry route: PG/FT/1 year
Awards: PGCE QTS
Intended intake: Primary - 160, Secondary - 183
Application route: Apply through the GTTR.
Enquiries: Please use the contact details provided.

Somerset Teacher Education Programme

Institution code: S31

James Wyatt
Somerset SCITT
SCIL
Taunton Academy (South)
Lyngford Road
Taunton Somerset TA2 7EF
t: 01823 368283
f: 01823 364698
e: scitt@somersetscitt.co.uk
// www.somersetscitt.co.uk

GENERAL INFORMATION

This is a collaborative venture between a number of Somerset primary schools, Early Years Settings, Somerset Local Authority and The University of Worcester. The Somerset SCITT Consortium has had ten years of successful training, and has been classified as a 'Category A' provider of ITT as a result of the latest Ofsted inspection report.

ACADEMIC AWARDS

PGCE Early Years (3-7)
PGCE Primary (5-11)
These programmes are divided between a centrally taught component (35%) and time spent in schools' settings (65%). The taught sessions focus on subject knowledge pedagogy as well as allowing opportunities for the exploration of current expertise in effective teaching, learning, and discussions of the latest research findings.

The Graduate Teacher Programme (GTP)
This is an employment route into teaching and further details can be obtained from James Wyatt at the above address.

We are seeking creative, energetic, enthusiastic and flexible people whose commitment to teaching is allied to a good sense of humour. You will need to be well organised with a genuine commitment to teaching to be successful in what is a very demanding as well as exciting and rewarding course.

Nationally, certain groups are under-represented. This is also true of our courses, These include men, people with disabilities and those from minority ethnic groups. If you are from one of these groups we would particularly welcome an application from you.

All the above programmes are one-year-full-time Primary postgraduate programmes at the end of which successful trainees will be awarded Qualified Teacher Status (QTS). In addition successful completion of the SCITT PGCE course achieves Postgraduate Certificate in Education (PGCE), awarded by the University of Worcester. Once you have achieved QTS you can work as a qualified teacher in any maintained school in England.

Entry requirements:
- Applicants must have a UK bachelor's degree or equivalent.
- GCSE in English language, mathematics and science.

Work experience: Evidence of working with children

Equivalence tests: Only arranged in exceptional circumstances.

OTHER INFORMATION

Validation to award a PGCE from The University of Worcester.

Entry route: PG/FT/1 year
Award: PGCE QTS
Intended intake: 85 PGCE (split between Primary and Early Years) 20 GTP
Application route: PGCE apply through the GTTR, GTP please see the Somerset SCITT website for application details. Early application is strongly advised.
Enquires: To SCITT Administrator at above address

Waldegrave Road, Strawberry Hill
Twickenham, TW1 4SX
t: 0208 240 4000
// www.smuc.ac.uk

GENERAL INFORMATION

St Mary's University College offers the best of all worlds. Founded in 1850, we have an excellent graduate employment record. We are renowned for having a modern outlook, friendly atmosphere and a caring student-centred approach. Our mission is to provide well informed, competent, committed and highly professional new teachers for denominational and state schools. We offer students the opportunity to obtain the Catholic Certificate in Religious Studies.

ACADEMIC AWARDS

The strengths of our courses lie in the 'Outstanding' quality of training and excellent partnership withschools as recognised by Ofsted in 2011.

BA Primary Education (QTS) - 3 years full-time
BA Primary Education (QTS) with an advanced subject elective - 4 years full-time
PGCE Primary - full-time and part-time
All programmes prepare trainees to teach 5 - 11 year olds across Key Stage 1 and 2 of primary schooling. Modules are provided in all foundation subjects of the National Curriculum. There may be an opportunity to participate in a short primary school placement in France, Germany or Spain. Experiences are gained in partnership schools where class teachers have been trained to support and assess trainees.

PGCE Secondary - full-time
Ours courses' strengths lie in the quality of training, as recognised in recent Ofsted inspection and our excellent partnership with schools.

The course aims to equip trainees with an understanding of how pupils learn, with training in managing learning and behaviour. School-based learning begins with observation, then blocks of experience within two partnership schools cover two thirds of the training year.

Main subjects offered
Applied ICT, geography, mathematics, modern foreign languages, physical education, religious education and science with physics, chemistry or biology.

Please see our PGCE Secondary Brochure on our website.

Entry requirements:
Undergraduate: We welcome students with a variety of qualifications, including A levels, AVCE, BTEC and Access. Offers are normally equivalent to BC at A level, including at least one six - unit award.

Postgraduate: For primary PGCE, normally an honours degree of 2.2 or better from a UK university or an equivalent qualification that has clear relevance to the National Curriculum. For secondary PGCE, a degree normally is required with a significant proportion of the content related to the subject to be undertaken. This degree should normally be at 2:2 or above. For PE only a 2:1 or above will be considered. We will consider those needing Subject Knowledge Enhancement courses for shortage subjects.

All entrants: GCSE English, maths and science grades A - C for all Primary PGCE candidates and for PE Secondary PGCE applicants. For applicants to other Secondary PGCE course a grade C at science is not required. ITT Primary candidates must have B grades at maths and English and a C at science. Please see our website for more details of GCSE equivalence. All applicants are required to have undertaken recent observation in a state school. All applicants must undergo medical and police checks (CRB enhanced).

Application route: Apply through UCAS or GTTR.

Contact:
Undergraduate: 0208 2404138
Postgraduate: 0208 240 4027

South West Teacher Training (SCITT)

Institution code: S66

West Exe Technology College
Hatherleigh Road
Exeter EX2 9JU
t: 01392 686165
e: swtt@westexetc.devon.sch.uk
// www.swtt.net

What course does South West Teacher Training offer?

- PGCE course for secondary teachers in: Design and technology, Modern foreign languages, Biology, Physics, Chemistry
- 40-week course starting in September.
- 75% of training takes place in Devon schools alongside experienced teachers.
- Opportunity to gain 60 master's credits.
- Specialist subject pedagogy and general teaching pedagogy delivered in the lead school in Exeter.
- Validation by Roehampton University in Surrey.

What qualifications will I need?

- A UK degree or recognised equivalent, 2:2 or above, related to the subject.
- GCSE grade C or above (or equivalent) in English and maths.

Other requirements

- Strong commitment and passion for a career in teaching.
- Enthusiasm and passion for the subject.
- Some experience working with young people in any context.
- Resilience and ability to self-motivate.

What funding is available?

- Physics, chemistry and MFL trainees receive a tax free bursary of up to £20,000 depending on degree classification.
- Biology and design and technology trainees receive a tax free bursary of up to £9,000 depending on degree classifiction.
- Tuition fees apply for all trainees.
- Trainees are eligible to apply for a student loan to cover tuition fees.

How do I apply?

- Via the Graduate Teacher Training Registry (GTTR)

South Coast SCITT Consortium

Institution code: S70

SCITT Learning Centre
Bransgore Primary School
Ringwood Road
Bransgore, Christchurch
Dorset BH23 8JH
t: 01425 674625
// www.scscitt.co.uk

GENERAL INFORMATION

This is a one-year full-time programme offering two specialisms, one in Early Years Education (3-7) and one in General Primary (5-11). The SCITT Learning Centre is situated within an outstanding partner school in the New Forest. Training takes place in a consortium of schools in Hampshire, Bournemouth, Dorset and Poole.

Trainee teachers spend 70% of their time in school supported by an experienced mentor. The mentor works closely with the trainee to help him/her develop the competences required to qualify as a teacher.

Trainees learn to plan, teach and assess children's learning. They learn to organise and manage a classroom to create a secure and effective learning enviroment.

Trainees spend 30% of their time in centre-based training, where specialist lecturers support the synthesis of theory and practice appropriate to trainees' chosen specialisms.

Our trainees are very successful in gaining subsequent teaching jobs.

We welcome applications from all candidates irrespective of race, colour, nationality, national or ethnic origins, gender, marital status, sexual orientation, disability or religious beliefs, in accordance with South Coast SCITT's equality and diversity policies.

ACADEMIC AWARDS

Qualified Teacher Status (QTS) and Postgraduate Certificate in Education (PGCE) offering 60 M level credits awarded by the University of Bedfordshire).

Entry requirements:
- A suitable academic profile including GCSE grade C or above in English language, mathematics and science.
- A degree - preferably 2.2 or above, but we consider all applicants on their merits.
- Evidence of work experience with children in schools as appropriate to the specialist age range.
- An informed professional reference containing a strong recommendation of suitability to train to teach.

OTHER INFORMATION

Entry route: PG/FT/1 year
Award: PGCE (University of Bedfordshire), QTS
Intended intake: 35
Application route: Apply through the GTTR

Enquires:
e: **gthurgood@scscitt.co.uk**
// **www.scscitt.co.uk**

Admissions Office
College Road
Stoke on Trent ST4 2DE
t: **01782 292753**
f: **01782 292740**
// www.staffs.ac.uk

ACADEMIC AWARDS

Main subjects offered:
- Business education
- Business and economics education
- Design and technology
- ICT
- Mathematics.

The course
The course aims to develop high quality, thoughtful teachers of: design and technology, ICT and mathematics for the 11-18 age range; plus two business courses for the 14-19 age range. It provides an opportunity to develop the professional knowledge, skills and attitudes expected of a qualified teacher. School experience runs throughout the year in parallel with the university programme of lectures and seminars to maximise integration between the two elements of the course and provide a richer learning environment. The course is built on very close relationships with partner schools and has a small scale, friendly feel with an emphasis on personalised provision for all trainees.

Entry requirements:
For all courses: An honours degree at 2:2 or above, at least 50% of which is in a subject related discipline.

Business and maths courses: GCSE's in English and maths at grade C or above (O levels and CSE grade 1 also accepted).

For ICT and D&T: GCSE in English at grade C or above (O levels and CSE grade 1 also accepted). GCSE in maths at grade C or above or equivalent.

For details on equivalents contact the Award leader.

We strongly advise all applicants to gain secondary school experience.

OTHER INFORMATION

Intended intake: We have a combined intake of 11 for the PGCE in Business Education and Business & Economics and 10 each for the PGCE in Design and Technology, ICT and Mathematics.

Awards: Postgraduate Certificate in Education (60 M credits) and Professional Graduate Certificate in Education (30 M credits) offered in all our PGCE awards.

Enquiries: All business related courses
Guy Durden
Institute for Education Policy Research
Business School, Staffordshire University
Leek Road ST4 2DF
t: 01782 294909 e: g.durden@staffs.ac.uk

Enquiries: Design and technology, and mathematics
Clyde Redfern
Faculty of Computing, Engineering and Technology
Technology
Beaconside
Stafford ST18 0AD
t: 01785 353830 e: c.k.redfern@staffs.ac.uk

Enquiries: ICT
Paul Maddock
Faculty of Computing, Engineering and Technology
Beaconside
Stafford ST18 0AD
t: 01785 353830 e: p.maddock@staffs.ac.uk

Stratford-upon-Avon College

Institution code: S74

The Willows North
Alcester Road
Stratford-upon-Avon
Warwickshire
CV37 9QR
t: 01789 266245
f: 01789 267524
e: college@stratford.ac.uk
// www.stratford.ac.uk
// www.facebook.com/stratforduponavoncollege
// www.twitter.com/stratfordcoll

GENERAL INFORMATION

We will make your study time with us a memorable
and rewarding experience. Our HE programmes are
designed to develop your skills and knowledge to
enable you to either progress to other HE courses or
find suitable employment.

We work in collaboration with City College Coventry,
Thames Valley University and the University of
Warwick to ensure that our academic standards,
assessments and materials are equivalent to those of
our partner institutions.

State-of-the-art facilities
The college has learning resource centres, an
excellent library, lecture theatres, a superb IT centre,
media suite, drama studios, training kitchens and
much more.

Accommodation
We help our students to find a secure and happy place
to live while they study with us. We offer campus
accommodation in purpose-built self-catering
apartments or homestay accommodation can also be
arranged.

COURSES

Our excellent achievement rates will give you every
chance of success in the following courses:

Foundation Degree in Early Years
This programme is offered in partnership with the
University of Warwick. It has been designed to meet
the professional needs of employees in the Early Years
Sector.

The FdA provides an opportunity for people who are
working with young children in an education child care
setting to develop their professional understanding,
knowledge and key skills whilst working.

International (Heart of England International Academy)

English as a Foreign Language Programme (EFL)
The college offers year-round EFL and summer
programmes. Our EFL programme runs from
September to June and offers 20 hours of tuition per
week. There are three separate modules: General
English, Skills Training and Academic English.

For further information please visit our website,
www.stratford.ac.uk

University of Stirling
Stirling FK9 4LA
t: 01786 467 044
f: 01786 466 800

ACADEMIC AWARD

The University of Stirling is distinctive among Scottish universities in offering concurrent programmes to prospective primary and secondary school teachers. These degree programmes enable you to gain a degree in Professional Education with an appropriate teaching subject or specialism in four years. These qualifications are recognised throughout the UK and the world. Successfully completing the programme enables you to provisionally register in the appropriate sector with the General Teaching Council for Scotland and enter the probationary scheme.

For Secondary Education, the main subjects offered are:

- a Bachelor named degree in one subject (excluding modern languages) (3 years)
- an honours degree in one or two teaching subjects (including modern languages) (4 years)
- in either case there is no need to go to another institution for further teacher training.

Main subjects offered:
- Biology
- Business studies
- Computing science
- English studies
- Environmental geography
- French
- Mathematics
- History
- Philosophy
- Physical education
- Modern studies
- Religion
- Spanish
- Sociology & social policy.

When studying two teaching subjects, only certain combinations of the above are available. Please consult the undergraduate prospectus for additional information.

The University of Stirling now offers three Primary Education courses. These are BA Professional Education (Primary) with specialism in either Modern Languages, the Environment or the Early Years.

Entry requirements: Education
(Concurrent Secondary Teacher Training) - entry requirements are normally those of the main teaching subjects with which it is combined, together with English Higher at C grade or GCSE English literature and GCSE English language or equivalent.

For Primary Education, maths at Standard Grade 2, INT2 C or GCSE C is also required. For specialism in the Environment, a science at Higher Grade B is required. For specialism in Modern Languages, a language at Higher Grade B is required. For specialism in the Early Years, a science or psychology at Higher Grade B is required. Please refer to the undergraduate prospectus for more detailed information. These specialised degrees also require certain subjects at Higher or A level. Please refer to undergraduate prospectus.

OTHER INFORMATION

Application route: Apply through UCAS.

ITE Support Centre
School of Education
Faculty of Humanities and Social Sciences
Jordanhill Campus
76 Southbrae Drive
Glasgow G13 1PP
t: 0141 950 3224
f: 0141 950 3717
e: itesupportcentre@strath.ac.uk

GENERAL INFORMATION

For further details of accommodation, leisure, sports, student union and campus facilities visit our website:
www.strath.ac.uk

Glasgow is a brilliant city to live in and Scotland is an exciting place to be. Glasgow is the home of Scottish Ballet, Scottish Opera and the Royal Scottish NationalOrchestra. It provides a base for the National Theatre of Scotland and houses the Mitchell Library, the largest public library in Europe, and Kelvingrove Art Gallery and Museum, Scotland's most popular visitor attraction. Glasgow's diverse cultural scene is celebrated with a vast number of festivals filling the calendar.

ACADEMIC AWARDS

B.Ed (Hons) in Primary Education
The B.Ed in Primary Education is the largest undergraduate programme in Primary Education in Scotland and our reputation is worldwide. Equipping graduates with the skills to meet all the demands of the changing primary teaching profession, our staff undertake innovative educational research which they integrate into the teaching programme. Technology and problem-based learning are integral to the course and reflective learning plays a critical part in students' progress. Please follow this link
www.strath.ac.uk/bed for course details.

PGDE (Primary and Secondary)
For information on the Professional Graduate Diploma in Primary Education please go to:
www.strath.ac.uk/pgdeprimary/fulltimepathway

For details on the Professional Graduate Diploma in Secondary Education please go to:
www.strath.ac.uk/curricularstudies/courses/pgde secondary

Stranmillis University College

Institution code: S79

Stranmillis Road
Belfast
BT9 5DY
t: **028 90381271**
f: **028 90664423**
// **www.stran.ac.uk**

Enquiries
t: **028 90384263**
e: **Registry@stran.ac.uk**
// **www.stran.ac.uk**

GENERAL INFORMATION

Stranmillis University College is located in south Belfast. Its students enjoy a purpose-built campus in a conservation area, occupying an enclosed site of 46 acres of woodland rich in wildlife. It is within walking distance of shops, restaurants, clubs and theatres.

Education at Stranmillis
- New state-of-the-art building.
- Designated as a Centre of Excellence in Teaching and Learning by the Department for Children, Schools and Families
- Ranked highly for overall student satisfaction in the National Student Survey
- Recent Higher Education Statistics Agency figures indicate a 94% success rate in relation to the employment of leavers.
- New student and learning support centre
- High quality facilities
- The delivery of academic excellence

ACADEMIC AWARDS: UNDERGRADUATE

BEd (Hons) Primary
BEd (Hons) Post-Primary:
Post-primary academic subjects offered:
- Business and enterprise with education
- Mathematics and science with education
- Religious studies with education
- Technology and design with education

Entry requirements for BEd:
Please see our current prospectus or website for specific information at **www.stran.ac.uk.**

Applications must be made through UCAS.

University Campus Suffolk (UCS)

Institution code: S82

Waterfront Building
Ipswich
Suffolk
IP4 1QJ
t: 01473 338000
e: info@ucs.ac.uk
// www.ucs.ac.uk

ACADEMIC AWARDS: UNDERGRADUATE

BA (Hons) Early Childhood Studies (UCS Ipswich)
FdA Children's Care Learning and Development
(UCS Ipswich, UCS Bury St Edmunds, UCS
Lowestoft, UCS Great Yarmouth)
BA (Hons) Children's Care Learning and
Development (Progression Year) (UCS Lowestoft)
BA (Hons) Early Learning (Progression Year) (UCS
Ipswich)
FdA Teaching, Training and Development (QTLS
Option) (UCS Otley)

ACADEMIC AWARDS: POSTGRADUATE

MA Learning and Teaching (UCS Ipswich)
Professional Graduate Certificate in Education
(Post Compulsory) (UCS Lowestoft, UCS Great
Yarmouth, UCS Bury St Edmunds, UCS Otley)

Certificate in Education (Post Compulsory) (UCS at
Suffolk New College, UCS Lowestoft, UCS Great
Yarmouth, UCS Bury St Edmunds, UCS Otley)

PGCE Suffolk and Norfolk Secondary SCITT (UCS
Ipswich)

PGCE Suffolk and Norfolk Primary SCITT (UCS
Ipswich)
PGCE North Essex Secondary SCITT (UCS Ipswich)

INTRODUCTION TO TEACHING AWARDS

Award in Preparing to Teach in the Lifelong
Learning Sector (PTLLS)
This course provides a basic introduction to
teaching/training/tutoring in the Lifelong Learning
Sector.

Certificate in Teaching in the Lifelong Learning
Sector (CTLLS)
This course is for the associate teacher role in the
Learning and Skills Sector. The programme includes
at least 30 hours of teaching.

Application routes: full-time undergraduate and
foundation degrees, apply through UCAS.

For part-time and Professional Graduate Certificate in
Education/Certificate in Education/PTLLS/CTLLS
courses, apply direct to University Campus Suffolk.

For Suffolk and Norfolk SCITT apply direct at
www.snitt.co.uk

For North Essex SCITT apply direct at
www.coastalscilt.co.uk

All candidates offered and accepting a place will be
subject to an enhanced Criminal Record Bureau
check.

For entry requirements and further information, please
visit our website at
www.ucs.ac.uk.

The University of Sunderland

Institution code: S84

Faculty of Education and Society
David Goldman Informatics Centre
St Peter's Campus
St Peter's Way
Sunderland SR6 0DD
t: 0191 515 2395
e: ell.enquiries@sunderland.ac.uk

ACADEMIC AWARDS

BA (Hons) Primary Education (5-11) - 3 years
full-time
Entry requirements: 300 UCAS points. (For full entry
requirements please see **www.sunderland.ac.uk)**

BA (Hons) Secondary Education (11-18) - 3 years
full-time
Main subjects offered:
- English
- Information communication technology

Entry requirements: 260 UCAS points. (For full entry
requirements please see **www.sunderland.ac.uk**)

BA/BSc (Hons) Secondary Education (11-18) - 2
years full-time
Main subjects offered:
- Information communication technology
- Mathematics
- Science

Entry requirements: HNC/D in an appropriate
subject area. One successful year of a higher
education programme in an appropriate subject area
(120 credits). (For full entry requirements please see
www.sunderland.ac.uk)

PGCE Primary Education (5-11) - also available
with French specialisim - 1 year full-time

PGCE Secondary Education (11-18)
Main subjects offered:
- Business studies
- Design and technology
- English
- Further education (post-16)
- Geography
- Information technology
- Mathematics
- Science with biology
- Science with chemistry
- Science with physics

SUBJECT ENHANCEMENT PROGRAMMES:

We also offer subject enhancement programmes in
design and technology, mathematics and science for
those students who lack the necessary subject
background to enrol directly onto a one-year PGCE.

OTHER INFORMATION

For full entry requirements for each programme please
refer to **www.sunderland.ac.uk**

School of Education and Social Work
University of Sussex
Falmer
Brighton
East Sussex BN1 9QQ
t: 01273 678405 (admissions)
f: 01273 877534
e: iteadmissions@sussex.ac.uk
// www.sussex.ac.uk/education/

GENERAL INFORMATION

The School of Education and Social Work is situated on a modern campus set in leafy parkland on the edge of the Downs. It is conveniently located on the south coast of England with easy access by road and rail to London, Gatwick and Heathrow airports and to Europe from the Channel Tunnel and ports.

We have always prided ourselves on partnership: partnership with schools, with local authorities and with our sister universities. Our way of strengthening the practice of school-based teacher training, which has existed in Sussex for over 40 years, is by working within a consortium of partnership schools. The Sussex Consortium for Teacher Education and Research takes an increasingly significant lead in the development of teachers throughout their professional lives. Our recent Ofsted reports have been very good, confirming that we offer high quality provision.

The Sussex campus

The university has a medium-sized campus, small enough to be friendly and welcoming, but large enough to offer a lively social life and a wide range of extracurricular activities. The campus is only a few minutes away from the centre of Brighton.

Accommodation

The university's housing office can offer advice on accommodation. Most PGCE students find their own accommodation in the private sector. Please contact: housing@admin.sussex.ac.uk.

Students' union

The students' union is the focus of student life at Sussex. It organises social events and runs shops and bars on campus. It also provides welfare advice and represents its members on university committees, to the public and in wider campaigns.

Leisure facilities

Brighton is a lively, friendly seaside city with great leisure facilities, whatever your taste. There is a great choice of gigs, theatre, sporting activities, clubs and shops. Visit www.tourism.brighton.co.uk to explore one of England's newest cities.

ACADEMIC AWARD

PGCE programmes

A Postgraduate Certificate in Education is awarded to all candidates who successfully complete academic components of the programme to master's level. This PGCE (M) currently provides candidates with a total of up to 90 M level credits and offers progression opportunities for professional development through a flexible part-time Master of Education (MEd). A Professional Graduate Certificate in Education (PGCE (H)) is provided as an exit award. Both the PGCE (M) and PGCE (H) are recognised nationally as professional qualifications and lead to the recommendation of Qualified Teacher Status.

University of Sussex

continued

Main courses offered: Sussex offers the PGCE in the following secondary subjects:

- English
- History
- Mathematics
- Modern foreign languages
- Music
- Science: with named specialisms in physics, chemistry and biology.

A PGCE is also offered at Primary (7-11 years).

In addition mathematics and modern foreign languages are offered at Key Stage 2/3 (7-14 years).

Programmes are one year, full-time.

Entry requirements:
In order to qualify for admission to the PGCE programme, you must be a graduate of an approved institution of higher education or validating body or hold some other qualification which is recognised as equivalent to an undergraduate degree.

You must also have passed the equivalent of GCSE English language and mathematics (grade C or above) and science for the Primary and 7-14 options.

Equivalence tests: Equivalence tests are available, but candidates are advised to revise the relevant GCSE syllabus in preparation for them.

Application route: PGCE apply through the GTTR.

OTHER INFORMATION

We also offer a route into QTS through our Graduate Teacher Programme (GTP). This employment-based route into teaching can be taken in a range of subjects at secondary level. GTP trainees also have an opportunity to gain a PGCE award.

Assessment and combined assessment of Overseas Trained Teachers is also available.

We also offer a range of courses designed to prepare teachers for entry onto QTS programmes including:

3,6 and 9 month Subject Knowledge Enhancement courses in chemistry, mathematics and physics.

We welcome candidates from the Schools Direct route.

Swansea School of Education
Townhill
Swansea SA2 0UT
t: 01792 481 010
f: 01792 481 061
e: enquiry@smu.ac.uk
// www.smu.ac.uk

GENERAL INFORMATION

Swansea Met is a member of the University of Wales Alliance, with three campuses situated in and around the city centre.

Our Swansea School of Education is part of the South West Wales Centre for Teacher Education.

Teaching courses are based at our Townhill campus. The Townhill campus is only two miles from the Gower Peninsula and has breathtaking views over Swansea Bay.

Swansea itself is a lively and attractive city on the South Wales coast, combining seaside, countryside and a thriving city centre.

The university has an excellent and longstanding reputation for teacher education, offering several PGCE and MA programmes.

ACADEMIC AWARDS

BA Educational Studies - 3 years
The degree is designed to provide students with an understanding of how young people learn and how schools provide the support to develop pupils' learning. It is possible to study educational studies as part of a joint honours degree with the following subjects: psychology, counselling and drama. Students who wish to become primary school teachers may be offered a guaranteed interview for the School of Education's Primary PGCE programme

before they have obtained their degree provided that certain criteria are met. Places will be offered to students who meet the requirements of the PGCE Primary programme.

PGCE Secondary (11+) - 1 year full-time
Main subjects offered: Art and design, biology, business, chemistry, design and technology, English, history, geography, information technology, mathematics, modern languages (including Welsh), physics, religious education, science.

Entry requirements: GCSE grade C in English language and mathematics. Relevant degree.

Work experience: Evidence of work with young people an advantage.

PGCE Primary (3-8/7-11) - 1 year full-time
PGCE Primary
Entry requirements: GCSE grade B in English language, C in mathematics and C in science.

- Applicants should be graduates of a UK university, polytechnic or college of higher education, or have qualifications that are equivalent to a UK degree.
- Applicants are also expected to have either an A level (or equivalent) or a degree in a National Curriculum subject suitable for primary teaching in order to offer a curriculum specialism.
- It is normal practice for all applicants to be interviewed before acceptance. Applicants are expected to have gained recent experience of primary schools before attending interview.

Application routes: Undergraduate apply through UCAS. PGCE apply through the GTTR. The programme can be followed through the medium of either English or Welsh.

Swindon College

North Star Avenue
Swindon
Wiltshire SN2 1DY
t: 01793 491591
f: 01793 641794
// www.swindon-college.ac.uk
Enquiries:
t: 0800 731 2250
e: studentservices@swindon-college.ac.uk
// www.swindon-college.ac.uk

GENERAL INFORMATION

The main campus is in central Swindon, five minutes from the town centre, rail and bus stations, with easy access to the M4. Swindon is thirty minutes from Bristol, Bath, Oxford, Reading and one hour from Birmingham, Cardiff and London.

FACULTY OF EDUCATION

- The largest provider of higher education in the area.
- New campus building with state-of-the-art facilities.

ACADEMIC AWARDS: UNDERGRADUATE AND POSTGRADUATE

These courses are Oxford Brookes University programmes delivered at the Swindon College campus.

BA (Hons) Education and Lifelong Learning
BA (Hons) Early Childhood Studies

Foundation Degree in Early Years
Foundation Degree in Support for Learning

Professional Graduate Certificate in Education (PGCE)

This is a two year in-service part-time Post-Compulsory teacher training course for appropriately qualified professionals to teach students aged 14+ in an FE setting. All candidates need GCSE grade A-C in English and maths or equivalent and preferably IT.

Once qualified, teachers in the Post-Compulsory sector can gain QTLS (Qualified Teacher Learning and Skills) via the IfL (Institute for Learning) with proof of 30 hours of CPD. This must be completed every year to retain QTLS status.

Entry requirements: Minimum entry qualifications apply. Please see our current prospectus or website for specific information: **www.swindon-college.ac.uk.** For any further information, contact student services on Freephone 0800 731 2250 or email: studentservices@swindon-college.ac.uk

Application route: Applications for degrees and foundation degrees should be made via UCAS.

There is a direct application process for PGCE courses.

OTHER INFORMATION

Candidates for undergraduate and PGCE programmes will undergo a compulsory interview.

Candidates offered and accepting a place will be required to complete a medical questionnaire and a 'clearance to work with children' declaration.

St Joseph's Catholic College
Ocotal Way
Swindon SN3 3LR
t: **01793 716970**
e: **b.harrison@swindonscitt.org.uk**
c.moon@swindonscitt.org.uk
// **www.swindonscitt.org.uk**

GENERAL INFORMATION

Swindon SCITT offers a School-Centred Initial Teacher Training course for those wishing to teach in secondary schools. Training is provided in local secondary schools with two local colleges. It is delivered by professional tutors and subject mentors in the schools. To support your development of teaching skills and subject expertise, there is an academic programme of lectures, seminars and group activities based at St Joseph's Catholic College. Here trainees have access to a unique blend of practising teachers, local authority specialists and University of Bath consultants.

Course structure

This is a full-time course which will run from early September until July. Precise dates will vary from year to year depending upon school terms and other factors. Up-to-date information can be obtained by contacting Swindon SCITT directly.

Intended intake: 34

Main subjects offered: 11-16 (with limited option for 11-18)

- Design technology
- English
- ICT
- Mathematics
- Modern foreign languages
- Science with biology
- Science with chemistry
- Science with physics.

ACADEMIC AWARDS

The course leads to the award of Qualified Teacher Status (QTS) and either the Professional Graduate Certificate in Education (at honours level) or Postgraduate Certificate in Education (at master's level). To be awarded QTS, trainees need to compile an e-portfolio of evidence throughout the course to demonstrate that they have met the national standards. To be awarded either PGCE, trainees are required to achieve at least a satisfactory grade in a subject-based assignment and an educational study.

Further details are available on our website **www.swindonscitt.org.uk.**

Application route: Apply through the GTTR.

The Thames Primary Consortium

Institution code: T25

Runwell Primary School
Canewdon Gardens
Runwell
Wickford
Essex SS11 7BJ
t: 01268 570215
e: jo@thamesprimaryconsortium.com

GENERAL INFORMATION

The Thames Primary Consortium is a substantial
group of well-established and successful primary
schools situated in south Essex on the north side of
the River Thames. Under experienced professional
leadership, the schools are responsible for teaching
30 graduates each year to become primary school
teachers. The course has a strong emphasis on the
development of the student's practical teaching skills
in such areas as behaviour management, lesson
preparation, planning and delivery, as well as in the
use of well-organised assessment, recording and
reporting skills. A major feature of the course is that
more than two thirds of the student's time is spent in
schools. The course provides Qualified Teacher Status
and a Professional Graduate Certificate in Primary
Education, the latter validated through the University of
Bedfordshire. Many of the most recent group of
successful students decided to stay in the Essex area
for their initial teaching post.

Local interests and activities

The schools are centred in Southend and Basildon,
which are lively and interesting towns with plenty of
facilities and social activities. In addition the local
railway lines provide easy access to the heart of
London and to its theatres, cinemas, museums, art
galleries, shops, clubs and restaurants.

Accommodation

Plenty of rooms, flats and houses are available for rent
in the area and students are provided, before the
course, with lists of relevant estate agents, and lists of
other students who may be pleased to share such
accommodation. Prices are markedly lower than
London prices and do not appear to be a barrier to
students. Students on the course normally qualify for
the £4,000 bursary, which is helpful in this context.

Students' union

Students are full members of the University of
Bedfordshire's students' union. Although they may
never use its facilities, they have a right to do so and
will receive all of the student discounts, as well as
useful access to restricted internet sites and major
libraries.

ACADEMIC AWARD

Successful students will receive Qualified Teacher
Status and the Professional Graduate Certificate in
Primary Education at either pass, merit or distinction
level. Students will have to choose whether to spend
most of their time in infant classrooms or junior ones.
Students will also need to specialise in one main
subject chosen from English and mathematics.

Entry requirements: The consortium is very pleased
to welcome applications from graduates and
prospective graduates and will happily consider
applicants whose degrees do not seem to have any
major immediate relevance to primary education.
Entrants must have the usual GCSE English language,
mathematics and science qualifications (in line with
national requirements) and should have imagination,
determination, humour and the general intellect
necessary for prospective members of a demanding
profession.

St George's Community Hub
Great Hampton Row
Birmingham
B19 3JG
t: 0121 212 4567
e: teachertraining@titan.org.uk
// www.titan.org.uk
// www.titanteachertraining.co.uk

GENERAL INFORMATION

Titan is a long standing SCITT (school-centred initial teacher training) programme. The Titan SCITT consists of high-achieving inner-city primary and secondary schools. The schools offer a variety of contexts in which trainee teachers are able to develop the necessary competences to meet the challenges of teaching effectively. Trainees teach in two of the partnership schools, gaining experience both in the classroom and the wider life of a school.

"Coherent, good quality training which results in high levels of satisfaction from trainees and enables them to gain employment in local schools".
(Ofsted June 2010)

The course has two major components: practical classroom teaching and taught sessions concerned with subject specific knowledge and broader educational issues.

Trainees are allocated a school-based trainer (SBT) in each school placement who supports and guides them. The trainee receives at least two hours per week of structured professional mentoring. However, the support is ongoing.

"SBT sessions are outstanding. Really helped me to develop teaching skills and will continue to further my development as a teacher"
(trainee February 2011)

On successful completion of the course all trainees will be awarded QTS and PGCE. In addition to this trainees will have the opportunity to study towards a master's level qualification.

ACADEMIC AWARD

PGCE Secondary (11-16) - 1 year full-time
Main subjects offered:
- Design and technology
- Information and communication technology
- Mathematics
- Physical education
- Religious education
- Science (chemistry and physics)

PGCE Primary (Key stages 1 and 2) 1 year full-time

Entry requirements:
- GCSE grade C or above in English language and mathematics (or equivalent) and science (Primary only).
- Degree related to the subject you wish to teach.
- Classroom experience (minimum of two days).

Training bursaries may be available, see our website for further information.

Our success rates are high with a large number of trainees securing employment in Titan schools.

Entry route: PG/FT/1 year
Awards: QTS, PGCE
Intended intake: 25 Secondary, 20 Primary
Application route: Apply through the GTTR.

'It's fantastic. Titan is the best way to train.'
(Design and Technology trainee July 2011)

Course fees are £9,000.

Marian Thomas
College Road
Carmarthen SA31 3EP
t: 01267 676 646
e: m.thomas@trinity-cm.ac.uk
// www.trinitysaintdavid.ac.uk

GENERAL INFORMATION

The campus is an ideal place to study. Teaching facilities, information services, student accommodation and the Students' Union help to create a safe and welcoming environment for the community of students. Sports facilities include a sports hall and health suite, an all-weather training pitch, tennis court and swimming pool on-campus as well as playing fields for rugby, soccer, hockey and cricket nearby.

West Wales is indeed the land of plenty. From the bustle of town life to the quiet tranquillity of the countryside and breathtaking beauty of its sandy beaches, the area offers the opportunity for a diverse and varied lifestyle. Carmarthen is the commercial centre for a large and thriving area. A busy market town, it has a good mix of traditional and modern shopping facilities, excellent leisure facilities and nightlife.

Trinity Saint David offers a range of affordable student accommodation for which prices vary according to the type of accommodation and catering services preferred.

ACADEMIC AWARDS

BA Primary Education with QTS or BA Addysg Gynradd gyda SAC (Welsh medium programme)
Intended intake: 119 (first year)
Entry requirements: Applicants are required to have a grade B at GCSE in at least two of the core subjects - English/Welsh language, mathematics and science. Exceptions will be considered if the general profile of the results across all subjects is predominantly high. Extensive experience of working with children is an advantage.

If invited to attend an interview, you will be required to complete a form to confirm that you meet the requirements of the 'Fitness to Teach' document published by DIUS.

In addition, you must be able to offer any of the following qualifications for entry to our degree programmes:

- Normally between 240-360 UCAS Tariff points. At least 240 points (12 units) should be attained from qualifications larger than three units. The remaining points may be attained from a variety of qualifications within the National Qualifications Framework, including a maximum of 20 points in Level 3 Key Skills.
- A levels (pre 2001): Ten points from at least two A levels, one of which would normally be related to your chosen area of study.
- Advanced GNVQ: Overall merit in an appropriate subject.
- BTEC Higher National Certificate: In an appropriate subject with at least five merits.
- BTEC Higher National Diploma: In an appropriate subject with at least five merits.
- New BTEC National Certificate (12-unit award): merit/merit in an appropriate subject.
- New BTEC National Diploma (18-unit award) merit/merit/pass in an appropriate subject.

Application route: Apply through UCAS.

Also available
BA Early Years Education
BA Physical Education
BA Primary Education Studies (without QTS)
BA Religious Education
BA Social Inclusion
BA Youth and Community
Please contact the Registry on 01267 676767 for further details.

College Road
Truro College Cornwall
TR1 3XX
t: 01872 267091
f: 01872 267526
e: heinfo@trurocollege.ac.uk
// www.trurocollege.ac.uk

GENERAL INFORMATION

Truro and Penwith College is one of the newest and fastest growing colleges in the country and has received a Training Quality Standard which acknowledges the college as a leading training provider. Boasting state of the art facilities housed in 11 buildings. The Truro campus is based just outside the picturesque Cathedral City of Truro and is easily accessible by car, train and bus. The local airport is also a short journey away. Truro College has a second campus, Tregye,a 15 minute drive from the main site. Opened in 2006, Truro College's university-level provision is situated in the Fal building. This is a purpose-built facility housing higher education, teacher training and education studies. The Fal is an adult-only environment and has a true HE ethos.

Newly merged Truro and Penwith College has received massive investment to redevelop the Penwith campus site with up-to-date, purpose-built accommodation. These new buildings allow expansion of existing courses and the introduction of new courses, whilst taking advantage of the fantastic position of the current college, both in terms of proximity to the town centre, bus and rail links and also to the fabulous views that the college enjoys over Mounts Bay.

Truro and Penwith College offers a wide range of education programmes to suit the needs of each learner, from the experienced teacher to someone embarking on a career in teaching. We have initial teacher training programmes for both secondary and post-compulsory sectors and CPD opportunities at certificate, intermediate, higher and master's levels.

ACADEMIC AWARDS: UNDERGRADUATE

Plymouth University
BA (Hons) Education and Training
FdA Early Childhood Education
FdA Education and Training in the Lifelong Learning Sector
FdA Outdoor Education
FdA Children and Young People's Workforce
Certificate in Education
The Diploma in Teaching in the Lifelong Learning Sector (incorporating full-time and part-time).

University of Greenwich (flexible learning)
Professional Certificate in Education and Professional Graduate Certificate in Education
Post-compulsory education and training, incorporating PTTLS, CTTLS and DTTLS) part-time.

ACADEMIC AWARDS: POSTGRADUATE

Plymouth University
Postgraduate Certificate in Education
The Diploma in Teaching in the Lifelong Learning Sector (incorporating full-time and part-time).

University of Cumbria
Postgraduate Certificate in Education with QTS (11-16 years) full-time

Cornwall School Centred Initial Teacher Training (See C79)
www.cornwallscitt.org

Battle Hill Drive
Wallsend
NE28 9NJ
t: (0191) 229 5000
f: (0191) 229 5301
e: enquiries@tynemet.ac.uk
// www.tynemet.ac.uk

GENERAL INFORMATION

Teaching courses are based at our Coast Road Campus in Wallsend, which is set within spacious grounds. The campus is close to Newcastle upon Tyne, the city of Sunderland and the A1 and A19, giving direct road links to Tyne and Wear, Northumberland, County Durham and Cleveland. The campus has easy access to airports, national and local railway stations and bus routes.

Higher education at TyneMet
There is a great demand for appropriately trained and qualified teaching staff in the Post-Compulsory sector and TyneMet College is well placed to prepare individuals to meet this demand.

TyneMet has a long tradition of delivering high quality teacher training, both for their own staff and for teachers and trainers from elsewhere in the sector. As well as a range of level 3 courses, the following are offered at higher education level and in the case of the Certificate of Education, lead to fully qualified teacher status in the Post-Compulsory sector.

COURSES

Certificate of Education in Post-Compulsory Education and Training (validated by University of Sunderland)
This Cert Ed is for practising teachers, lecturers and trainers who work in the field of post compulsory education and training. It is practical in its focus, builds upon the diverse experiences of course members and relates these to issues in teaching, learning, assessment and professional development.

Entry requirements: a professional qualification equivalent to NVQ3 or above, advanced craft qualification or an HND/C. In order to satisfy the practical teaching requirements of the course you will need to organise a minimum of 60 teaching hours in year 1 and 90 hours in year 2.

Duration: 2 years
Attendance: part-time
Assessment: There are no examinations. Assessment includes written assignments, group activities, presentations, teaching observations and peer assessment.

Professional Graduate Certificate in Post-Compulsory Training (PGCE) (validated by University of Sunderland)
This PGCE course is for practising teachers, lecturers and trainers who work in the field of post-compulsory education and training. It is practical in its focus, builds upon the diverse experiences of course members and relates these to issues in teaching, learning, assessment and professional development.

Entry requirements: A degree in the subject you wish to teach. In order to satisfy the practical teaching requirements of the course you will need to organise a minimum of 60 teaching hours in year 1 and 90 hours in year 2.

Duration: 2 years
Attendance: part-time
Assessment: There are no examinations. Assessment includes written assignments, group activities, presentations, teaching observations and peer assessment.

Diploma in Professional Learning and Development (leading to BA (Hons) Education and Training)
This course is for professionals across the public and private sector who are engaged in, managing or facilitating learning.

Duration: 2 years
Attendance: part-time
Assessment: All assessment is assignment-based.

For further information about any of our courses, please contact our Gateway Student Advisors on (0191) 229 5000, key option 2.

School of Education
University Avenue
Ayr KA8 0SX
t: 01292 886000
f: 01292 886006

ACADEMIC AWARDS

BA Hons Education

This new programmes is offered for entry in 2013/14 at the Ayr Campus. In addition to gaining the degree, successful completion of the course will provide applicants with the formal teaching qualification necessary for provisional registration with the General Teaching Council for Scotland.

Entry requirements

SQA Higher BBBB including English, plus maths at Standard Grade (credit) or equivalent.GCE A level BBC or BCC, plus four GCSEs including maths at A or B and English language and English literature. An offer of a place is conditional on a successful interview.

Childhood Studies

This programme is designed to allow students entering Year 2 to deepen their understanding of a variety of issues related to childhood and services for children and their families.

Entry requirements: HNC Early Education and Care or HNC Childcare and Education. In addition a Higher at C or above (or equivalent) in English is preferred. Applicants with similar childcare qualifications and qualifications pre-dating HNC should contact the university for advice on RPL.

Community Learning and Participation (subject to university approval)

This degree programme prepares students to work in a variety of community contexts through academic study and work based learning.

Year 1 entry requirements: SQA Highers at BBCC or GCE A levels at CCC.

PGDE Primary

The PGDE (Primary) also covers the main area of the primary curriculum and professional studies. School experience placements comprise 50% of the 36-week course. The application deadline is 15 December 2012.

Entry requirements: For the PGDE (Primary), applicants should normally hold a degree from a UK university, along with passes in English language at Higher Grade and mathematics at Standard Grade (credit level), or equivalent.

PGDE Secondary

Students currently undertake one or two of the following subjects, depending on qualifications: art and design; biology with science; chemistry with science; English; mathematics or physical education. The university reserves the right to confirm which of the above subjects are available in any one session. Please contact the university if you wish to confirm the availability of your subject before applying. During their university-based studies, PGDE (Secondary) students study cross-curricular school and professional studies, in addition to their specialised subject study. School experience placements comprise 50% of the 36-week course.

Entry requirements: Applicants currently should hold a degree which contains one third of the academic workload in each of a minimum of two academic sessions directly relevant to the secondary subject or subjects to be taught. A pass in Higher English language or equivalent is also required. Further clarification on the acceptability of degree qualifications can be obtained, before applying, from the School of Education or the Scottish Executive's Memorandum on Entry Requirements to Courses of Teacher Education in Scotland.

Application routes: For BEd (Hons) Education, Childhood Studies and Community Learning and Participation - apply through UCAS. For PGDE courses - apply direct to the university by visiting **www.uws.ac.uk/apply** to obtain an application form.

The University of West London

Faculty of Professional Studies
Crescent Road
Reading
Berkshire RG1 5RQ
e: **learning.advice@uwl.ac.uk**
// **www.uwl.ac.uk**

GENERAL INFORMATION

We have two campuses, West London (Brentford and Ealing), and Reading (Berkshire). The teacher training provision is located at Reading, where an established team offer a range of in-service and pre-service qualifications, endorsed by Standards Verification UK (SVUK) and leading to the award of Qualified Teacher Learning and Skills (QTLS).

Local interests

Reading is a large and thriving town with good nightlife, a varied sports and arts programme and one of the largest shopping centres in the south. There are good road and rail links to London, Heathrow and the rest of the UK.

Accommodation and student services

The university offers a range of support services to students, including advice on finance and careers, as well as a professional counselling service. Accommodation is available in halls of residence.

ACADEMIC AWARDS

PGCE (Lifelong Learning): full-time
Diploma for Teaching in the Lifelong Learning Sector: part-time
All applicants are required to attend for interview.

Entry requirements:
Pre-service route: PGCE (Lifelong Learning): A first degree in your subject (minimum 2:2), or equivalent qualification, together with a good general education background, including level 2 qualifications in English and mathematics. Commercial or industrial experience in appropriate vocational subject areas is also useful. Applicants should also be aware of the diversity of students encountered in the Learning and Skills sector, and are encouraged to observe lessons, prior to interview.

In-service route: Diploma for Teaching in the Lifelong Learning Sector: This is an in-service route for teachers currently employed in the Learning and Skills sector for which level 2 English and mathematics, plus level 3 in your subject specialism are required.

Application route:
PGCE: All applications should be made through the Graduate Teacher Training Registry **www.gttr.ac.uk**.

All other courses: Call: 0800 036 8888. Email: learning.advice@uwl.ac.uk. Website:
www.uwl.ac.uk

Follow us on Twitter:
http://twitter.com/#/westlondonguru

Swaffield School
St Ann's Hill
Wandsworth
London SW18 2SA
t: 020 8874 1442

From September 2012 Wandsworth SCITT will be in new premises elsewhere in the borough. Full details of the school where our training will take place will be published as soon as possible.

GENERAL INFORMATION

The Wandsworth Primary Schools' Consortium

- started in 1996 and has twice come third in national league tables for excellence in teacher training.
- has had a 100% employment success for its trainees.
- is a group of high-achieving, south-west London schools that provides first-class Foundation Stage and KS1/KS2 teacher training, leading to the award of a PGCE.
- provides a balanced course with an emphasis on practical work in schools.

The taught course

- is small and allows extensive group and tutorial work with acknowledged experts in the field of education.
- supports trainees in their subject knowledge acquisition through lectures, by tutorial help and through peer tutoring. Working in teams is strongly encouraged.
- delivers the curriculum through lectures, workshops and seminars.
- provides opportunities for trainees to build individual strengths by exploring new ways of looking at established practice.

School experience

- The London Borough of Wandsworth is a diverse area with a vibrant mix of cultures and a strong sense of community.
- Its schools are committed to equal opportunities and to raising the levels of achievement for all its children.
- The consortium's schools deliver personalised, one-to-one tuition in a classroom setting.
- All our school-based mentors are experienced practitioners who receive expert training in the teaching of adult learners.

We seek to recruit trainees who are keen to succeed, enthusiastic and hard-working. Our trainees enjoy being part of a small, close-knit team of people whose aim is to raise the standards in inner-city schools. The collaborative atmosphere that is fostered on the course enables trainees to develop their teaching skills and forge networks for their future career. Visit our website at **www.scitt.co.uk** for further information.

ACADEMIC AWARDS - POSTGRADUATE CERTIFICATE IN EDUCATION

PGCE Early Years (3-7) - 1 year full-time
PGCE General Primary (5-11) - 1 year full-time
Courses validated by Kingston University.

Entry requirements

- An honours degree in any subject at 2:2 or above.
- English language, mathematics and science GCSE or equivalent at grade C or above.
- Previous work experience with children desirable but not essential.

Enquiries: email wpsc@swaffield.wandsworth.sch.uk

University of Warwick

Institution code: W20

Institute of Education
Coventry CV4 7AL
t: 024 7652 8148
// www.go.warwick.ac.uk/education

GENERAL INFORMATION

Warwick is one of the UK's leading research universities. The Warwick Institute of Education is one of the UK's leading centres for teacher education, education research and professional development. The ethos of the institute is created through a lively interaction of teaching and research, together with a close partnership with local schools, early years settings, colleges and local authorities.

Local interest
The university is on the border of Coventry and Warwickshire, so attractions in both the city and the countryside are within easy reach.

Accommodation
For information on accommodation, visit
www.go.warwick.ac.uk/accommodation.
Unfortunately, on-campus accommodation is unavailable to PGCE trainees.

Students' union
Warwick has one of the biggest students' unions in the country. It hosts excellent social events, including major national and international music events.

Leisure facilities
The university has generous facilities for a wide range of sporting interests. It also boasts one of the largest arts centre complexes outside London.

ACADEMIC AWARDS

PGCE Early Years - 1 year full-time
Intended intake: 30

PGCE Primary - 1 year full-time
Intended intake: 131

PGCE Primary - 2 years part-time
Intended intake: 25

PGCE Secondary - 1 year full-time
Intended intake: 178

QTS is awarded upon successful completion of government skills tests.

Secondary main courses offered:
- Business education (14-19)
- Drama with English
- English with drama
- History
- Mathematics
- Modern foreign languages (French, German or Spanish)
- Modern foreign languages with business education
- Science (biology, chemistry and physics)

For more information, please visit
www.go.warwick.ac.uk/pgce

Application route: Apply through the GTTR

Graduate Teacher Programme (GTP) - secondary subjects only

For more information, please visit
www.go.warwick.ac.uk/gtp

Entry requirements: Applicants to all courses must have, or expect to gain before the start of the course: a GCSE grade C or equivalent in English language and mathematics. Applicants to Early Years and Primary courses must also have a GCSE grade C or equivalent in science.

Please note that applicants to Early Years and Primary courses are expected to have GCSEs or equivalents before applying.

Thomas Telford School
Old Park, Telford TF3 4NW0
t: 01952 200000
f: 01952 293294
e: wmc@ttsonline.net
// www.wmc.ac

GENERAL INFORMATION

The one-year PGCE programme, validated by
Staffordshire University, is based at Thomas Telford
School. Thirty excellent secondary schools combine
with the lead school to form the consortium. One of
the distinctive features of this school-centred initial
teacher training (SCITT) programme is that all of the
students' time is spent in school. It is a dynamic
programme, able to provide individualised training to
meet the needs of each student teacher. Excellent
quality assurance procedures are in place to secure
high standards of training and support.

Assessment

Students are assessed against TDA and PGCE
requirements by a variety of techniques. All students
compile an evidence log to record where QTS
standards are met. There are a series of written
assignments in which students are required to
consider both theoretical and practical issues linked to
their school-based practice.

Location

Thomas Telford School is located close to Junction 5
on the M54. The BR main line station is just over a
mile from Thomas Telford School.

ACADEMIC AWARD

Professional Graduate (30 masters' credits) and
Postgraduate (60 masters' credits) awards are
available. The 40-week PGCE is an 11-16 programme
with enhancement at post-16 in the following
subject areas:

Design and technology (D&T)

- The programme is able to train teachers of D&T in
  any combination of specialisms to meet the Design
  and Technology Association's (DATA)
  competencies.
- Health and Safety training is an integral part of the
  programme.

Intended intake: 12

Information communication technology (ICT)

The programme provides opportunities to
developstudents' knowledge, skills and teaching
capabilitiesusing a wide range of IT applications.
Training ensuresstudents gain a good
understanding of ICT as a subjectand also a variety of
curriculum models for teachingNational Curriculum
requirements.

Intended intake: 12

Physical education

- The programme provides training in all six activity
  areas of the National Curriculum.
- A large number of Governing Body award courses
  are built into the programme, some of which
  are held at weekends.

Intended intake: 19

Entry requirements: Standard Teaching Agency
requirements.
Equivalence tests: Equivalence tests are available
for suitable applicants in both English language
and mathematics.
Application routes: Apply through the GTTR.

Conway Park Campus
Conway Park
Birkenhead
Wirral CH41 4NT
t: 0151 551 7777

Enquiries
0151 551 7777
www.wmc.ac.uk

GENERAL INFORMATION

As a further education college we are the largest provider of post-16 learning on the Wirral. The area is closely connected to Liverpool by ferry, train or bus and has easy access to M53/M56 and M62 motorways. We pride ourselves in ensuring that learners receive the individual support necessary to complete their course successfully.

We offer both degree courses and all levels of professional qualifications and apprenticeships. Our aim is to provide access to higher education for a wide range of people through full-time and part-time courses and work place learning, which are designed to be flexible and challenging.

ACADEMIC AWARDS

Foundation Degrees - recruited through UCAS
FdA Early Years Senior Practitioner (sector endorsed)
FdA Information Advice and Guidance

We also offer the following teacher training and supporting teaching & learning courses - part-time

Professional Graduate Certificate in Education (Post Compulsory)
Certificate in Education (Post Compulsory)
Certificate in Teaching in the Lifelong Learning Sector (CTLLS)

C&G Award Preparing to Teach in the Lifelong Learning Sector (PTLLS)
Level 4 Award in Internal Quality Assurance - V1
Level 3 Certificate in Assessing Vocational Achievement
NVQ 3/4 Advice and Guidance
Advanced Apprenticeship in Children's Care Learning and Development
Advanced Apprenticeship Supporting Teaching and Learning in Schools/Playwork
CACHE Level 2/3 Diploma Playwork
CACHE Introduction to Eatrly Years/Caring for Children
CACHE Level 2/3 Diploma for the Children and Young People's Workforce
Mentoring

Entry requirements: Entry criteria apply to all our courses. Please see our website for details **www.wmc.ac.uk** or call Learner Services on t: 0151 551 7777.

University of Wolverhampton

Institution code: W75

School of Education
Gorway Road
Walsall
WS1 3BD
t: 01902 518412
e: sed@wlv.ac.uk
// www.wlv.ac.uk/sed

GENERAL INFORMATION

The School of Education is located in the vibrant town of Walsall. The campus has accommodation, sports and learning facilities. 2008 saw the opening of a new teaching building for the school, including specialist facilities for science teaching and ICT teaching. The building has a social computer area where students can drop in to access the internet or work on assignments. Excellent inspection scores from Ofsted and QAA indicate that the teaching at the School of Education is of high quality; in 2010 the primary and secondary teaching divisions attaining an Outstanding Ofsted rating - 93% of 2008 University of Wolverhampton teacher training graduates are employed in teaching and education roles.

Course Information

The extensive array of courses available at the school includes:

- BEd Early Primary (leading to QTS)
- BEd Primary Education (leading to QTS)
- Childhood & Family Studies
- Special Needs and Inclusion Studies
- Education Studies
- PGCE Primary (leading to QTS)
- PGCE Secondary (leading to QTS). Subjects include business education, design and technology, English, information communications technology, mathematics, modern foreign languages, physical education, psychology, science, biology, chemistry and physics)
- PGCE Post Compulsory Education
- Graduate Teacher Programme (leading to QTS)

Local interest and activities

Birmingham and Wolverhampton are a bus ride away and both the M5 and M6 are easily accessible from any part of the country. The campus is based in close proximity of the town centre, which boasts many high street names, not to mention the wealth of pubs, bars and eateries. With the redevelopment of Town Wharf, a newly created square and canal basin, Walsall is now home to a £21m art gallery. The university's Transport Department runs a free intercampus bus shuttle service for its students from Monday to Friday, connecting all campuses and town centres.

Accommodation

The halls of residence at the Walsall campus were opened in 2005. All rooms on Walsall Campus are inclusive of basic contents insurance, and launderette facilities. Wireless Internet access is available. There is also accommodation to meet the needs of those with disabilities.

Leisure facilities

The campus boasts excellent sports facilities including a multi-gym, large indoor heated swimming pool, a dance studio, tennis courts, numerous sports pitches, an athletics track and two gymnasiums; our facilities are also being used to train Judo hopefuls for the 2012 Olympics!

For more information about studying at the University of Wolverhampton, or for our entry requirements visit
www.wlv.ac.uk/sed

University of Winchester
West Hill
Winchester
Hampshire SO22 4NR
t: 01962 827234
f: 01962 827288

GENERAL INFORMATION

The University of Winchester stands on a pleasant site overlooking the city of Winchester. It is a ten-minute walk from the city centre where there is a well-equipped leisure centre, pubs and restaurants to suit all tastes and budgets.

Accommodation

There are a number of halls of residence on campus as well as an award-winning student village, which is a five-minute walk from the university campus.

ACADEMIC AWARDS

BA (Hons) Primary Education

This is a four-year (or three-year for those assessed as suitable at the end of year one) modular course in initial teacher training, leading to a BA honours degree with the recommendation for the award of QTS. Students are prepared to teach either Early Years 3-7 or Primary 5-11 with a specialist subject. The current specialist subjects are art, drama, early years, English, French, geography, history, mathematics, physical education, religious education, science, special educational needs and media and ICT.

Entry requirements

These vary according to the specialist subject, but generally we require between 260-300 points at A2 level, including C in a relevant subject at A2 level, or 60% at Access, including a main option subject. All applicants must have GCSE English language, mathematics and science at grade C or above, or equivalent. See our prospectus for details. Applicants are expected to demonstrate recent relevant work experience in a primary school.

Application route: Apply through UCAS.

PGCE Primary

The course prepares students to teach within the age range 5-11 years.

Entry requirements

An honours degree normally 2:1 or higher, advanced level study and qualifications, and GCSE English language, mathematics and science at grade C or above. Recent relevant experience in a maintained primary school is a key factor both to success in selection for interview and for subsequent acceptance on the programme. Please see our prospectus for further information.

The full-time course covers three terms and last 38 weeks, of which 18 are spent on school experience.

Application route: Apply through the GTTR.

The part-time course can be completed over a period of two to three years. The course should suit those who wish to continue with part-time work, for example as a teaching assistant. There is an 'assessment only route' to QTS for those applicants who already have substantial teaching experience, and qualifications which may not be recognised in this country.

Application route: Apply direct to University of Winchester.

PGCE Secondary Religious Education

This is a part-time flexible course offered at our Basingstoke campus.

Application route: Apply through the GTTR.

University of Worcester

Institution code: W80

Henwick Grove
Worcester WR2 6AJ
t: 01905 855111
f: 01905 857542
e: admissions@worc.ac.uk
// 01905 857542

ACADEMIC AWARDS

BA (Hons) in Primary Initial Teacher Training with QTS- 3 years full-time
Intended intake: 125

This course is designed for those who wish to teach all areas of the Primary Curriculum. There is some choice of curriculum area to specialise in during the final year through a research project including: English, mathematics, information and communication technology, history, geography, special educational needs (SEN), music, art, design technology, science, physical education, forest schools, behaviour management, philosophy for children, RE and creative arts. These areas are continually updated and reviewed to reflect current issues and priorities in primary education.

Students follow a common programme during term 1, spanning the 3-11 age range, and then opt for the 3-7 years or the 5-11 years route for the remaining course of study. School experience, both serial and block practice, is a substantial and integral part of the course.

For information on our current entry requirements, please visit our website: **www.worcester.ac.uk**

PGCE Primary - QTS with 60 master's credits - 1 year full-time
Intended intake: 206

This full-time 38 week PGCE Primary course will prepare you to teach across the primary age range and in all Foundation and Primary Curriculum subjects. You will be equipped to meet the National Standards for the Award of Qualified Teacher Status (QTS) upon successful completion of the course. Before commencing, you will decide whether you wish to focus on teaching Early Years (pupils 3 to 7 years old), or Early/Later Years (pupils 5 to 11 years old) within the PGCE programme.

This course includes a significant professional pedagogy and management element, which covers the role of the professional teacher, the child as a learner and wider issues associated with school and society, in particular the Every Child Matters agenda.

You will develop an advanced understanding of child development and classroom relationships, as well as the skills in classroom organisation, behaviour management, SEN assessment, recording and reporting that are essential to effective teaching. To fulfill part of your master's level work, you will choose an extended subject study from a range of 14 Primary Curriculum subjects and themes.

For information on our current entry requirements, please visit our website: **www.worcester.ac.uk**

PGCE Secondary with QTS with possible 60 master's credits - 1 year full-time
Intended intake: 147

This postgraduate course prepares you to teach pupils aged either 11-16 or 11-18 (14-19 for courses marked with*), depending on subject qualifications, in: design and technology (food and textiles), English, history, home economics, mathematics, languages, physical education, psychology* or science (biology, chemistry or physics).

For information on our current entry requirements, please visit our website: **www.worcester.ac.uk**

GTP route: There are also graduate teacher places in both shortage and other subjects.

* The university organises alternative examinations in English language and mathematics for students without the appropriate certificates.

Application route: Undergraduate apply through UCAS. PGCE apply through the GTTR. GTP applicants should apply via the TDA website.

Department of Education
Heslington
York YO10 5DD
t: **01904 323454**
f: **01904 323459**
e: **educ21@york.ac.uk**
// **www.york.ac.uk/pgce**

GENERAL INFORMATION

Founded during the period of university expansion in the early 1960s, York has established a national and international reputation for the quality of its courses and its research, and can be reliably found in the top 10 of most measurements of quality. York was awarded an Ofsted grade one 'Outstatnding' in March 2010. York has about 10,000 students and combines the advantages of a university large enough to provide a vibrant social and cultural environment with those of a smaller community able to be welcoming and friendly to its students.

Local interest/activities
The campus and nearby village of Heslington provide a welcoming community atmosphere complemented by the proximity and obvious attractions of the city.

Accommodation
A range of university accommodation is available to postgraduate trainees at competitive costs. Full details about accommodation and prices can be found at: **www.york.ac.uk/admin/accom.**

Students' union
The students' union represents student interests at the university. It coordinates the activities of the academic, cultural, religious, political and recreational clubs andsocieties, provides a link with outside organisations and concerns itself with all aspects of student welfare within the university.

Leisure facilities
The university has extensive provision for sports of all kinds with 40 acres of playing fields and two sports halls. Excellent facilities are also offered for the enjoyment and performance of music.

ACADEMIC AWARDS

PGCE and QTS
York offers the one-year PGCE course at postgraduate (M) level leading to QTS in five secondary subjects (11-18).

Main subjects offered and intake:
- English (with drama) - 16
- History - 12
- Mathematics - 31
- Modern foreign languages (French, German, subsidiary Spanish) - 25
- Science (biology) - 9
- Science (chemistry) - 17
- Science (physics) - 9

Entry requirements:
- All entrants must have qualifications in English language and mathematics at GCE O level or GCSE (grade C or above) or hold equivalent qualifications in these subjects.
- Normally, offers will be made conditionally on gaining a degree in a relevant main subject. Queries about the suitability of a degree should be made to the department.

Equivalence tests: The department is able to offer equivalence tests in English language and mathematics.

Application route: Apply through the GTTR.

OTHER INFORMATION

Enquiries: Please e-mail or telephone for further information or for a prospectus.

York St John University

Institution code: Y75

Lord Mayor's Walk
York YO31 7EX
t: **01904 876598**
f: **01904 876940**
e: **admissions@yorksj.ac.uk**

GENERAL INFORMATION

York St John University has been training teachers since 1841. We've been at it a long time and we're good at it. Recent Ofsted reports have verified the quality of our programmes. We have an excellent reputation in the teaching profession. Our students succeed - they get good teaching jobs and achieve positions of responsibility because they exemplify the knowledge, concern and careful preparation that are central to our tradition in teacher education. You will leave our Teacher Education Programme fully prepared for professional practice as a teacher.

Local interest and activities

What better place to train as a teacher than York? We're very close to the buzzing heart of York city centre and just a stone's throw from the world-famous Minster. Some of the best views of York can be seen from the medieval city walls by our front gates. York is one of the UK's top tourist attractions. It's an amazing mix of magical sights, cultural venues, thriving business, excellent shops and brilliant cafes.

Accommodation

Semi-catered and self-catering accommodation is available.

Students' union

The union supports a whole range of clubs and societies, increasing in number every year. We offer everything from dance to rugby, rowing to drama, skiing to trampolining, even a curry club! And, if we're still not offering what you're looking for, all you need is ten like-minded individuals to start up your own club.

ACADEMIC AWARDS

BA (Hons) Primary Education (3-7)
BA (Hons) Primary Education (5-11)
Application route: Apply through UCAS.

PGCE Primary (3-7) - full-time
PGCE Primary (5-11) - full-time
PGCE Secondary Religious Education (11+) - full-time
Application route: Apply through the GTTR.

PGCE Primary (3-7) - part-time
PGCE Primary (5-11) - part-time
PGCE - flexible route
Application route: Direct to York St John University.

Entry requirements: For all teacher education courses, GCSE grade C or above in English language, mathematics and science (excluding secondary PGCE). A satisfactory medical certificate and Criminal Records Bureau enhanced disclosure are also required. For Postgraduate Primary programmes, a recognised degree, preferably in a National Curriculum subject area, is required and for Secondary PGCE a degree in, or closely allied to, the subject to be taught is necessary. Upper second class degree required, although strong candidates with a lower second class result may be considered. Candidates should have at least ten days' recent experience (ie in the past year) in a UK primary school or EYFF setting before applying for the courses.

Equivalence tests: York St John may accept an equivalence test in lieu of mathematics and science GCSEs and also offers a mathematics equivalence test. Please contact the institution for more details.

PS

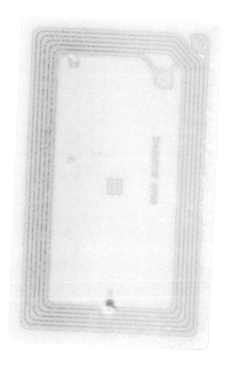